RED RIVER GIRL

RED RIVER GIRL

THE LIFE AND DEATH
OF TINA FONTAINE

JOANNA JOLLY

VIKING

VIKING

an imprint of Penguin Canada, a division of Penguin Random House Canada Limited

Canada • USA • UK • Ireland • Australia • New Zealand • India • South Africa • China

First published 2019

www.penguinrandomhouse.ca

LIBRARY AND ARCHIVES CANADA CATALOGUING IN PUBLICATION

Jolly, Joanna, author
    Red River girl : the life and death of Tina Fontaine / Joanna Jolly.

Issued in print and electronic formats.
ISBN 978-0-7352-3393-5 (softcover).—ISBN 978-0-7352-3394-2 (HTML)

    1. Fontaine, Tina, 1999-2014. 2. Murder—Manitoba—Winnipeg. 3. Murder—Investigation—Manitoba—Winnipeg. 4. Cormier, Raymond (Raymond Joseph)—Trials, litigation, etc. 5. Native women--Violence against—Canada. I. Title.

HV6535.C33W55 2018   364.152'309712743   C2018-902411-9
    C2018-902412-7

Cover and book design by Rachel Cooper
Cover image © Wwphoto/Dreamstime.com

Printed and bound in Canada

10 9 8 7 6 5 4 3 2 1

Penguin
Random House
VIKING CANADA

To my family,
without whose love and support
this book would not have been possible.

CONTENTS

PROLOGUE   1

1.   "The Red Is an Unforgiving River"   7

2.   "Tell Momma and Papa I Love Them"   29

3.   O'Donovan   50

4.   "Not Like *CSI*"   62

5.   The Low Track   75

6.   Tessa Twohearts   89

7.   Life on the Instalment Plan   106

8.   22 Carmen   123

9.   "I Did Not Kill That Girl"   141

10.   The Chloe Green Duvet Cover   157

11.   Project Styx   175

12.   Jenna   197

13.   Whistler   214

14.   "Not a Case of Tunnel Vision"   236

15.   Justice for Tina   253

EPILOGUE   273

ACKNOWLEDGMENTS   279

INDEX   283

RED RIVER GIRL

PROLOGUE

I n 2016, in the early hours of a mid-September morning, a guard led me into a secure interview room inside a jail in Manitoba and handed me a red panic button to press should I need assistance. Sitting opposite from me at a table was a prisoner still in the process of finishing his breakfast cereal and toast. Raymond Cormier demanded to know which media outlet I was from. When I explained I was a BBC journalist but was there to interview him for a book, he threw his toast at my head and screamed that he was only interested in speaking to the local press. For a second, I considered pushing the panic button but instead adopted the submissive pose advised by BBC hostile environment trainers— head bowed, palms open and visible—and waited for him to calm down. After a few minutes, he did, and he instructed me to turn on my recording equipment. Over the next two hours he spoke without pause, detailing his childhood, adult life, sex life, drug addiction, and, most of all, how he had become the prime suspect in one of Canada's most notorious murder cases. At times he was angry, at times contrite, as he remembered the person he was accused of killing: the fifteen-year-old Indigenous schoolgirl Tina Fontaine. His speech was mumbled, repetitive, and often confused, but he stayed firm on one point: "I did not kill Tina Fontaine."

My journey to Cormier's prison cell had begun two years earlier. At the time, I had been working as a BBC journalist for over a decade, specializing in reporting on Asia. Exploring the continent was my passion. Asia was literally in my blood, as my father was an Indian doctor who had settled in the United Kingdom and married my English mother. I had reported from Japan to the Indian subcontinent, where I was based in Kathmandu as the BBC correspondent. Before this, I had spent three turbulent, gripping years covering Timor-Leste's violent struggle for independence. As I travelled I found myself coming back to the same issue time and again. Violence against women was a problem in every country in which I worked. In 2013, horrified by the brutal gang rape and murder of a young woman in Delhi months before, I made a documentary on Indian attitudes towards sexual violence. I wondered whether there was any society where attacks against women weren't seen as inevitable and accepted with complacency.

In the summer of 2014, my career took a different tack when I became the BBC online feature writer covering the US and Canada based in Washington, DC. I arrived to find the news cycle dominated by the police killing of the unarmed black teenager Michael Brown and the beheading of the American journalist James Foley by Islamic State terrorists. In our morning editorial meetings we would pick over the previous day's developments and try to find lesser-known stories we thought important to cover. It was at one of these meetings, in mid-August, that a Canadian colleague said the words that would eventually lead to this book. She was referring to the recent discovery of Tina Fontaine's body in the

Red River in Winnipeg, a story that had made headlines in her own country but had been barely covered elsewhere. "There's been another murder in Canada," she told the group of assembled journalists. "Canadians are *so* racist."

I found her remarks surprising. My personal experience of Canada was slim, but my impressions had been overwhelmingly positive. Canada seemed an enlightened country, home to an inspiringly multicultural Olympic team, a safe haven for refugees, and consistently top of the list of best places to live. It was a shock to hear that it had a problem with racism and violence against Indigenous women.

Among the great many Canadian articles on the issue, there was one story that disturbed and puzzled me. In February 2014, Loretta Saunders, a twenty-six-year-old Inuk student, had been attending university in Halifax, Nova Scotia. She had been working on a thesis on the reasons behind the disproportionately high number of missing and murdered Indigenous women when she herself was murdered. Studying photographs of Loretta's face, I struggled to understand how this attractive, intelligent young woman had become a target. Loretta was murdered by her roommates over rent money. As I continued to read up on the subject, I began to grasp the extent of the violence and its connection to poverty, historical racism, and marginalization. I learned that over the past few decades, hundreds of Indigenous women had been murdered or gone missing and that many of their cases had not been solved.

A few months later, in November 2014, there was more news from Winnipeg. A second Indigenous schoolgirl had been brutally attacked. This time, the girl survived, but her assault renewed calls for the federal government to do more to stem the violence. I started to plan a reporting trip to Winnipeg, feeling that the city encapsulated the issue with its large but segregated Indigenous population, its high number of missing and murdered women, and the very public failure of its police to protect Tina before her death. I began to negotiate with Winnipeg's deputy chief of police, Danny Smyth, for access to the Homicide Unit and its detectives. It was a delicate task that took nearly three months to organize, but by the end of January 2015 my colleagues and I were on a flight to the city.

Our report, "Red River Women," was published in April 2015 as a multimedia article and radio documentary. The reaction from the BBC's huge worldwide audience was one of shock and surprise, highlighting how little was known about the violence outside of Canada. The idea of writing a book about Tina Fontaine began to form in my mind, but I was conscious that without an arrest it was a story with no conclusion. Then, in December 2015, the head of the Winnipeg Police Homicide Unit, Sergeant John O'Donovan, emailed to say that Raymond Cormier, a drifter and convicted felon, had been charged with Tina's murder. When I asked O'Donovan how much information he was prepared to give me about his investigation, he replied cryptically that he would only speak face to face. Taking a chance, I bought a ticket to Winnipeg, hoping he would open up. I was not disappointed. Over lunch on a snowy January day, the detective detailed the extraordinary lengths to which he and his team had gone to catch the man he firmly believed was responsible for killing the Indigenous teenager. It was at this point that I resolved to write a book that would tell Tina's story.

Nine months later, I was interviewing Raymond Cormier in his prison cell. Afterwards outside in my car, I remained chilled despite the warm September sun. The enormity of the project ahead of me was beginning to sink in. The afternoon before, I had been in Ottawa, interviewing Carolyn Bennett, then the minister for Indigenous and Northern Affairs. She had told me that Tina Fontaine—"a real person with a real family and real experiences that we as a country need to learn from"—had given a face to the issue of missing and murdered women. Over the next year and a half, I continued to work on building up a picture of Tina's final weeks. But it wasn't until Raymond Cormier's trial, in January 2018, that I fully understood many of the details. Even then, the picture was incomplete. We still don't know how Tina Fontaine died. The case against Cormier, described to me by O'Donovan as compelling and conclusive, proved to be circumstantial and weak. When Cormier was found not guilty, I felt my work needed to explore why the police investigation had taken the path it had. I wanted to understand the pressure officers were under to find a name and face to fit this crime, when so many other killings of Indigenous women and girls had gone unsolved.

The story in this book is based on extensive face-to-face interviews, police notes, transcripts of recordings, and trial testimonies. I interviewed Tina's family and friends, O'Donovan and his team of detectives, undercover officers, the Crown and defence lawyers, community members from Sagkeeng First Nation, Indigenous politicians and activists, medical and legal experts, and Raymond Cormier himself. The dialogue is pieced together from recorded intercepts of conversations, trial testimonies, and interviews. In some cases, I have changed the names of those involved to protect their identity. I've tried to build up as accurate a picture as possible. In the few instances where I've been unable to locate witnesses, I've relied on the reporting of the Winnipeg press corps, which has been generous and supportive throughout this project.

In particular, I want to thank two people for their invaluable help. John O'Donovan has been my main source of police information, sharing notes and information and answering endless questions about procedure and developments with unfailing patience and clarity. He has also become adept at describing his emotions, something

I suspect he initially found quite difficult. When I interviewed members of his team, they unanimously told me that O'Donovan was an excellent boss, consistently supportive and understanding. Having worked closely with him for the past three years, I can easily see this to be true.

I am also extremely grateful for the cooperation of Tina's guardian, Thelma Favel. Thelma welcomed me into her family at a time of acute grief and when she was under pressure to speak to many journalists. She was always generous with her time, and I was moved by her courage and open-heartedness. Thelma and I shared a grim joke that whenever we were together, it was only a matter of minutes before one of us would cry. In truth, I was grateful for the chance to share her grief, as the emotional strain of researching this book took its toll. Her kindness remains with me to this day.

Finally, I want to say a few words about the person I did not have the chance to meet: Tina Fontaine. The details of Tina's final weeks were painful to piece together. But as I wrote this book, I developed a strong sense of Tina's teenage character and spirit. Fierce, funny, protective, brave, risk-taking, she was a young woman trying to forge her identity and make difficult choices in what was often a dangerous world. It is a tragedy that Tina did not live to fulfill her potential, like hundreds of other Indigenous women who have met a similar fate. One small consolation is that Tina's legacy lives on as the face of a movement for much-needed change. As her guardian, Thelma, said of her, "She carried her message strong."

1.

"THE RED IS AN UNFORGIVING RIVER"

I t starts with a river. The Red River plots a wandering course north across the Canadian Prairies, snaking its way through the city of Winnipeg. It curves through the urban landscape, spawning towering glass structures and grand-pillared offices at the point where it meets its tributary, the Assiniboine. The Red is Winnipeg's lifeblood and the reason for its existence, a highway for the European colonizers who came in search of fur and an ancient gathering place for the Indigenous peoples they traded with. In summer, it hosts fishing trips and dragon boat races. In winter, its frozen waters become skating trails and hockey rinks. Beside its banks are the rail lines that brought Winnipeg its immigrants and wealth, and the suburban gardens where its citizens now relax. But the Red has a darker, more complex role. The river is a drain, a muddy artery clogged with secrets. The homeless build shelters on its banks, waste pollutes its waters, and the desperate choose it as a place to die by suicide, surrendering their lives to its brown, silty depths.

On the morning of August 17, 2014, the Red River was witnessing an unusual clamour of activity as police dive boats motored into position under the metal trusses of the Canadian National Railway bridge. Onlookers gathered to watch as police divers lowered themselves backwards into the water, causing ripples to glint gold in the morning sun. They weren't looking for the fifteen-year-old Indigenous schoolgirl who had been reported missing the week before. The reality was that in Winnipeg young Indigenous women often disappeared into the underbelly of the city. It rarely warranted such a thorough river trawl. Instead, the boats were searching for the body of Faron Hall, a local hero who had, two days earlier, walked down to the river's edge, removed all his clothes, placed them neatly in a pile, and waded into the warm, muddy water.

Hall was a homeless alcoholic who had shot to national fame in 2009 after performing two rescues in the river. The first was of a teenage boy who had fallen from a bridge while dodging traffic on a cold May evening. Hall had dived into the icy water and pulled the boy out of the strong current, which was dragging him under. Hall didn't see anything special in the rescue. He had learned to swim during his childhood on the Dakota Tipi First Nation reserve, and he felt it was his duty to help those who weren't so able. A few months later, he was called on to use his swimming skills again. After a day spent drinking with friends by the river, a woman had slipped and fallen in. Her boyfriend jumped in to help, and Hall, realizing that they were both in trouble, quickly followed. He managed to save the woman but not the man, a failure that weighed heavily on his conscience. "The Red is an unforgiving river," he later told a local reporter. "It can take your life and spit you out."

For his actions, Hall was rewarded with a medal and money, some of which he donated to a local homeless shelter. But fame sat uneasily on his shoulders. On one occasion, he was beaten up after being recognized as the "homeless hero." On another, he faced public shame when the press reported how he had been arrested for drinking and begging. Like many Indigenous men, Hall encountered an excess of violence and sadness in his life. His mother died young, his sister was fatally stabbed, and Hall himself struggled with addiction. He served time for assault and eventually returned to living rough in a makeshift tent on the riverbank, within sight of the sweeping cables of the Esplanade Riel pedestrian bridge.

On the day Hall walked into the Red, it wasn't clear if he was trying to cool off, attempt a third rescue, or had something more melancholy on his mind. Whatever his motives, he was soon seen flailing in the strong current that swept beneath the bridge. A water taxi sped to the rescue, and the boat pilot tried to grab on to the homeless man. But the pilot suffered a heart attack in the process and was dispatched to a nearby hospital for treatment. By Sunday morning, the dive teams knew they were looking for a body.

At the same time that the divers were combing the riverbed, Alexander Cunningham, the captain of the pleasure cruise boat MS *River Rouge*, was finishing a late breakfast and returning to where he'd moored his vessel the previous night. Cunningham had taken the boat out on Saturday evening for a birthday party cruise. After motoring up and down the river, he had come to a stop at the wooden structure of the Alexander Docks, a kilometre north of where Hall was last seen. Decades before, river cruising had been a glamorous activity in Winnipeg, attracting tourists from around the province and from the US cities of Grand Forks and Fargo. The *River Rouge* had once been a fancy boat, its interior decorated with oil paintings, run by a man who liked to be known as the Commodore. It could even boast that Princess Margaret had been a passenger, back in the 1970s, when going on board meant formal dress for women and a jacket and tie for men. Half a dozen similar cruisers plied the river then, some with ornamental paddle wheels harking back to the glory days of the early settlers. But by 2014, only the *River Rouge* was left, hiring itself out for parties and private events.

Cunningham was in his seventies and had a lifetime of sailing experience. That summer, he had returned to captain the *River Rouge* after a decade spent piloting boats in the Yukon. He compared coming back to the Red to reuniting with an old friend whose character he understood intimately. Cunningham knew exactly where the Red's currents ran strongest and how, if they combined with a strong offshore wind, his boat's five-hundred-tonne bulk would act like a sail and pull him off course. He understood how much the river could fluctuate with the seasons as it crossed the floodplain on which Winnipeg was built. The captain could calculate the precise angle and speed needed to approach each bridge, and knew exactly when to slow down where the water was shallower. He also knew the effect his boat could have on the debris that littered the riverbed. Once, years earlier, when he had turned the *River Rouge* around quickly at the confluence of the Assiniboine and the Red, a dead body had popped up in the water in front of him. He was pretty sure it was the sucking action of his two propellers that had pulled the corpse up from where it had been stuck on the muddy bottom.

In the early hours of August 17, Captain Cunningham had used those same powerful propellers in reverse to slow his boat down so he could swing it into position at the Alexander Docks. Hours later, as he watched the action on the river unfold from his boat deck, the secret his engines had inadvertently dislodged had already floated north in the current.

Among the onlookers and Sunday walkers who were watching the search for Faron Hall was Dwayne Oliver and his ten-year-old son. They had woken up early and parked near the Alexander Docks to visit the nearby Manitoba Museum. But discovering it wasn't yet open, they had headed to the riverbank to find a good place to fish later in the day. The pair had stood for a while staring out over the water, following the police boat and divers a few hundred metres away. As they began to walk north from the dock towards a point where long reeds and scrubby trees marked a bend in the river, they chatted about the person the divers were searching for. The boy found a discarded life preserver and picked it up, telling his father it could have been used to help. It was here, about four and a half metres from the shore, that Oliver saw something unusual half-submerged in the shallows. He told his son to hang back as he inched closer to what appeared to be the back of a human body slouched over on its knees and wrapped up in a tan-coloured blanket. His suspicion that he'd stumbled across something sinister was confirmed by the caustic smell of rotting flesh and a black cloud of flies.

Oliver and his son headed back to the dock, calling 911 as they ran. It was only a few minutes before they heard sirens and saw the flashing lights of a fire truck carrying a specialized rescue dinghy, which was quickly launched onto the river by a crew clad in wetsuits. The boat sped north to where the tourists pointed, closely followed by the police dive crews, who by now had abandoned their search for Faron Hall. The teams could easily spot the suspicious object: a large bundle, stained brown with river mud, that had become lodged in the long reeds. As they drew up alongside it, one crew member reached over and pulled the saturated mass towards them. It was a struggle to haul it on board, and only when it was safely secured could they see they were dealing with a human body. It was too small to be Faron Hall. The material the body was wrapped in had been knotted at the top, but a mottled, bruised-looking arm had worked its way out of the opening to hang exposed in the water. The recovery crews motored back towards the Alexander Docks, where police officers helped to bring the grim parcel ashore. At 1:50 P.M., faced with a potential crime, the officers alerted the head of the Winnipeg Police Homicide Unit, Sergeant John O'Donovan.

Across town, in the quiet residential neighbourhood of Charleswood, fifty-three-year-old O'Donovan had been enjoying a Sunday at home with his wife, Mary. The couple, originally from the west of Ireland, had just finished lunch, and O'Donovan was getting his two rescue greyhounds ready for a walk when his phone began to vibrate. As officers described their discovery to him, the detective was struck by the detail of the knots tied at the top of the bundle. This was no suicide or accidental drowning. Hastily apologizing to his wife, O'Donovan grabbed his jacket and headed out to his car, already mentally setting up the process of initiating a murder investigation.

During his thirty-minute drive to the Winnipeg Police headquarters, O'Donovan coordinated his investigation on speaker phone. First, he called the forensic supervisor to find out the sex, age, and condition of the body. Could she tell him how long it had been in the water? He phoned the street supervisor to ask about the exact location where the body had been found. Had any security cameras caught anything? Who might have seen something significant? And he spoke to the sergeant in charge of the district to find out what resources were available to seal off the area and interview possible witnesses. It was the height of the summer holidays, and his team was having difficulty finding enough officers to deploy to the scene. As O'Donovan reached Portage Avenue, in the city's downtown, he made a strategic stop at a Tim Hortons, figuring caffeine would help him concentrate after his heavy lunch. A few minutes later he parked his car behind Red River College and headed across the street into the 1960s purpose-built home of the Winnipeg Police Service, a vast concrete bunker known as the Public Safety Building.

Once at his desk, the detective began entering what he knew into a newly created computer file. He worked methodically, despite feeling pressure from the operation under way on the riverbank. O'Donovan enjoyed the work. The process of meticulously unravelling the tiniest details of a homicide still fascinated him, even after more than a decade investigating murders.

At the Alexander Docks, Constable Susan Roy-Hageman was the forensic supervisor O'Donovan had called for basic information. She had arrived not long after the rescue crew had secured the recovered bundle on the dock and covered it with a black tarpaulin. After years spent processing crime scenes and identifying bodies, Roy-Hageman knew her first task would be to remove the tarpaulin and take photographs. The bundle was holding too much water to handle easily, so she decided to make two small incisions into the fabric to drain some of it away. This was a gamble, as vital evidence could be lost as the water ran out. But she was confident that if she monitored the flow carefully, nothing significant would disappear. The next step was to take prints from the body's exposed fingers, which she emailed to her technicians to process. The result came back quickly: there was no match in the system. Realizing she could get nothing more on the dock, Roy-Hageman gave the order for the entire bundle to be placed in a zippered bag and moved to St-Boniface Hospital in Winnipeg's French-speaking district for a more thorough examination.

O'Donovan had already dispatched two investigators to the hospital's autopsy suite to take notes and send back photos. The forensic pathologist on duty that day was Dr. Dennis Rhee, who had only recently moved to Winnipeg from California, where he had completed his training and residency. Over the past decade Rhee had dealt with more than a hundred homicide victims, some of whom had been concealed in a similar way to the body now before him. The pathologist began his investigation by photographing the knots that held everything together at the top of the bundle, recording that there were two sets, each consisting of several simple knots tied on top of each other. As he removed the material around the body, he saw that it had been packed with several rocks, large and small, weighing 11.5 kilograms in total. Everything inside was coated with a layer of dark green river mud, so it was only after close inspection that Rhee was able to see that the material was double thickness. On one side it was embroidered with a leaf pattern, and he could see buttons and eyelets running along the bottom edge. The doctor recognized it as a duvet cover and handed it over to the police forensic team for further investigation.

Turning his attention to the body, Rhee saw that the victim was small, young, and female. He measured her height as 160 centimetres (5 feet 3 inches) and her weight as 33 kilograms (73 pounds) and concluded that he was probably looking at a very young teenager. She was wearing a short-sleeved T-shirt with the words "Born To Rock" printed across the front, a bra, a short skirt that looked like it had once been white, underwear, pink Adidas high-top sneakers, and short socks. From his experience, he noted the body's state of decomposition as "moderate." Because there was some bloating in her abdomen and limbs, the pathologist estimated that the girl had been in the water for more than a few days but not longer than a few weeks. His observation was confirmed by the marbled red-and-green hue of her skin, under which her blood vessels had broken down and become visible, like branches of a tree. On parts of her body her skin had sloughed off entirely and was lying detached in paper-thin sheets, another indication of a prolonged period of submersion.

Rhee tried to form a picture of what the girl had looked like. He could see that her hair was black and straight and of medium length, with the exception of the right side of her head, which was shaved very short. But he struggled to make out her facial features. The skin on her nose and cheeks had mostly slid away, and although the globes of her eyes were still present, they were unrecognizable in what had become a mask of red and pink. The pathologist knew it would be impossible to match the victim's face to a photograph. But he could see another way to identify her. She had a tattoo on her back, high up between her shoulder blades, that was still distinct despite the decomposition. It was a name, "Eugene Fontaine," and had two dates written beneath it: "01-03-1970 – 30-10-2011." On either side of the tattoo the pathologist could make out the delicately inked outline of angel wings.

In the autopsy room gallery, the police investigators emailed a picture of the tattoo to O'Donovan, who immediately contacted the city's Missing Persons Unit. In their files was the name of a fifteen-year-old schoolgirl, Tina Fontaine, who had run away from home in early July and had been listed as missing several times. She was described as being Aboriginal, five foot four (163 centimetres), and weighing one hundred pounds (45.4 kilograms). A recent photograph showed that her hair was black and shaved short on one side. The report also noted that she was the daughter of Eugene

Fontaine, who had been killed in 2011. At first, O'Donovan could not believe that the bloated body from the autopsy pictures belonged to the slim young girl in the missing persons photograph. But the tattoo was a definite confirmation of her identity.

O'Donovan needed to know if Rhee could identify any obvious injuries that had led to Tina's death. A full-body X-ray had already revealed that she had no broken bones. The pathologist had observed several shallow depressions on the skin of her face—on her right cheek and right forehead—and two more on her scalp. Some of the underlying nose cartilage was also missing, and he found more indentations on the back of her right thigh and the front of her left knee. But without conducting a full post-mortem, he could not say whether these marks were caused by injuries or decomposition. One thing was clear, though, O'Donovan thought as he read over Rhee's notes: Tina had not put herself in the river.

The detective's next task was to notify Tina's family and officially confirm her identity. After some deliberation, he asked his investigators to crop the autopsy photos so that only Tina's tattoo was visible. The pictures were some of the most distressing he had seen in his career, and he was loath to show them to Tina's family. His team felt the same. It was the first time many of them had seen the damage that warm, polluted river water could do to a body. It was especially difficult to see this happen to someone so young.

Later that Sunday evening, eight kilometres to the north of where Tina had been found, police divers finally recovered the remains of Faron Hall. They announced their discovery to the press, adding that they weren't treating his death as suspicious. The coincidence of finding two bodies in the river on the same day was already making headlines, and O'Donovan's boss, Danny Smyth, the superintendent of crime investigations, announced he would schedule a news conference for the following morning.

O'Donovan, who did not leave his desk until 10 P.M. that Sunday, was already back at work the following day when Smyth caught up with him. The detective had been in the office since 7 A.M., when he led the morning briefing to determine what was known about Tina's movements. Working with him was the team he had assembled: six pairs of detectives assigned to focus primarily on this case. After discussing their strategy to collect information, O'Donovan had just enough time to put on a jacket and make an attempt at straightening his tie before being brought out before the media to conduct his briefing.

At the front of the room, balanced on a wooden plinth the police press team had placed a poster of the most up-to-date picture of Tina they could find. It was a close-up portrait of the schoolgirl looking straight into the camera. She was wearing large gold hoop earrings, and her shoulders were tanned and bare apart from the flimsy straps of a summer top. Her black hair was short and swept across her forehead, showing clearly that it had been shaved on one side, and she was smiling. O'Donovan thought how young and fresh-faced she looked. She could easily have been mistaken for eleven or twelve rather than fifteen. As he placed his prepared list of case notes on the table and looked out over the packed room, the gulf between the image beside him and the autopsy photos provoked an unexpected wave of anger. The detective had been planning to present the facts calmly, point by point, but now he just wanted to speak.

"This is a child that's been murdered," he began, his Irish accent clearly detectable. "I think society would be horrified if we found a litter of kittens or pups in the river in this condition."

O'Donovan paused for a moment as the video cameras trained their lights on his face and the reporters digested what he was saying. A buzz had begun to ripple around the room. The Winnipeg press corps was used to announcements about dead Indigenous youth, especially after hot summer weekends when people had been out drinking and having fun on the river. But hearing a detective speak with such passion about an Indigenous victim was unusual. The journalists put up their hands to ask questions. Did O'Donovan know how Tina had died? The detective hesitated before answering. It was normal in investigations to keep those details quiet, he said, because revealing them could identify the person who had killed her.

"This is a child, so, I mean, society should be horrified," he continued. He sensed he was acting emotionally, but wanted to make his point again. Tina, he told his audience, had been tiny. He wanted to stress her vulnerability.

"She was barely in the city, for a little over a month," he said, his voice breaking slightly. "She's definitely been exploited, taken advantage of and murdered, and put into the river in this condition."

His colleagues, more used to O'Donovan's stoic leadership, absorbed his unusual display with quiet nods of support.

After the press conference, O'Donovan's administration clerk took him to one side to say she was proud of the way he had spoken up for the victim. There was, among his team and throughout the building, a collective revulsion at the thought of a child-killer lurking somewhere in their community.

More than two thousand kilometres to the east, in the town of Belleville, Ontario, Indigenous activist Nahanni Fontaine was enjoying a holiday visiting friends. She'd been sitting on their sofa, drinking coffee in her pyjamas, when the Winnipeg press conference came on TV. Fontaine, who had grown up on the same

Manitoba reserve as Tina and was distantly related to the teenager, watched O'Donovan speak with a heavy sense of resignation. The forty-three-year-old had spent years advocating for the family and friends of other Indigenous women who had gone missing or been found dead, and her first instinct was to grab her phone to start calling them. The girl in the river wasn't their relative, but they would still need help with processing the death. As the broadcast continued, however, Fontaine's sadness turned to astonishment. She had witnessed plenty of press conferences concerning the death of Indigenous women, but she had never seen anything like the one being given by O'Donovan. The typical explanation offered by authorities was that runaway girls like Tina were dying because they had chosen to follow a "high-risk lifestyle." But here was a police officer speaking about Tina with compassion and empathy, as if she were a true victim—as if she mattered. For once, somebody seemed to care.

Fontaine knew this wasn't always the case. She could cite numerous examples of official indifference to girls like Tina stretching back years. Most notorious was the case of the teenager found dead on frozen, snow-covered ground in 1971 on the outskirts of the remote Manitoban town of The Pas. Nineteen-year-old Helen Betty Osborne was originally from the Indigenous community of Norway House Cree Nation, but because her reserve didn't have a secondary school, she had moved to The Pas to continue her education. Her family said she had hoped to become a teacher. Late one night, while walking home, she was picked up by four young white men who had been cruising the streets looking for an "Indian girl" to have sex with. Osborne was forced into the men's car and driven to an isolated spot where she was sexually assaulted and stabbed more than fifty times with a screwdriver. She was so disfigured that police could identify her only by her fingerprints.

It took sixteen years before three of the men were charged with Osborne's murder, even though the identity of all four men was an open secret in The Pas. Only one of them was convicted.

In 1988, after a Winnipeg police constable shot dead the Indigenous leader J.J. Harper in a case of mistaken identity, the Aboriginal Justice Inquiry of Manitoba was established to investigate this and Osborne's killing. Commissioners spent a year visiting towns, cities, reserves, and jails to collect information on how the Indigenous community interacted with the police and judicial system. Its findings were stark. In the case of Helen Betty Osborne, it described a police culture defined by racism, sexism, and indifference, operating in a community where callous treatment of Indigenous people was the norm. The justice system as a whole, they concluded, had failed Manitoba's Indigenous population on a massive scale.

The commission's final report listed examples of how the white population of The Pas had ignored and belittled their Indigenous neighbours. There were rumours of white men throwing Indigenous men off a bridge into the Saskatchewan River, allegations that were never seriously investigated by the town's all-white police force. Officers were criticized for routinely stopping and interrogating young Indigenous men on the streets, and the report found that police had turned a blind eye when white men harassed Indigenous girls for sex. If the girls refused to cooperate, it was assumed that a bit of alcohol or violence would change their minds, and officers never thought to question whether the girls were being groomed or coerced into sexual activity. When they investigated Osborne's murder, some officers had threatened and intimidated her Indigenous friends though police had taken care to inform the parents of their white suspects of their rights.

"This discriminatory conduct was probably so inbred that the officers did not notice that their conduct displayed prejudice and discrimination," the report stated. It found that police behaviour reflected a hierarchy established by Canada's early settlers: white men at the top, Indigenous men beneath them, and Indigenous women at the very bottom. "It is intolerable that our society holds women, and Aboriginal women in particular, in a position of such low esteem," the report concluded.

Since Helen Betty Osborne's death, dozens more Indigenous women had been killed in Manitoba, some of them from Osborne's own family. In 2003, a cousin, sixteen-year-old Felicia Solomon Osborne, told her mother that she thought she had been followed by a car as she walked home from her Winnipeg high school. A few weeks later, she disappeared. Her mother immediately called the police, but she was told Felicia needed to be missing for twenty-four hours before a search could start. In fact, it was more than a week before the police interviewed her and almost two months before they issued a press release asking for help in finding Felicia. A month after that, the Winnipeg Police Service River Patrol was conducting routine maintenance at the Alexander Docks when they discovered a dismembered human thigh. A few days later, a man walking along the bank of the Red River found an arm. The police established that the body parts belonged to Felicia but learned nothing more about the fate of the teenager. Newspaper reports speculated that she had been killed because she was caught up with gangs and the sex trade. Her mother vehemently denied this, and Felicia's killing remained a mystery.

Five years later, another Osborne cousin, Claudette, also disappeared. The twenty-one-year-old was last seen in July 2008, heading to the low-budget Lincoln Motor Hotel, on one of Winnipeg's inner-city highways. Claudette, who had struggled with an alcohol and drug addiction, had given birth to her fourth child only weeks before. According to her sister, Bernadette Smith, Claudette tried to call relatives to say she was being hassled by a man she had just met, a long-distance truck driver from Calgary.

"She was still bleeding and this gentleman—I don't know if I'd call him a gentleman—this man was trying to have sex with her, and she was calling people at four in the morning asking for help," said Smith.

Claudette, frightened for her safety, left a phone message describing how the man was trying to push himself on her and pleaded for someone to come and get her. But the cell phone she was calling had run out of credit and her message did not immediately appear. It was days before the family heard her cry for help, and by then she was gone.

Smith reported her sister's disappearance to the police but felt it was a struggle to get them interested. She said it took them nearly a week to check the security cameras at the hotel, by which time any relevant footage had been recorded over. Detectives did track down the truck driver from Calgary, but they couldn't find any evidence to place Claudette in his vehicle. Smith said the police told her to let the matter go as he had a wife and kids and was embarrassed.

She responded with anger. "Our loved one is missing, and he's picking up women and he's got a family and a wife at home and children, and he's embarrassed? He should be embarrassed!"

To Smith, it seemed the police were treating the truck driver more like the victim. "I mean we're all human beings, but we really feel like because we're Indigenous people in Canada, we're not taken seriously. They just think that no one is waiting for us, that nobody cares about us, that we're disposable," she said.

Almost unbelievably, a fourth woman from Helen Betty Osborne's extended family was also killed. Hillary Wilson was eighteen when she went missing from her home in Winnipeg in August 2009. Her body was later found on a dirt path on the outskirts of the city.

A few weeks earlier, the body of one of her best friends had also been discovered, this time on nearby farmland. Raven Thundersky, whose own sister had been murdered and who was trying to raise awareness about violence against Indigenous women, spoke to the CBC after the girls were found. "I can't remember the last time— and I mean for Aboriginal women—when the last time was that we actually were able to see the face and have the name of one of the murderers responsible for taking one of our women," she said.

The Osborne women represented just a small segment of a much larger phenomenon happening throughout Canada. Nahanni Fontaine had counted more than 120 missing and murdered Indigenous women in Manitoba alone over the previous three decades. The Royal Canadian Mounted Police, which collated national figures on the problem for the first time in 2014, estimated that nearly 1,200 Indigenous women had been murdered or gone missing in Canada between 1980 and 2012.

The Native Women's Association of Canada had collected its own figures, which showed that the number of those murdered or missing nationally over the last forty years was closer to four thousand. Even taking the lower figure, the conclusions were chilling: Indigenous women made up only 4 percent of Canada's female population but were four times more likely to be murdered or go missing. In Manitoba, according to the RCMP figures, almost half of all women murdered were Indigenous.

The frustration for activists like Fontaine was in getting the wider population interested in a problem it didn't see as its own. In 2010 she had scored a victory when she was appointed the Manitoba government's special advisor on Aboriginal women's issues, the first such position in Canada. She was thankful for the official recognition but felt the support was not universal. At the core of the issue was the perception that the violence against women was confined within the Indigenous community. It was true that domestic violence and sexual assault were problems. This had been highlighted in Manitoba's 1988 Aboriginal Justice Inquiry, which found that one in three Indigenous women in the province had experienced abuse by their partners, a figure far higher than that for non-Indigenous women. But the more recent RCMP figures highlighted a different concern: whereas 74 percent of non-Indigenous women murdered between 1980 and 2012 were killed by a partner or close family member, for Indigenous women the figure was only 60 percent. Indigenous women were more likely to be killed outside the home by strangers or "casual acquaintances," a term often used to describe the sex worker and client relationship. When Indigenous women left their reserves and moved into cities, they were falling prey to random predators.

One of the most shocking illustrations of this trend was the Robert Pickton case in Vancouver. Pickton, a pig farmer, was known to have killed at least thirty-three women and bragged that he was one short of killing fifty. More than half of his victims were Indigenous. Pickton found his often drug addicted and sexually exploited victims in Vancouver's shabby Downtown Eastside. It was 1997 when police began to notice that an alarming number of women were disappearing, but it took another five years before they arrested Pickton, and only then because his farm was raided on an unrelated charge. The investigation had struggled because it fell between the jurisdiction of two police forces and because it took time to persuade senior officers that the women hadn't just drifted away. Pickton was ultimately convicted on six counts of second-degree murder.

Indigenous women had also been killed along what became known as the Highway of Tears. Between 1969 and 2006, there were eighteen recorded murders and disappearances along British Columbia's Highway 16, a remote road that stretches from Prince

Rupert, on the Pacific coast, through forests and logging towns to the city of Prince George. Locals said the number of missing was closer to fifty, and very few of the cases had been solved.

"We victim-blame," says Fontaine, describing how this violence was viewed in mainstream society, where she felt there was a misogynistic impression of what "Native women" were like. It was true that Indigenous women were more likely to live vulnerable lives dominated by drugs, alcohol, and sex work, but Fontaine saw nothing inevitable about it. To her, the real issues were abuse, poverty, and a lack of opportunities. But most of all, she felt women were suffering because of an intrinsic racism.

"Whereas Indigenous people understood Indigenous women and girls as life-givers, as sacred and equal, we saw that shift to 'They're whores, they're promiscuous, they're squaws,'" she says of their treatment by the early settlers in Canada. "*Squaw* is the Iroquois word for female genitalia. We have a swear word that starts with a *c* and ends with a *t*, and this is essentially what generations of Indigenous women and girls have been called."

Fontaine liked to tell the story of a civic project she commissioned, a mural showing the faces of murdered Indigenous women painted on a bridge over a highway in Winnipeg. The artist told Fontaine that while he was working, a young white man riding a bicycle had stopped to ask him what he was doing. When the artist told him, the man replied, "Oh, those fucking whores deserved what they got." It was unbelievable, Fontaine said, that he hadn't thought to blame the killers.

On the morning after Tina's body was found, as he assembled his team inside the Public Safety Building, O'Donovan was acutely aware of the political sensitivities surrounding the teenager's death.

The demand from the Indigenous community to do more to solve dozens of deaths and disappearances was something the city had already tried to address. In 2011, the Winnipeg Police Service had joined with the RCMP to form Project Devote, a special task force dedicated to investigating cold cases.

The task force's official objective was to reinvestigate long-standing unsolved cases of missing or murdered vulnerable people, regardless of the victim's race. The reality was that most of its twenty-eight cases involved Indigenous women, including all three of the unsolved Osborne murders. But although Devote had been running for a couple of years, it had made headway with just one case, and that was only after the main suspect confessed while in prison for another murder. Devote was located separately from the main Winnipeg Police headquarters, in an office crammed full of cold-case box files, a large map tacked on its wall pinned with the possible location of perpetrators. Detectives spoke of their struggle to track down witnesses and find evidence for crimes that had taken place so long ago. The victims' relatives, though grateful that the cases had been reopened, criticized the lack of results. Bernadette Smith had so little faith in Devote that she joined with friends to organize a private boat to drag the Red River for evidence in Claudette Osborne's disappearance. It was a small fishing boat that pulled single lines along behind it—barely effective, but at least she felt she was taking action.

But, by the summer of 2014, something seemed to be changing in Winnipeg. The anger and compassion for a dead Indigenous child that O'Donovan had so clearly articulated in his press conference was beginning to be felt across the city. Two days after Tina's body was found, Winnipeggers flocked to a rally in support of Indigenous peoples. More than a thousand gathered at the Alexander Docks to commemorate Tina Fontaine's and Faron Hall's lives. Indigenous men and women were joined by other Canadians who wanted to demonstrate their support. Office workers, students, and parents pushing children in strollers gathered together and walked down Main Street, holding up traffic behind them. Some carried placards on which they had written the names of other Indigenous women who had been murdered or gone missing and whose cases remained unsolved. It was only a few weeks after the unarmed black teenager Michael Brown had been shot dead by a white police officer in Ferguson, Missouri, an event that sparked a mass protest and the birth of the #BlackLivesMatter movement in the United States. The Winnipeg marchers spoke of wanting to ignite something similar that might fan out across all of Canada. Many called for the government to initiate a national inquiry into the violence.

On that warm summer evening, the marchers headed along Main Street towards the Forks, the spiritual heart of the city, at the confluence of the Red and Assiniboine Rivers. Only a few weeks earlier, on a grassy bank overlooking the water, Nahanni Fontaine had unveiled a monument to the missing and murdered. It was made from smooth white granite, its rounded contours echoing the shape of a woman's body. To Fontaine, it symbolized the Indigenous "female spirit, both beautiful and hard." Now the marchers converged around it, laying pouches of ceremonial tobacco at its base and settling down in the nearby Oodena Celebration Circle to listen to singing and drumming. Even as the sun went down and the sky turned a deep, inky blue they remained in place, lighting candles for the dead. Beside them in the dark, the waters of the Red River slid silently by.

A few blocks away, O'Donovan was still in the Public Safety Building. He regarded the vigil as an opportunity to gather intelligence and had assigned a surveillance team of plainclothes detectives to film those attending. A few years earlier, he had investigated a double homicide where the perpetrator had stood right at the front of a memorial held for the women he had murdered. The detective knew that killers liked to insert themselves into their dramas, and he suspected that the person who had murdered Tina could be at the Forks, acting in a telltale way. *I will find you*, he thought. Later he would review the footage, a task he would repeat many times in the coming months.

That night he headed home in time to catch up with Mary before bed. She noted that in all the years he had been a detective, her husband had never, until Tina, referred to a victim by her first name.

2.

"TELL MOMMA AND PAPA
I LOVE THEM"

On the Sunday that Tina Fontaine's body was found in the Red River, her great-aunt and official guardian, Thelma Favel, had been spending the afternoon at her house on the outskirts of Sagkeeng First Nation reserve. Outside, under a wide sky, the birch and aspen were turning yellow in the late summer sun. Thelma remained inside, too anxious to enjoy the good weather. Six weeks earlier, her baby, as she liked to call Tina, had gone missing after a trip to visit her biological mother in the city. Thelma had repeatedly tried to find the teenager, contacting the police and the provincial child welfare agency to register her as missing and in danger of exploitation. Now it was days since she had heard any news, and her concerns for her fifteen-year-old charge were mounting.

Thelma had Wi-Fi, something of a rarity in the neighbourhood, and her house was a popular hangout for her foster kids, young relatives, and their friends. Around mid-afternoon, her grand-niece alerted her to a post on Facebook written by a cousin in Winnipeg. It said that the body which had just been pulled out of the Red River had been identified as Tina. Thelma read it with a rising sense of panic. This was Facebook, she told herself, and you couldn't always believe what people wrote. When she went to bed that evening, she decided that as she had heard nothing from the police, she wasn't going to allow herself to think the worst. But the next day, two RCMP officers were standing at her door. Gently, they told her to brace for bad news. It was true that a body had been found, they said, and they could confirm it was Tina. As the first waves of grief flooded through her, Thelma felt like her heart was being ripped out of her body.

In the blur of days that followed, Thelma struggled to absorb the fact that Tina was never coming home. Sagkeeng First Nation had been Thelma's home for decades, and now her door was constantly swinging open as family and friends arrived to express sympathy and make sure she was looked after. Her home was officially "off-reserve," within the town line of neighbouring Powerview-Pine Falls, but she was still very much part of the Indigenous community and was grateful for its support. At the same time, she found herself fielding calls from journalists from across the country wanting to hear her reaction to the teenager's death. Tina's young and pretty face had sparked a national sense of out-rage and mourning, and Thelma was beginning to realize that her grief would never be only personal. "I don't understand why it had to take Tina's death to open everybody's eyes to the fact that there's a problem out there," she said with some bitterness.

Situated an hour and a half's drive north of Winnipeg, Sagkeeng was a world away from the city where Tina had died. Reaching there meant travelling north on Highway 59, past the city limits and into a landscape of flat fields and creek beds fringed by tall brown grasses. At the Brokenhead Ojibway Nation reserve, the highway passed the art deco façade of the South Beach Casino and continued on into forests of pine and birch, where billboards at the roadside advertised holiday resorts and warned drivers to be "bear smart." As the road neared the freshwater expanse of Lake Winnipeg, it cut right across low hills and to weave its way down to the southern bank of the Winnipeg River. Here, a dark wooden sign painted with white letters welcomed you to "Sagkeeng Territory, Signatory to Treaty 1."

Past the sign, the small, rundown homes of the reserve loomed into view. The buildings spread out in two straggly fingers along the north and south banks of the river, marking the point at which it emptied into the lake. The land was home to the Anishinaabe-Ojibway people, who had fished, hunted, and traded here for centuries. Treaty 1 was the name of the agreement that had established Sagkeeng back in 1871. It had been signed by the newly formed Canadian government and Indigenous leaders, the first of a series of treaties by which land was exchanged for money, goods, and what the Indigenous people hoped would be a prosperous life under colonial rule. The reserve was originally named Fort Alexander, after a nearby fur trading post. Later, its inhabitants chose to take the name "Sagkeeng" from the Ojibway word meaning "mouth of the river." By the time Tina was growing up here, the two names were still in use, with the older generation still referring to the settlement as Fort Alec.

Farther along the road the imposing structure of the Pine Falls hydroelectric dam dominated the landscape, serving as a bridge across the river. Nestled next to it was the small town of Powerview-Pine Falls, built in the 1920s to provide homes, a school, and a hospital for the workers at a large paper mill that had since shut down. The town's stucco-sided houses and tidy lawns fanned out in orderly roads named after trees—Holly, Poplar, Cherry, Birch—their neat geography in contrast to the sprawl of reserve housing. In the 1950s and 1960s, at the height of production, the mill employed Indigenous people from the reserve. But the town always maintained a separate identity. Indigenous children were banned from swimming in the communal pool, and families were forced to sit separately in the movie theatre and hospital waiting room.

In August 2014, when the news of Tina's death filtered through Sagkeeng, it provoked a deep sense of shock and grief, but not surprise. The reserve already held the dubious distinction of having the highest number of missing and murdered women and girls of any Indigenous community in Canada. Activists spoke of how poverty, a lack of jobs, and overcrowding were forcing women to leave to find work, separating them from their community and making them vulnerable. They pointed to the fact that one of the victims of the Vancouver killer Robert Pickton was originally from the reserve.

But it wasn't only when they left that Sagkeeng women faced danger. It was impossible to grow up on the reserve untouched by domestic violence, abuse, addiction, mental illness, or suicide. A hundred and fifty years ago, when Treaty 1 was signed, the hope was that the government would protect the Anishinaabe-Ojibway, enabling them to thrive. Instead, they had been subjected to decades of policies aimed at assimilating the "Indian" into a European and Christian way of life. Early colonial administrators believed that the Indigenous needed to be civilized, regarding them as ignorant, backward, and incapable of self-governance, an attitude that lingered well into the twentieth century. The central pillar of these policies was the establishment of the residential school system. Its purpose was to educate, but its legacy amounted to a cultural genocide that shattered communities, tore families apart, and frustrated the ability of generations of parents to raise their own children.

Sagkeeng had been home to the Fort Alexander Residential School, run by nuns from the Catholic order of the Oblates of Mary Immaculate. The school was an imposing white four-storey building that had towered above the grassland on the south bank of the Winnipeg River. When it opened in 1905, it had been welcomed by the community. But instead of nurturing the children, the nuns regarded them as savages. Students were treated harshly, forbidden from speaking their own language, isolated from their families, starved, and often sexually abused. For a long time the treatment meted out in residential schools was hidden from public view. But in 1990, Phil Fontaine, a distant relation of Tina's and head of the Assembly of Manitoba Chiefs, shocked Canada when he spoke out publicly about the abuse he had endured at Fort Alexander. His testimony spurred thousands of other residential school survivors to lodge what became the largest class action lawsuit in Canadian history, leading to a settlement agreement that included the creation of a Truth and Reconciliation Commission. Officials spent six years travelling across the country hearing testimony from 150,000 former students who had been taken from their families and forced to spend much of their childhood locked away. By the time Tina's body was found, in the summer of 2014, the commission was in its final stages. The following year it would publish a report detailing ninety-four recommendations, one of which was the establishment of a national inquiry into why so many Indigenous women and girls, many of whom had spent time in residential schools, were being killed.

———

Thelma Favel had always counted herself lucky not to have been one of the Sagkeeng children forced to attend Fort Alexander. Born in 1958, the seventh of nine siblings in an Ojibway family, she was too young to attend the school, which was closing down by the time she started lessons. But she had first-hand knowledge of the damage it could do. Both her parents had struggled through the residential system, and she watched her older brother George attend Fort Alexander as a day student. She remembered how George would row across the river to school each morning. He had gone there with a distant relative, Doug Fontaine, who used to tell stories about how the nuns would try to rub their breasts up against him and how he would wet the bed at night to protect himself from being molested.

By contrast, Thelma's early schooling at the newly built junior high school on the reserve had been easy and enjoyable. But that changed when she was sent to high school in Powerview-Pine Falls, where the children teased her for a medical condition that gave her seizures. Thelma's mother, who was raising her children alone after the death of her husband, solved the problem by sending Thelma to Winnipeg to lodge with another son and his family. Thelma was fourteen when she moved, in an arrangement supervised by the provincial government's child welfare body, then known as the Children's Aid Society. It was the beginning of a life-long professional and personal association for Thelma with the agency, which would later become known as Child and Family Services, or CFS. This close connection wasn't unusual in Manitoba, where CFS played a prominent role in the lives of Indigenous people. Despite a population of only one million, the province had the highest number of children in care in Canada, and the vast majority of these were Indigenous. Over the years, Thelma's view of the organization would darken, becoming bitter and angry when CFS failed to protect Tina. But in the early days, she was grateful that they had facilitated her move into what would become a happy home environment.

Winnipeg was a new adventure. Thelma settled into the inner-city North End, where she found a strong sense of community in the working-class neighbourhood of wooden houses and tree-lined streets. After a brief interlude away to complete a nursing qualification, she was offered a job in a home for abused girls, many of whom were Indigenous. She had become friends with the boy living across the street, Joseph Favel, who was a couple of years older than her. Unlike Thelma, Joseph was not a "status Indian," a person legally recognized as an Indian by the Canadian government. He was Métis, descended from the children of European settlers and Indigenous women. After a few years of getting to know each other, Joe proposed, and in 1978, when Thelma was twenty, the couple were married.

A year before their wedding, Thelma's life had changed dramatically when her sister asked her to help raise her eight children. It marked the start of Thelma's long career as a professional foster mother and the beginning of a relationship that would bring Tina Fontaine into her life. One of the children she cared for was her nephew Eugene Fontaine, or Geno, who would later become Tina's father. Thelma remembered him as a bright, funny child who would always say "I know" when asked a question, even if he didn't have a clue what was going on. He joined a household full of other foster children and, by now, Thelma's own two daughters and adopted son. Joe, a truck driver, was often away, so Thelma was left alone in a small apartment surrounded by children. "It was hectic," she said. Some of her foster children had children of their own, leaving her with several babies to look after while they were at work. But she also remembered it as being fun.

In the 1990s, after two decades living in the North End, Thelma and Joe began to notice that the neighbourhood was changing. It was busier now. The area's cheap housing was popular with new Asian and African immigrants as well as young Indigenous people who were moving into the city to look for work. The bonds of community that Thelma had cherished were breaking down and the crime rate was increasing. The streets were becoming the drug, sex work, and gang hangouts that Tina would experience twenty years later, when she went missing. The breaking point for Thelma was when her children were robbed at a local store three weeks in a row. She told her husband that if the children couldn't go shopping without her having to worry, it was time to leave.

It was a few years after this that Tina arrived in her life. Thelma and her family had returned to Sagkeeng, but her nephew Eugene, now in his twenties, had remained in Winnipeg, pursuing what Thelma called the "party lifestyle." She knew he drank too much, had an addiction to prescription drugs, and had drifted away from his family. When he was twenty-three, Eugene formed a relationship with a twelve-year-old girl from the Cree community named Valentina Duck, who was living in foster homes and who was known to have been sexually exploited from a young age. Valentina was fourteen when she became pregnant with their first child, a boy, who was quickly taken into care. The couple remained together and, on January 1, 1999, when Valentina was seventeen, she gave birth to Tina Michelle. A year later she had another daughter, Sarah. Thelma remembered vividly meeting Tina as a baby at a family event and noting how sweet and well-behaved she was. But her parents' relationship was unstable. Eugene's addiction worsened and his behaviour towards Valentina was violent and unpredictable. In

2001, the couple split. After spending some time with Child and Family Services, Tina and Sarah were returned to their father's care. Eugene was still drinking heavily and, in 2004, he discovered he had cancer of the lymph nodes. He didn't think he could manage alone, so he asked Thelma if she would consider raising his daughters.

At first Thelma was hesitant. She was older now and had decided to foster only teenagers, because she no longer had the energy for young children. But Eugene persisted, telling her that he probably didn't have much longer to live. Both he and Thelma hated the idea of his girls being raised in the child welfare system. Thelma was developing an ambivalent attitude towards Child and Family Services. On the one hand, they had provided her with a job and income as a foster mother. On the other, she found them too eager to put Indigenous children into care. The agency seemed to prefer to do this, often taking children when they were babies rather than providing long-term support for families. Thelma suspected they relied on these placements to secure their funding, and she regarded their attitude as a continuation of the colonial belief that Indigenous families couldn't take care of their own children. But she knew the problems weren't one-sided. She told her husband, "There's a lot of foster homes out there that are only doing it for the money and not really caring." In the end, it was Joe who made the decision to take in the girls, telling Thelma they needed a proper home and that the months they had already spent with CFS were enough. When Tina was five and Sarah four, Thelma became their guardian through a private family arrangement.

It had been a while since Thelma had looked after young children, and at first, she struggled. They had been sent to her with just the clothes they were wearing, but the Sagkeeng community rallied round, bringing over bags of children's clothes, pyjamas, and toys.

On the first night, at bath time, Thelma wasn't sure if she should stay in the room with the girls, but they called out to her to wash their hair. Afterwards, she sat on the side of the tub and splashed cold water on them, laughing at how much they loved it. Although Tina was the older of the two, she was smaller than her sister. But Thelma could see she was confident and strong. Her father had nicknamed her Monkey and her sister Chubby. Monkey was a curious child who was not afraid to ask questions, grilling Thelma and Joe early on as to why her father referred to them as Momma and Papa as well as Aunt and Uncle. She quickly developed a special bond with Joe, teasing him and making him laugh. It wasn't long before Monkey and Chubby were calling the couple Momma and Papa themselves.

Thelma, a devout Catholic, had the girls baptized at the St. Alexander Roman Catholic Church in Sagkeeng First Nation. She had fond memories of how she and Joe would sit with Tina and Sarah on their laps and ask them, "How come Momma and Papa love you so much?" to which Tina would reply, "Because we have Jesus in our hearts." The girls were enrolled in nursery school, and from there grade school and Sagkeeng Junior High. Tina was interested in her Ojibway heritage, and Thelma tried to teach her a few words. But her own knowledge was rusty, so they would usually end up speaking English. Thelma was more successful in showing Tina how to cook, and she remembered how the schoolgirl would bake blueberry muffins to share at family gatherings.

As Tina grew older, it was clear she had a love for small children, especially babies. In the summer, when Thelma and Joe would gather their relatives together on a beach by Lake Winnipeg, Tina would splash in the water with her younger cousins. Whenever Thelma's great-grandson was brought to the house, Tina would immediately scoop the baby up into her arms. She held him so much that he became known as her baby, and whenever Thelma couldn't find him, she knew he would be in Tina's room. Tina confided in Thelma that she wanted to work looking after children, possibly for CFS, as Thelma had done. A few years later, when Tina was a teenager, she and Thelma would sit on the sofa and watch the nightly TV news reports on the Phoenix Sinclair Inquiry. Phoenix was a five-year-old Indigenous girl who had been kept in a basement, starved, and finally beaten to death by her mother and her partner. "I want to check on every one of those kids," Tina had cried when she heard the details of the abuse.

If there was one issue that could still cause Tina and Sarah pain, it was that they didn't see enough of their father. The girls understood he was gravely ill and couldn't live with them, but they missed him deeply. He had tried to keep their relationship going, visiting Thelma's home on Sundays to eat supper with his daughters. He brought them presents for Christmas and birthdays and spoiled them with their favourite candy and treats when he cashed his monthly welfare cheques.

But in 2011, this family routine ended abruptly. On October 31, when Tina was twelve, Thelma was at home when her sister called to say she was with the police. She said officers had found Eugene's body on the reserve. Thelma immediately jumped in her car and drove to her sister's location: the old road that ran along the south side of the river. "That's Geno," her sister had shouted when Thelma arrived, pointing towards a shed at the back of a property which had been cordoned off with yellow crime scene tape. Thelma could make out the shape of Eugene's body lying on the ground outside. She later found out that her nephew had been on a three-day drug and alcohol binge with two friends and had fallen into an argument with them. The friends had ganged up on Eugene, kicking him in the head, and tying him up behind a shed where he died from his injuries. He was forty-one. Thelma had known his illness would take him early, but she wasn't expecting to lose him so violently and so soon.

She collected Joe to make the short journey to Sagkeeng Junior High and wait for Tina and Sarah to be taken out of class. Finding the words to tell the girls was an impossible task. All Thelma could manage was, "Your dad's not going to come around anymore." Sarah asked why, and Thelma carefully explained that some men had beaten him up and killed him. At first the girls screamed. Joe held tight to Tina and Thelma hugged Sarah. Then Tina became quiet before asking why anyone would do that to her father. Thelma could find no answer. She tried telling the girls that Eugene wouldn't suffer anymore and that he was at peace, but that only made Tina ask, "How can he be at peace if I'm not with him?" Hearing the girls' screams, the school counsellor, Cindy Guimond, had come into the room to see if she could help. She found the two girls hanging on to Joe and Thelma, looking pitifully small and vulnerable, their faces still covered in the green paint they had put on that morning to dress as witches for the school Halloween party.

In the weeks that followed, Thelma was proud of the way the girls held themselves together as she planned Eugene's wake and funeral. The proceedings were a mixture of Christian and community traditions. An Indigenous elder lit a sacred fire in her garden before Eugene's body arrived to lie in her house for four days prior to the funeral. As friends and family members filtered in to pay their respects, Tina and Sarah busied themselves serving drinks and sandwiches. After the funeral, they helped make up a plate of food for their father so they could share a last meal, burning it on the fire according to the Ojibway tradition.

Though the girls appeared strong, Thelma could see they had been changed by the tragedy. On the brink of adolescence, Tina had already begun to distance herself from family life. Sometimes, when the reality of losing her father sank in, she would break down and cry. Other times, she withdrew into her own world. In Winnipeg the Crown was preparing its case against the men who had killed Eugene, and Thelma learned that, in their defence, they wanted to speak about the abuse their parents had suffered at residential school. This provoked an explosion of anger. "You can't keep putting the blame on everything," she complained to Joe. "Sometimes you have to take the blame yourself and learn to try to change yourself." She knew plenty of people who'd been to residential school, including her own parents, who had not gone on to be violent or commit murder.

Tina wanted to attend the preliminary hearing, but the lawyers advised that the details were too graphic for a child to hear. Instead, she was asked to write a victim impact statement for the court. She struggled to find the words to express her grief. "How can I tell the judge what those guys did to us?" she asked Thelma, and crumpled up the paper she was supposed to be writing on. Thelma told Tina that she would write the statement instead.

Tina was also struggling with anger, and for her the pain was directed inwards. Despite repeated calls to victim services, the teenager received no counselling for her grief. She had always been reserved at school, and the strain of her father's murder was beginning to affect her studies. Cindy Guimond remembered how Tina already stood out because of her protective relationship towards her little sister. Now the schoolgirl's reputation was becoming fiercer. She lined her eyes with black makeup and projected a tough girl image. "If she acknowledged you," said Guimond, "you felt like you were one of the lucky ones." Guimond remembered a time when she was called in to mediate between Tina and a group of girls who Tina thought were picking on Sarah. She had been impressed by the way Tina was willing to work through the problem and reconcile her differences, but this wasn't the last of the arguments. Tina complained to Thelma that kids were saying they were glad her dad had been murdered. She was sent home from school for fighting, and Thelma felt the teachers were ignoring her side of the story. Tina was also being kept back in classes, even though she was clearly an intelligent child. After a few months of strained relations, Thelma decided the best thing to do was take both girls out of the reserve and put them into the mixed environment of the high school at Powerview-Pine Falls.

It was a decision that quickly paid off. Tina flourished in class, excelling in math and science. Thelma noted how, in her new school, Tina amassed a group of friends who were themselves outcasts who had been bullied. It was as if she wanted to extend her natural protection of her sister to everyone in need. But the sadness that followed her father's murder remained, manifesting itself in bouts of crying and isolation. Tina was no longer the happy girl who would skip down the hall and bake muffins for her family. Her moods remained dark. Sometimes her aunt, Thelma's daughter Laurie, would take her on a drive to talk about her problems, and Tina would open up and cry about her father. It was still possible to cheer her up by giving her a baby or a small child to look after, but she was never quite the same joyful girl that Thelma had come to know.

On New Year's Day 2014, Tina turned fifteen. She was increasingly asserting her independence but was physically small and could easily be mistaken for an eleven- or twelve-year-old. For her birthday, she had asked for two special presents. The first she gave to herself. It was a tattoo of her father's name, his birth and death dates, and angel wings inked on her back between her shoulder blades, a tribute that would become crucial in confirming her identity later that year. The second present was something she requested from Thelma. She asked to be allowed to go to Winnipeg to reconnect with her biological mother.

Valentina Duck had not seen Tina or Sarah since Eugene had taken them to live with Thelma. But she had reappeared in their lives after Eugene's funeral when she phoned Thelma's house to speak with her daughters, having managed to prise the number from the funeral directors. This had annoyed Thelma, who would have preferred to be the one in control of reintroducing Valentina to the girls. But Tina had welcomed the call and the two spoke regularly. Even though she was settled with Thelma and Joe, Tina desperately missed having a relationship with her biological mother. While at school on the reserve, she had told her counsellor that her feelings for her mother were confused, alternating between anger and love. She didn't understand why her mother had given her up, but she also wanted to be part of her life.

Valentina's call came at a sensitive point. Tina was grieving her father's death and at the same time was beginning to experiment with life beyond the sheltered confines of the reserve. The teenager was pushing back against authority, both at home and at school. In the fall of 2013 she ran away for the first time, finding her way to Valentina's house in Winnipeg. Back in Sagkeeng, Tina struggled with the discipline expected from Thelma and Joe. The couple had always run an orderly household, with strict rules about finishing homework and chores before being allowed out. They had also banned alcohol. There had been a time when they drank socially, but they'd quit after Thelma suffered a stroke at the age of forty and was confined for months to a wheelchair. Tina rebelled by smoking marijuana and was suspended from school. "I just wanted to try it," she protested when Thelma grounded her and confiscated her iPod in punishment. Thelma could see that the teenager was making new friends online. She had posted sexually provocative selfies on her Facebook page and was chatting to adult men in Winnipeg she'd never met. Tina's moods remained dark, and during one family argument she slashed into her forearms with a pen. She was desperate to spend time in the city and begged Thelma to let her go for her fifteenth birthday in January. She explained that it wasn't just that she wanted a taste of city life: Valentina had told Tina that she had younger half-sisters. Tina, whose love of small children had not diminished, was thrilled at the prospect of meeting them.

Thelma hated the idea of Tina and Sarah staying with Valentina but didn't think it fair to say no. But before giving permission, she sought to reassure herself that the girls would be safe. For the first time since Tina had come into her life, Thelma called Valentina directly. She asked about her circumstances and whether she had a social worker she could check in with. Valentina was open in her responses, replying that she was in the process of getting her other children back from foster care and giving Thelma the name of her CFS case worker. Thelma said she called the case worker, who told her she was confident that Valentina was sober and no longer funding her drug habit by selling sex on the streets. And so Thelma agreed to let the girls go. Later, CFS staff said they had no record of this interaction.

By all accounts, it was a successful visit. The weekend coincided with one of Valentina's younger children's birthday, and Tina and Sarah helped organize a party with balloons and a cake. Tina's Aunt Laurie picked the girls up, noting that Valentina was living with an older man in a well-maintained house in the North End. When they returned home, Thelma observed how excitedly they spoke about their new little sisters, hardly mentioning Valentina at all.

But the visit stirred a restlessness in Tina. On the morning of March 2, Thelma went into Tina's bedroom to hurry her up for school only to discover the teenager was missing. The previous day had been her father's birthday. Thelma immediately called the police, then Valentina, and was relieved to find out that Tina was safe at her house. When the police brought the teenager home, Thelma wanted to know how she'd managed to reach Winnipeg on her own, but Tina just shrugged off the question. In April, she went missing again. This time she was brought home by a friend, Larry Dumas, a deaf young Indigenous man she had met in Winnipeg. Thelma was reassured by Larry's demeanour, finding him polite and well-mannered. Again, she asked Tina to explain why she had run. Tina promised to talk about it, but somehow she avoided the confrontation.

When Tina went missing in April, Thelma had contacted Child and Family Services to ask them to take the teenager into care because she was having difficulty managing her behaviour. In May, a social worker met Tina and arranged counselling. However, the sessions were booked at a location seventy-five kilometres away, and Tina was unable to attend. Instead she asked Thelma to allow her to spend more time with her biological mother and half-sisters. Thelma disliked the idea, but fearing the teenager would take off again, she struck a deal. Tina would be allowed to visit Valentina for one week in the summer holidays if her grades were good enough. Even though school records showed the teenager was absent from classes that summer, Thelma believed that Tina had done well in her exams so kept to her side of the bargain. On June 30, Thelma's daughter Samantha and son Brian volunteered to drive Tina and her sister down to Winnipeg. When the day arrived, as the girls were walking out the door, Sarah suddenly changed her mind saying she didn't feel comfortable with Valentina. So Thelma loaded just Tina's bag into the back of the car and hugged her tight before waving goodbye. She could not have known it would be the last time she would ever see her.

As a precaution, Thelma had given Tina sixty dollars and a pre-paid phone card, telling her that if things didn't work out she was to call anytime and she would pick her up. In a decision she would later regret deeply, Thelma chose not to ring Valentina's social worker again, assuming she was still doing well. If she had, she would have discovered that Valentina's life had begun to spiral downwards and she had lost custody of her younger children. Brian and Samantha had an inkling of this when they reached Valentina's house and found it locked up. But Tina insisted everything was fine and asked them to drop her off at Valentina's sister's, where she said she would be safe.

A week passed and Thelma heard nothing from Tina. She tried phoning the number at Valentina's house but discovered the line had been disconnected. Finally, she and Joe drove down to Winnipeg, only to find Valentina's house deserted. Thelma was terrified that Valentina had abducted Tina and would try to keep her, so she called the regional CFS office to say she had lost control of the schoolgirl. The worker noted her concern and was able to locate Valentina and assure Thelma that she didn't have Tina. Thelma then contacted her local RCMP station to report Tina missing. She was in the process of pleading with CFS to arrange counselling for when Tina returned when Sarah showed her a Facebook message Tina had sent. It was a selfie of Tina with a black eye and scratched face. Underneath the photo, the message read, "Chubs—look what our MOM did to me."

Thelma later heard that Valentina had got Tina drunk, beaten her, and thrown her out, though Valentina always denied abusing her daughter. Tina was now on her own in the city, and Thelma was extremely worried. The police put out a missing persons alert on TV for the teenager, but it was only shown once, and Thelma felt it would have little impact. Meanwhile, Sarah had come to her with another message from Tina, which read, "Tell Momma and Papa I love them but I'm not ready to come home." It prompted Thelma and Joe to drive to Winnipeg again to search the malls and shopping areas where they thought the teenager might be. They believed Tina was in danger of sexual exploitation and were desperate for more help from CFS. But when Thelma called the agency, she faced confusion over which branch was looking after Tina. She felt as if she was going around in circles. Finally, she was told that CFS in Winnipeg had taken on Tina's case.

In the seven weeks between June 30 and August 17, when her body was found, Tina was registered as "missing" five times by the authorities. The last time was on August 9, when police reported that Tina had disappeared from the city centre hotel where she'd been placed by CFS. Thelma said she was not informed of this development and it wasn't until she called the agency on August 15 that she was told Tina had been officially missing for a week. It was three days later that RCMP officers arrived at her door to inform her that Tina's body had been found in the Red River.

In the first intense days of grief, Thelma found herself asking the same question over and over. How could it be that no one was able to keep her precious teenager from being "thrown away like garbage" into the polluted waters of the Red?

As Tina's death became the focus of intense media scrutiny, Thelma struggled to recognize the schoolgirl portrayed on television and in the newspapers. The Tina who was reported to have been living on the streets and taking drugs was very different from the girl who, only a few months before, had hung on to her arm when they were out shopping and forced her to cross the street if they saw anyone drunk or behaving strangely. The photograph Sergeant John O'Donovan had shown of Tina, with her hair shaved short on one side, broke Thelma's heart. "It was her pride and joy," she cried, describing how Tina's hair used to reach all the way down her back. Thelma had loved to brush it for her. Tina's grandfather, a medicine man, used to say that Indigenous girls got their strength from their hair. It made them who they were, and if they kept it long, they would always be special. Thelma wondered if, when alone in Winnipeg, Tina had stopped feeling special.

As the city mourned Tina's death, Thelma refused to join the crowds who gathered at the Alexander Docks. "I'm not going to worship where she was killed and where she was found," she said. Instead, at the end of August, she and Joe arranged for Tina's funeral to be held at St. Alexander Roman Catholic Church in Sagkeeng, the same place where the teenager had been baptized. As they had done with Eugene, they first kept Tina's body at home for four days while friends and family paid their respects. When it came time for the service, Tina's cousins carried her coffin, each wearing her picture printed on feathers made of purple felt, her favourite colour. Some family members cut off locks of their hair and placed them on her casket so she would still have strength in heaven. As with her father, Thelma hosted a feast, burning a plate of food for the teenager on a sacred fire.

Later, when Thelma received Tina's ashes, she kept them close to her at home for a week. Then, on a bright day in September, chosen because it was the birthday of her great-grandson, the baby Tina had looked after as her own, Thelma buried the schoolgirl in the same plot as her father. As Tina was laid to rest in St. Alexander graveyard, on the banks of the Winnipeg River, Thelma felt a sharp wind blowing across the water, signalling the end of summer. High

above her, in the cloud-streaked sky, long lines of geese were preparing to migrate south for the winter. *All seasons change*, she
thought as she watched the birds fade to a smudge on the horizon.
She comforted herself with the thought that perhaps God had sent
Tina for a reason and that she was only meant to stay for the brief-
est of times.

3.

O'DONOVAN

For Sergeant John O'Donovan, the blue sky days of winter were the worst. Driving through Winnipeg's suburbs in sub-zero temperatures, he would sometimes see sun dogs on the horizon, the strange illusion of lights hanging next to the sun caused by light bouncing off ice in the atmosphere. When the wind stirred the snow into clouds of white powder, he would think back to his childhood in Ireland. It had been months since he'd last seen grass and it would be months before he'd see it again, so he'd comfort himself with memories of green hills rolling into the distance and the smell of dark, peaty earth. On those days, he would wonder why he had chosen Winnipeg and the frozen prairies as his home. But the thought never lingered. There was always too much work to do, or too little time to spend with his children, who loved to be out in the numbing air, dragging him skating or tobogganing.

As a child, O'Donovan had planned neither to emigrate nor to become a policeman. He was born in 1961, the middle son of a carpenter and housewife living a modest life in a terrace house tucked away in the cobbled streets of Cork. School and lessons bored him, but he found his passion in horses, thrilled by the power of a gallop with the wind in his face and clods of earth churning up beneath him. As a skinny teenager, he had been dedicated to competing in point-to-point races and had collected a shelf full of trophies to show for it. His formal education ended at seventeen, when he left school to become an office clerk. When he was nineteen, his mother asked him to drive an old school friend and her family on a day's excursion as a favour. O'Donovan had been happy to oblige, ferrying them on a two-hour trip up the coast. The eldest daughter, Mary, had sat next to him in the front, and somewhere along the way, amid the chatter and the laughter, he had fallen in love. Within two years, they were married and living in a tiny house in the town of Ballincollig, on the outskirts of Cork.

For a while, they were settled. O'Donovan continued to travel to the city to work while Mary stayed at home to care for their growing family. But by the mid-1980s the Irish economy was in free fall, with political uncertainty and high unemployment. When O'Donovan's job came under threat, the couple considered the possibility of leaving. At first they thought of Australia, but Mary felt its reputation for beach life was too glamorous for the serious task of raising children. New Zealand was more attractive, but the distance seemed daunting. In the end, Mary declared Canada the best option. It seemed more like home, and, more importantly, O'Donovan's mother knew someone who knew someone in Toronto who might give him a job. The couple sent their applications to the Canadian embassy in Dublin and waited for news. Knowing Canada was bilingual, they bought a French dictionary to practise a few phrases for the interview. "We were young and we didn't have a clue," said Mary.

O'Donovan was twenty-eight when, in 1989, he left Ireland. His father and brothers accompanied him to Shannon Airport to say goodbye, none of them knowing when they would see him again. Mary and their three sons followed six weeks later. The couple had sent their belongings ahead by ship and carried with them the $13,000 they had raised by selling their house. O'Donovan's mother's friend had come through with a job in Toronto and advised them to rent a cheap townhouse in the commuter city of Burlington, at the western end of Lake Ontario. It was a distribution and sales job, which meant O'Donovan was away for days at a time. When his family arrived, they spent just two nights together before he was back on the road. Mary was so terrified at being left alone that she wedged their sofa against the patio doors for safety.

After a few months, O'Donovan found a new position selling suits in a men's clothing store. The income was decent and there was no more travel, but the job was dull and he was keen to find something more challenging. Most of all, he wanted to buy a home for his family. He could see that, even with overtime, a house in Burlington was out of his reach. As the family prepared to celebrate their first Canadian Christmas, he heard a friend mention that property in Winnipeg was cheap. O'Donovan had never heard of the city, but the idea took root and by January he was spending his evenings researching in the library.

O'Donovan had been looking for a reason to choose Winnipeg, and in its history he found a story that inspired him. The prairie city had always been a frontier, a magnet for the adventurous, ambitious, and hard-working. The early immigrants had come from his own country, as well as France and Scotland, working in the fur trade under the control of the Hudson's Bay Company. Intermarriage with Indigenous women had given birth to the Métis people and a leader, Louis Riel, who fought for self-determination before Winnipeg became part of the new Dominion of Canada. O'Donovan was drawn to the story of rebellion, finding in it a parallel with Ireland's struggle against the British. Modern Winnipeg appealed for its mosaic of nationalities attracted by the railway and the promise of land. In the early twentieth century, the city had grown so quickly that it was known as the Chicago of the North. Immigrants from Poland, Ukraine, Germany, Sweden, Hungary, and Iceland had flooded in. They were joined by Jews from Eastern Europe and German-speaking Russian Mennonites fleeing persecution. Decades later, Winnipeg was becoming home to immigrants from Africa, Asia, and the Middle East. All embraced the chance to start over, just as O'Donovan was considering now. Although the odds of easy prosperity had diminished as the city cycled through periods of boom and bust, it still had a need for new people.

That summer, John and Mary packed up their belongings and took a three-day road trip with the boys through the American Midwest before heading north towards Winnipeg. O'Donovan had never experienced anywhere as empty as the great North American prairies. As he drove, he found himself looking out for grain elevators, anything to break up the monotony of farmland lying low against the massive dome of sky. A few hours out from the town of Marquette, in northern Michigan, on a long stretch of arrow-straight road, a wolf jumped out in front of the car and ran ahead of them for a hundred metres before casually hopping away over a fence. The ease with which the animal moved through its surroundings unnerved him. The countryside in Ireland had been a cozy patchwork of village, wood, hill, and pasture, where people and nature had coexisted for an eternity. Here, the low-level towns and strip malls felt like tiny afterthoughts dropped into an endless expanse of flatness. He wondered how he would ever fit into this unfamiliar landscape.

In Winnipeg, the family drove straight to Charleswood, the neighbourhood O'Donovan had chosen as a safe place to raise children. The family rented a small home, and O'Donovan found a job selling suits in a local mall. They struck up friendships at the neighbourhood pool and noted how open and unpretentious Winnipeggers seemed. A few weeks after arriving, Mary declared it was time they ventured downtown to get a feel for their new city. They drove in past the elegant edifice of Union Station and the enormous French-château-like façade of the Fort Garry Hotel towards the intersection of Portage and Main. O'Donovan had read that this was the famous crossroads at the heart of Canada, the meeting point of roads from north, south, east, and west, notorious for being the coldest and windiest corner of the country. But the Irishman found it an underwhelming mix of concrete and traffic. The couple looked for shops and cafés but were disappointed to find only sterile-looking bank buildings and soulless office blocks. The city centre seemed past its best, worn down and broken by the passage of time. Mary noticed men panhandling on street corners and drunks arguing at bus stops. It was nothing like the cheerful downtown shopping she'd known in Toronto and Cork.

By late October, O'Donovan was discovering why his new city was nicknamed Winterpeg. His first prairie winter squeezed the air from his lungs, and he marvelled at how it was possible to live in a place that could get colder than the North Pole. He loved that Winnipeggers embraced the weather, walking and skating to work on ice trails carved into the Red and Assiniboine Rivers. But he hated how the wind sliced his face and the freezing temperatures dragged on for months. In Ireland, if there was any snow at all, it was wet and mushy and melted quickly on the ground. Here it was fine and dry, like powdered sugar, reflecting the brightness of the strong prairie sun. As winter progressed, the snow was shovelled into huge banks stained with salt and sand that would flank every road. When spring approached, these would melt and freeze over, glazing the sidewalks with a hazardous sheen of ice. When the piles finally disappeared, they would release a gritty film of dust that settled everywhere, turning the city a dull shade of grey.

In March 1991, after Mary had given birth to a daughter, the O'Donovans bought the house they were renting. The demands of a mortgage and the needs of four children were becoming a struggle. Mary was making a small income as a child minder, and at Christmas John had earned a little extra by hanging festive lights at the mall. But he needed something more reliable. Out of the blue, he told his wife about an advertisement he'd seen for new recruits for the Winnipeg Police Service. She was surprised. Their family was more familiar with having relatives in the outlawed Irish Republican Army than in the security forces, and Mary worried that John's lack of a college education might hold him back. But O'Donovan was determined, believing his ability to work hard and an innate sense of right and wrong would see him through. He was thirty-two when he applied. "You're definitely too old to get in," Mary told him, not wanting him to be disappointed.

She was right. O'Donovan was not accepted. But he reapplied the next year and was successful. Coming home for the first time in his new police uniform was a moment of intense pride. His starting salary wasn't much more than he'd made selling suits, but he now had the security of a pension and benefits. Most of all, he had an identity he could be proud of and a renewed sense of purpose. The passion he had known galloping the Irish hills was coming alive again.

The police service O'Donovan joined was a descendant of the force established in Winnipeg in the early 1870s, when the city was earning the reputation of being "the wickedest" in the newly formed Dominion of Canada. Winnipeg was the last large civilized settlement before the remote and undeveloped North West Territories, the final chance to drink, gamble, or sleep with a woman. The city was notorious for public drunkenness, barroom brawls, and kidnapping, and the arrival of the newly expanding railways only made this worse. Prostitution was a particular issue. Men outnumbered women dramatically, inspiring the government to launch a campaign in Toronto and Montreal that urged nice girls to move west with the slogan "So great is the demand that anything in skirts stands a chance." The city's newly formed council attempted to control the problem of prostitution by confining brothel owners to the area around the rail tracks. But there were complaints that things were getting out of hand and that the sex trade was becoming so brazen that nude women were riding bareback in the street. Winnipeg's early police officers had not been beyond temptation. The first chief, John Ingram, was fined and suspended for being found in a state of undress in a "house of ill-fame."

Over time the police force grew, modernizing first with uniforms, then bicycles, and then patrol vehicles. The police department became the first in Canada to purchase radio equipment to broadcast directly to its cars and could boast that the first Canadian women to work in law enforcement had been hired as matrons to its female prisoners. In 1927, Winnipeg's city officers grabbed the attention of North America when they captured Earle Leonard Nelson, an American serial killer who had murdered an estimated twenty-eight women, including two in Winnipeg. Nelson was tried and eventually hanged in the city, cementing the force's reputation for daring and ingenious police work.

By the time O'Donovan joined the police, Winnipeg was no longer referred to as the wickedest city in the country, though it had maintained its reputation for lawlessness and violence. It consistently held the record for the highest number of homicides per capita in Canada, an honour that resulted in the unhappy moniker "Murderpeg." Just as in the 1870s, vice and crime centred around the Point Douglas area—a rectangle of blocks stretching east of Main Street between the railway tracks and the Red River—within the larger North End. It was the same area Thelma Favel moved to in the 1970s and left twenty years later as more immigrants and Indigenous people settled into its cheap housing. Over the decades, the immigrant makeup of the North End had changed, with more prosperous groups moving out to be replaced by newer arrivals. But the Indigenous population remained and continued to grow. In 2014, when Tina found herself homeless on the North End's streets, this inner-city district boasted the highest urban population of Indigenous people in the whole of North America.

The North End was where O'Donovan's police career began and where he completed his training and first job placement. He was happy to be posted here, preferring the area's grittier streets to the polite boredom of the suburbs. In the North End, he witnessed poverty, illness, despair, a chronic lack of services, and drug and alcohol abuse. The vast majority of victims and perpetrators of crime were Indigenous. To the Irishman, they reminded him of the rural people who would sometimes drift into the city back home. "They lead a simpler life, and when they come here, they're a little shy, a little quiet," he would say. But he could also see that their lives were plagued by drugs, sexual exploitation, and gangs. O'Donovan found the violence so disturbing that he told Mary and his children not to go anywhere near the district, certainly not at night. Mary hadn't minded. She already knew that many in the city felt the North End was a no-go area.

O'Donovan soon learned that the relationship between the Winnipeg Police and the Indigenous community had been strained for many years. He had not yet joined the force when the Indigenous leader J.J. Harper was mistakenly shot by an officer, a case that stirred cries of racism within the Indigenous community. Manitoba's 1988 Aboriginal Justice Inquiry had agreed with their accusation, describing the Indigenous experience of the police as a "problem of considerable magnitude" and stating that there had been systemic racism within the service for years. Officers were alleged to have used racist language and shown a disproportionate readiness to stop and search Indigenous people and were accused of an overzealous use of the drunk tank to detain anyone who displeased them. There was also talk of the police conducting "starlight tours," a name given to the practice of picking people up and dropping them off in remote locations to find their own way home, often without appropriate clothes or shoes and often in freezing winter temperatures. By the time O'Donovan joined, the Winnipeg Police Service was running mandatory training in cultural sensitivity in response to its past failings. The new recruit heard rumours of patrolmen who'd had sex with girls they booked for prostitution and stories of how, after weekly drinking sessions, or "choir practices," off-duty officers would look for homeless Indigenous men to beat up. But O'Donovan's personal experience was more positive. The senior officers who mentored him appeared to be good, diligent workers who cared about their jobs and were respectful of the community. O'Donovan could see there had once been a time when becoming an officer meant falling in line with an all-male white hierarchy. He hoped those were the bad old days, long since behind them.

In 2005, after training in forensics and intelligence, O'Donovan was promoted to the Homicide Unit as a detective constable. Here, he helped investigate the twenty to thirty murders that were committed in the city each year, many related to Winnipeg's burgeoning gang problem. Some cases stayed with him for years, like the 2007 murder of Anthony Woodhouse. Woodhouse was a young man who had got drunk one night, come home late, and argued with his wife. Storming out of his house, he had decided to walk to his mother's place, a few blocks away in the North End. He arrived just as dawn was breaking but found she was out, so had sat on her front porch to wait for her to return. While he was there a gang member had walked by, mistaken him for a rival, and shot him in the face. His mother arrived home half an hour later to find her son bleeding on her doorstep. An ambulance had rushed him to hospital, but he was pronounced dead shortly after arriving.

O'Donovan, who by then had been promoted to detective sergeant, interviewed Woodhouse's mother before she knew her son had died. She repeatedly asked the detective for an update, but O'Donovan decided to stall on telling her that Woodhouse was dead, feeling it was the best tactic to find out what she knew. It was only after the interview was over that he admitted her son hadn't made it. When she heard the news, she had broken down with a grief so acute that O'Donovan immediately regretted holding back the information. Two years later he had solved the case with the testimony of another gang member, who helped convict eight other suspects wanted for five different murders. It was a triumph for the police, but for O'Donovan the strong sense of failing Woodhouse's mother remained a lingering regret.

By 2014, after being promoted to the senior rank of sergeant, O'Donovan was again working in the Homicide Unit, this time as a supervisor. It was a role he embraced with confidence. The detective had built a reputation for being a calm and generous mentor as well as an original and unorthodox investigator. The year before, while supervising the Major Crimes Unit, he had been tasked with finding a serial robber who had raided several banks in Winnipeg. The offender, who he believed had committed a string of similar crimes in Calgary, was a violent man who would chase customers and bank tellers with a knife before making off with the cash. O'Donovan gathered the surveillance footage from Calgary and Winnipeg and found that it showed the robber moving through the banks but didn't show his face. He put forward the idea of filming their chief suspect as he walked through the police station and giving this and the bank footage to a professor of kinesiology at the University of Manitoba. The professor was an expert in assessing the gait of world-class runners and was able to prove scientifically that the man in the police station had the same distinct way of walking as the robber in the banks. Faced with this evidence, the man confessed.

But there had also been cases where, despite his most creative efforts, O'Donovan had failed to bring his suspects to court. These were the ones where he was convinced of the identity of the offender but lacked the evidence that would convict them. They had left him feeling conflicted—not quite a failure, but not a success either. They played on his conscience, taunting him with doubts about his methods and whether he had done everything he possibly could to get his man.

His worst regrets were reserved for the investigations where he had confidently declared to a victim's family that he would deliver justice but failed to do so. Weighing heavily on his mind was the case of a seventeen-year-old Indigenous girl found murdered in a field outside Winnipeg in 2007. The victim had been identified as Fonessa Bruyère, a young woman who had been in and out of Child and Family Services for most of her life. Shortly before she died, Bruyère had been removed from foster care by the provincial authorities and handed over to a family member despite the authorities having information that she would be exposed to drugs and the sex trade if she was placed there. Her body was discovered soon after two other murdered women were found on the outskirts of Winnipeg, a coincidence that led Indigenous leaders, including Nahanni Fontaine, to call for a special investigation into whether a serial killer might be operating. O'Donovan had the job of liaising with Fonessa Bruyère's father, and he promised him that the police would find his daughter's killer. But the investigation drew a blank, and O'Donovan deeply regretted giving the father hope. He had only "added to his grief and frustration," he said.

Seven years later, O'Donovan was reminded of Fonessa Bruyère when he received news of the body found in the Red River. On the hot August afternoon when the Missing Persons Unit identified Tina Fontaine, he thought carefully about what he would say to her family. Patrol officers had already informed her next of kin, and O'Donovan planned to visit them in person, mentally preparing himself for the difficult conversations. He knew he couldn't promise a result, but he would assure them that he would do the best he possibly could.

4.

"NOT LIKE *CSI*"

In the days immediately following the discovery of Tina's body, O'Donovan would catch himself gazing at the view from his office window over the tree-lined streets beyond City Hall. He would watch the traffic stopping and starting and let himself breathe in the ordinary rhythms of city life. If he looked the other way, out through his office door into the open-plan hub of the Homicide Unit, he could sense the energy and intensity of his team members as they attempted to pin down the basic facts of the case. The start of any investigation could feel overwhelming, but this one was proving exceptionally difficult. The only piece of definite information they had was that Tina had been officially reported missing on August 9 after running away from the care of social services the day before. Beyond this, her whereabouts in her final days remained a mystery. Detectives were used to relying on cell phone records, security camera footage, and forensics to tell them where victims were killed, how they had died, and who was responsible. Here, they were working in the dark. Tina did not own a cell phone, there were few security cameras where her body had been found, and even if there had been, detectives did not know exactly when she was put in the river. Hardest of all was that there was no crime scene to analyze. O'Donovan's instinct told him that the only way to make progress was to slow down and take stock. If he showed confidence his team would follow, even if the odds of solving the case were against them. This meant using every possible means to answer the fundamental questions: How had she died? And where had she died? O'Donovan hoped the pathologist would be able to give answers.

After his preliminary examination of Tina's body, Dr. Dennis Rhee returned the following day to complete his work. He had already concluded that Tina had no broken bones or obvious injuries, save the shallow depressions on her face and body that may have been caused before death. Now he turned his attention to exploring the underlying tissue of her face, nose, and forehead to look for further evidence of trauma. He began by removing layers of skin and muscle and found that the structure was mostly intact apart from the cartilage of her nose, which was missing. This was puzzling, as the skin around her nose was still in place, leading Rhee to consider a number of theories. While the irregularity was not severe enough to have been caused by a major blow, it could have been caused by a lesser attack, such as a punch or slap in the face. But the pathologist could not be sure that the cartilage had been destroyed before death. It was possible that one of the rocks placed inside the duvet cover to weigh it down had hit Tina's face as she lay submerged. Or perhaps the Red River's catfish population had been responsible for the damage. Either way, the injury had not been fatal. Rhee noted its presence, unsure of what it revealed.

The pathologist continued to examine Tina's skull, looking for areas of bleeding that could indicate a significant blow to her head.

There were none. Moving down her body, he paid careful attention to her neck. His experience told him that strangulation was a common cause of death in female homicide victims, and assailants typically used more force than necessary to kill. This tended to leave evidence in the form of bruising, spots of blood, or damage to the larynx. He carefully dissected each layer of skin and muscle, looking for something out of the ordinary, but again found nothing unusual. There were no fractures or dislocations in Tina's vertebral column, and the tiny C-shaped bone in the front of the neck, the hyoid bone, which is often broken under pressure, remained intact. Rhee knew it was possible for a perpetrator to strangle a victim and not leave a mark, but that was rare. He concluded that he couldn't rule out the possibility that Tina had suffered a minor assault to her neck, but he could not say with any certainty that it had happened.

Moving on to the internal examination, Rhee saw that Tina's internal organs were still mostly intact, with the exception of the soft tissue of the brain, which had already disintegrated from being submerged in water. The teenager's heart was healthy, and her cardiovascular system appeared to have been functioning normally. He examined Tina's lungs, considering that she may have been unconscious but not dead when she entered the river. As there was no specific autopsy finding to confirm drowning, he knew it would be a diagnosis of exclusion, made only if all other possibilities were ruled out. But the lack of evidence left him unsure. There was also the possibility that she had been suffocated, but again he could find nothing to prove it definitively.

Rhee's next task was to look for evidence of sexual assault. The fact that the teenager had been found fully dressed with no rips in her clothing suggested she had not been involved in a struggle before death. But knowing that Tina had been a young runaway at risk of exploitation, he considered it likely that her killing was sexually motivated. Examining her, he found nothing to suggest she had been raped or sexually assaulted, but the pathologist knew that river water may have washed vital evidence away. Wanting to be sure, Rhee took swabs to be analyzed in the RCMP forensic laboratory in Ottawa to see if DNA from a second person could be identified.

With no anatomical injuries on Tina's body, Rhee considered the possibility that she had died from an alcohol or drug overdose. Testing would normally mean collecting vials of blood for analysis, but the state of Tina's body made that impossible. Instead, Rhee collected samples of fluid from the chest cavity and removed a section of liver, sending everything to the RCMP lab in Vancouver for analysis. The findings came back promptly. Tina's blood alcohol level was moderately high, just over the legal limit for driving. But the lab urged caution in interpreting the result, explaining that it may have been falsely elevated because of decomposition. Even if the reading was accurate, the alcohol in Tina's blood would not have been enough to kill her.

The lab conducted a second test for THC, the active component in cannabis. The results showed the presence of cannabis but this would not have been lethal. Tina tested negative for crystal methamphetamine and cocaine, and there was no evidence that she had used opioid prescription drugs. Nor was there any trace of gabapentin, a drug originally developed to treat epilepsy, which had become popular on the streets for its ability to give a mild cannabis-like high.

In his final report for the Winnipeg Police, Rhee concluded that the cause of Tina's death was "undetermined." There was nothing in his examinations or the toxicology results that gave a clear indication of how she had died. The pathologist agreed that the circumstances in which she had been found suggested that she had been killed at the hands of another person, but he could not with any certainty say she had been murdered. "There are possibilities other than homicide, such as accidental death from drowning, after which someone could have concealed her body," he wrote, adding that his senior colleagues agreed with him.

Reading Rhee's report, O'Donovan felt a deep sense of frustration. The detective had hoped that at the very least, the pathologist would conclude that Tina's death was suspicious. He asked Rhee to consider ruling that the schoolgirl had died from "homicidal means," pointing out that she "didn't put herself in the duvet cover, fill it with rocks, tie a knot at the top, and hop into the river." But Rhee maintained his position, and O'Donovan was not able to bring any pressure to bear.

The detective moved on to his next question. Could the pathologist give an opinion on the post-mortem interval, the time between Tina's death and her discovery? A precise answer was impossible, but Rhee was able to give an estimation based on his understanding of decomposition. He knew that the environment surrounding a body—the temperature, the surface on which it rests, its exposure to oxygen, and whether it's in water—affects the speed at which it decays. He was aware of Casper's Law, an observation used by doctors since the 1800s, which holds that a body left in the open air will decompose twice as fast as one immersed in water and eight times faster than one buried in the ground. Following this, he concluded the decomposition rate would have been slower than normal because the body was submerged.

The water temperature may also have been significant. O'Donovan asked the Winnipeg harbour master for a record of the temperature at the time Tina was found. He was told that it wasn't recorded in Winnipeg but measured two hundred kilometres upstream, due south across the US border in Grand Forks. There, the water had been 24°C to 25°C, not cold enough to have significantly slowed the rate of decay. Putting those factors together, the pathologist estimated a post-mortem interval of between three and seven days, with the caveat that it could be as little as two days or as much as nine. Rhee also told O'Donovan that he didn't think Tina's body had been lying exposed in the shallows for long.

At home after work, O'Donovan conducted his own research on rates of decay by reading papers written by scientists and FBI agents working on "body farms," research facilities where the decomposition of human bodies was studied in a variety of environments. He also turned to Kevin Pawl, a fellow sergeant in the Winnipeg Police Service and an expert in underwater search and recovery. Pawl had been a member of the unit for almost twenty years and had worked on numerous cases, including once recovering the body of a woman who was weighted down with ropes and patio blocks in the Assiniboine River. He had been the supervisor in charge of the dive team searching for Faron Hall the day Tina was found. Pawl had directed his divers to look in the area where Hall was last seen, because he knew bodies could sink and resurface quickly in the same place. This was known as a "first float" or "gastric float," and it happened when gases trapped in the stomach expanded and dragged the body back to the surface. It normally took between two and five days, but warm temperatures could accelerate the process to as little as one day, which was why Pawl had sent out a team for Hall as soon as he could. It was also possible for a body to remain submerged for longer until it had reached the "full body float" stage, which happened when the limbs and abdomen bloated up from decomposition, typically seven to ten days after being submerged.

Looking at the autopsy photos, Pawl could see that Tina's body looked far larger than her death weight of 35 kilograms (77 pounds), suggesting that she had been at the "full body float" stage when found. Pawl knew that the weight needed to hold a body underwater in this advanced state of decomposition would need to be equal to half its body weight. The 11.5 kilograms of rocks placed inside the duvet cover with Tina would not have been enough to keep her submerged beyond a week. It was possible that her body had been trapped for a few days in the heavy silt at the bottom of the Red, but at some point her body would have become too buoyant to remain weighted down and she would have broken free. Knowing this, Pawl told O'Donovan he was certain that Tina had been in the water for no less than seven days, and more likely around ten.

O'Donovan was keen for Pawl to tell him where on the riverbank Tina had been put in the water. But the sergeant was unable to give an answer. Putting together all the information from the river search and autopsy, O'Donovan believed the most likely entry point was the wooden wharf of the Alexander Docks. His theory was that Tina had been thrown into the water there and that her body stayed weighted on the riverbed until the combined factors of bloating and the churning action of the *River Rouge*'s engines had set her free. She would have floated with the current until becoming snagged in the reeds in shallow water less than a hundred metres away.

From the start of the investigation, O'Donovan's detectives had been collecting security camera footage from around the Alexander Docks area. Not all the cameras had been helpful, with many set to overwrite within a day or two. The most promising was on the Mere Hotel, pointing towards its parking lot next to the docks. O'Donovan had already assigned the task of going through its footage to an enthusiastic young constable. Now he was able to tell the junior officer the time frame within which to search for suspicious activity.

Meanwhile, the Forensic Identification Unit, more commonly known as Ident, had begun its work. Constable Susan Roy-Hageman had been the original Ident officer on the scene when Tina's body was recovered, and now she would coordinate the forensic examination. Roy-Hageman had been with the Winnipeg Police Service for twenty years and had spent the last eight of them building up an expertise in crime scene investigation. In real life, forensic work was never as quick and conclusive as people thought, "not like *CSI*," the popular TV drama. If anything, she would describe her work as painstaking, slow, laborious, and often inconclusive. It was normal for teams to go to great lengths to gather and preserve evidence only to find it too damaged to be useful. Test results rarely came back within the hour, and DNA was not always identifiable. In fact, Roy-Hageman had worked on several homicides where her team found no trace of a perpetrator at all.

In this case, without a crime scene, Roy-Hageman and her team knew they had little to go on. Even with what they did have—a body, some rocks, and a duvet cover—it was likely the river had washed away evidence or it had become overwhelmed by decomposition. Nevertheless, the officer ordered a meticulous examination of everything found. Her team's first task was to identify exactly where the rocks had come from. In total, they counted four large pieces of stone, a piece of brick, and a number of smaller stone fragments. Roy-Hageman recognized the stone as Tyndall limestone, which was native to Manitoba and used as riprap along the length of the Red River to protect its banks against erosion. The stone was present just north of the Alexander Docks but was also common farther upstream and so not much help in placing where the duvet cover had been loaded.

The cover itself was saturated with mud, river water, and organic debris from Tina's body. Roy-Hageman realized she would not be able to process it unless it was washed, which was not ideal for preserving evidence. But the officer figured she could limit the damage by washing the outside only and making sure that any evidence caught inside remained. When it was clean, she could see that it had once been white or pale beige, decorated with a pattern of embroidered leaves in gold, brown, and rust that ran along its bottom edge, rising up towards its centre. Roy-Hageman positioned it face down on a large sheet of paper and used a scalpel to cut it open into three panels. Her team carefully checked each of these for hairs and fibres, marking and photographing their finds in situ before lifting them off with clear tape. In total, they found twenty-nine individual hairs, seven of them grouped within a small cluster. They also identified four kinds of fibre that had come from elsewhere, coloured red, black, and red-and-blue.

Before sending the hairs to the RCMP forensic lab in Ottawa for DNA testing, Roy-Hageman examined them under a microscope and selected the ones most likely to have a root from which she hoped a nuclear DNA profile could be extracted. It was the same RCMP lab to which the swabs from Tina's autopsy had been sent. During the process of examining these exhibits, lab technicians had found a hair in the vaginal swab, which they had added to their list of items to be tested. Keen to move his investigation forward, O'Donovan asked the lab's senior management to expedite the analysis, explaining that the case was particularly sensitive because it involved a child. The lab obliged. But when the results returned, they were disappointing. There had been too little biological material on any of the hairs or from the swabs to extract a profile.

Frustrated, O'Donovan made the decision to send the material to a private lab in Laval, Quebec, that specialized in testing for mitochondrial DNA. This type of testing had been used by crime scene analysts around the world since the 1990s as a complement to nuclear DNA testing, but it was still regarded as a somewhat imprecise science by the Canadian justice system. Mitochondrial DNA was more abundant than nuclear DNA and easier to find, making it useful for cases where samples were damaged or degraded or there was limited biological material. But the profile it gave was based on a shared maternal lineage rather than matched to one individual, and this meant that results were less conclusive and often challenged in court. It also came with a hefty price tag. O'Donovan would be spending close to $200,000, which meant he needed approval at the highest level. He explained to his superiors that, with so few leads, this testing was their best and perhaps only option. They agreed, and the preliminary results were promising. The lab was able to prove that the hair found in the vaginal swab had the same maternal lineage as Tina and so belonged to her. They were also able to match three of the hairs found in the duvet cover to the teenager. But from the remaining hairs they were able to identify at least eight different unknown profiles. There was no suspect to match these to yet, but O'Donovan considered this a significant development.

Later, Roy-Hageman sent the lab pieces of the duvet cover that had fluoresced under an ultraviolet light, believing they might show seminal fluid, saliva, or urine. The results, when they arrived, showed that the biological material on the cover matched Tina and no other profiles could be found.

With the forensic testing exhausted, the next step was to find out where the duvet cover had been sold. The manufacturer's label identified it as being from Costco Canada, a stroke of luck for the investigation team as the company was a members-only store that kept a record of each item bought by its registered customers. The barcode showed they were dealing with a queen-sized duvet cover in a pattern called Chloe Green. O'Donovan believed he could use Costco's records to track down every Chloe Green cover sold in the city. It would be a laborious task, but his detectives would be able to check whether the owners were still in possession of the bedding and whether any had the sort of background that might make them a suspect.

The search was complicated by the fact that the item barcode used to identify the Chloe Green cover was shared by three other duvet designs, and it wasn't possible to identify them separately. Company records showed that from February 2013 to the date of Tina's discovery in the Red River, Costco's Winnipeg stores sold 864 duvet covers of all four patterns. In addition, twenty-nine duvet covers with the same identification code had been marked as surplus and sent to a discount store on Main Street. Again, it was impossible to say how many of these had been the Chloe Green pattern.

Feeling he had no choice but to try to track down all 864 duvet covers, O'Donovan began to plan the most ambitious canvassing operation of his career. He comforted himself with the thought that although the search would probably take months, it would still be possible to complete and the situation would have been worse if Tina had been found wrapped in a plain white sheet. Dozens of detectives and police shift workers were drafted in to help. Teams working in pairs were assigned names of duvet cover buyers and asked to visit them personally to make sure they still had the bedding in their possession. Owners were not told why they were being asked, and for the most part the teams themselves did not know that the effort was connected to Tina Fontaine. The media had reported that the schoolgirl was found in some sort of bag, which over time became widely assumed to have been a plastic bag. It was a discrepancy that suited O'Donovan, who felt the detail could be useful when a suspect was finally found.

Despite the odd request, duvet cover owners were more than happy to help. In cases where the bedding had been sent out of town—to friends or relatives living elsewhere or to summer cabins—purchasers went out of their way to make sure they could still account for it. One drove to his lake house specifically to take a photo of the cover with a copy of that day's newspaper lying on top of it. Others emailed pictures from as far away as Greece and the Philippines. Slowly, the Homicide Unit was able to build up a picture of how many of the 864 duvet covers were Chloe Greens and where they were in the city. Out of all those canvassed, only one hundred customers had bought the Chloe Green pattern. Of these, eighty-nine were able to show the police that they still had the cover. Five said they had returned it to Costco. Four said it was at a cabin or elsewhere but couldn't confirm that, and two said they had given their bedding away to the thrift store Value Village, where donations were left outside in large steel bins that were often picked through by the homeless.

Detectives had less luck identifying the owners of the twenty-nine covers sold at the discount store on Main Street, which didn't keep records. Nor could they guarantee that the cover used to wrap Tina had not been brought into Winnipeg from another province. But even with these unknowns, O'Donovan considered the exercise successful in eliminating potential suspects. His teams checked names against the police register for serious offences or previous convictions for sex crimes and found no one of potential interest. And the project established that the Chloe Green design was relatively rare, a fact that was likely to become important later in the investigation.

As results filtered in, O'Donovan reflected that he was still no closer to knowing how Tina had died, where she had died, and who had killed her. But the detective was satisfied that, regarding the forensic operation, his team had left no stone unturned. "Let's get back to basics and start beating the bushes," he told his team as they gathered for their regular morning briefing. He believed that knocking on doors and identifying potential witnesses would be the only way to uncover what Tina had done after leaving Sagkeeng and arriving in the city.

5.

THE LOW TRACK

On June 30, after Tina had hugged Thelma goodbye and jumped into the car to be driven south to Winnipeg, the plan had been that she would spend one week catching up with her biological mother, Valentina, and her younger half-sisters. But while this had been the official aim of the visit, there were no doubt other possibilities on the teenager's mind. Her previous escapes to Winnipeg had given her a brief taste of what it was like to live the unsupervised life of an adult, free to make her own choices. After the constrictions of home and school, the city presented opportunities to be explored with an anonymity impossible in the small, closed world of the reserve. When Thelma's son and daughter, who were driving Tina that day, found Valentina's house locked and empty, the teenager had insisted that she would be fine. She persuaded them to drop her at Valentina's sister's house nearby, reminding them that there were plenty of other relatives and family friends who could keep an eye on her. Her confidence had been reassuring, and they had seen no reason to worry.

The Winnipeg where they parted company was the complicated, colourful, and dangerous world of the inner city, more specifically the North End, just blocks away from where Thelma had lived twenty years previously before packing up and leaving because of rising crime. It was the same district where O'Donovan had enjoyed training as a rookie cop and later cut his teeth as a homicide detective. For the teenager, these streets were the only Winnipeg she knew, and they would, just a few weeks later, become the site of her death.

The North End was a short walk up Main Street from the rich commercial heart of the city, and barely a few blocks away from the elegant and gentrified buildings of Winnipeg's historic Exchange District. But it was a different world. The change began a few streets south of where the Canadian Pacific Railway line crossed Main Street, where office blocks and civic buildings gave way to pawn shops, seedy-looking hotels, and the six-storey hostel of the Salvation Army. After the rail bridge and underpass, which felt menacing even in the middle of the day, there were more graffiti-sprayed low-budget hotels with boarded-up windows and chicken wire strung across their doorways. This was no accommodation for tourists. The guests who stayed here were, in the main, funded by social welfare cheques paid directly to the hotel management. Inside were dark, decrepit bars serving as crack houses. Outside, groups would loiter on the sidewalks, especially on warm summer nights. Young men in hoodies, drunks on bicycles, girls pushing strollers—all poor, mostly sick, and mostly Indigenous. If you didn't belong here, there was no reason to stop. Most Winnipeggers sped by quickly in their cars.

Because of the railway lines, which ran into a huge, sprawling rail yard to the south of the area, and the natural boundary of the Red River to the east, the North End felt cut off from the rest of the city. At its heart were eight to ten blocks of old clapboard and vinyl-sided houses that had become a predominantly Indigenous enclave. Farther north were immigrant communities: Ukrainian and Filipino families who had settled generations before and passed their houses down to children and grandchildren. The strong sense of community that Thelma remembered still existed and was visible in youth projects, walk-in health clinics, church meeting halls, and a wide range of help centres dotted throughout the area. But no amount of community support could shake the North End's reputation for violence and vice, which it had held since the rail line arrived a century before. The district remained Winnipeg's dark underbelly, a hub for organized crime run by gangs. Gang membership reflected the area's mix of nationalities and was dominated by Indigenous leaders. The Manitoba Warriors dealt in drugs and prostitution. The Indian Posse made a living from armed robbery. Both frequently stole from homes and businesses to fund drug purchases. There were also mixed gangs. The North End Blood had Indigenous and Asian members; the Filipino and Vietnamese, in particular, were known for their violence. Somalis, Sudanese, and West Africans ran the Mad Cow gang and the African Mafia. Despite repeated attempts by law enforcement to clean them out, their dominance continued and had spread across the Prairies to Calgary, Saskatoon, Regina, and Edmonton.

The North End was also notorious for sexual exploitation. In the early twentieth century, when rapidly growing Winnipeg was becoming the Chicago of the North, its street prostitution was split into two districts. The "high track" operated around the ornate turn-of-the-century offices and theatres of Market Avenue, in the Exchange District. This was the more expensive trade, catering to an upmarket clientele. In contrast, a "low track"—rougher, riskier, and cheaper—had sprung up in the area running along the railway tracks. In more recent years, the high-track trade had moved away into massage parlours and onto online escort sites, while the low track had continued to operate and had extended out towards the city's West End district, close to the University of Winnipeg. Here, on residential streets, sex workers waited at night for cars to slow down and drivers to call them over. Young and middle-aged women stood alongside transgender women and grandmothers. Most worked to fund an addiction. The police who patrolled the area estimated that 90 percent of those selling sex were Indigenous.

From his years working the inner city, O'Donovan knew how easy it was for women to become mired in sexual exploitation, especially if they had been groomed from a young age. He had heard plenty of depressing stories. Like that of Jennifer, an Indigenous girl who had grown up in the North End in the 1990s. When she was fourteen, she and a friend had been walking to a 7-Eleven to buy Slurpees when they were stopped by two older Filipino men who asked if they wanted to party. Usually she would have said no or thrown rocks or sworn at them, but this time she agreed to go. Her decision led to her being used by a sex ring selling underage girls and being raped, at fourteen, by a man who gave her crack cocaine. It was the first time she'd had sex, and she was petrified, but she didn't think to report it to the police because what had happened was quite normal among her friends. Nor could she tell her parents. Her home life was chaotic. She had run away several times from a mother who beat her when drunk. Some of her friends had even worse domestic situations to escape, and for them the sex ring became a place of safety. Jennifer knew they were severely abused at home, and that having sex with older men didn't really faze them; they would just blank out. Now, as a mother herself, Jennifer refused to let her twelve-year-old daughter walk the streets alone for fear she might be sucked into a similar lifestyle.

O'Donovan knew many more Indigenous girls like Jennifer. Samantha had been sexually abused by her grandmother's boyfriend and had run away from home at eleven. At first, the older men she met on the streets had been kind to her, giving her gifts and taking her for rides in their cars. But they had also fed her drink and drugs and expected her to steal, deal, or sell sex for them. Many of her friends were raped, and she thought she had been too, but couldn't be sure because it happened after she had passed out from drinking. As bad as it was for her, she said, it was far worse for the Indigenous girls who had drifted into Winnipeg from isolated rural reserves and weren't as street smart as the city kids. These girls were often placed in foster homes or hotel rooms by Child and Family Services, but tended to escape. It didn't take long before they were addicted to drugs and selling sex to fund their habit. In Samantha's opinion, Indigenous girls were particularly prized by immigrants to Canada, who found their dark hair attractive. Even when she was heavily pregnant, men would proposition her for sex.

Once on the streets, the women would struggle to turn their lives around. O'Donovan knew of an Indigenous woman in her forties, Candace, who had been selling sex since the age of fourteen. She told him how the girls had developed their own safety system, warning each other about dodgy customers, watching out for each other as they worked. It was easy money if the dates were good and the men didn't try to harm them. But there had been plenty of bad dates. Candace and a girlfriend had once been locked inside a house for two days and fed water laced with sedatives. They had escaped by prying open a bathroom window and jumping down from the second floor. Another time a customer had pulled a gun on her. Now she carried a weapon. The abuse came from everywhere. She remembered how a group of young men had once stopped their car and thrown eggs and rocks at her, calling her a dirty little Indian and telling her to get off the streets.

For O'Donovan, trying to protect women like Jennifer, Samantha, and Candace meant targeting not only the pimps, gang masters, and drug pushers, but also the men who bought sex from them. The Winnipeg Police had joined forces with the Salvation Army, which had been running a "johns" program since the late 1990s to re-educate men arrested for buying sex. The program was open only to first-time offenders who did not already have a record of sex crimes. In the year before Tina went missing, its records showed that most men picked up were either Caucasian or Asian. Very few were Indigenous. They were all ages, white-collar professionals and blue-collar workers from throughout the city, the suburbs, and rural Manitoba. Part of their education was to understand that the women they purchased sex from weren't doing it for pleasure or out of choice. They were doing it to survive, and for them it was a dangerous business.

On the warm day in June when Tina arrived in Winnipeg, she seemed oblivious to these threats and her own vulnerability to them. As she told Thelma's son and daughter, she wasn't alone in the city. She knew plenty of friends and family who could look out for her if needed. So it was here that O'Donovan instructed his team to start their questioning, asking them to gather information on how often Tina's relatives had met the teenager and when they had last seen her alive.

Detectives began by interviewing Tina's aunt, Angie Duck, who had taken Tina in when she arrived. Duck was hazy about the details. Tina had come over on "a cloudy and rainy afternoon," she said, and had immediately wanted to contact her mother. Duck had obliged, and soon after, Valentina arrived to pick Tina up. O'Donovan already knew from Thelma that it was a few days after this that Tina sent Sarah the selfie showing her scratched and bruised face, saying their mom had beaten her up, though the detective had not seen the picture himself because it had apparently been deleted. Another relative later told reporters that Valentina had got drunk and "kicked the shit" out of her daughter.

The next time Angie Duck remembered seeing Tina was a week or so later. Tina had been with Larry Dumas, the deaf friend who had brought her back to Sagkeeng after she had run away. On July 22 Tina came to her house again, this time with a new boyfriend she introduced as Cody. Duck was able to give a precise date of the meeting because Tina posted a picture of a family gathering on Facebook. In all the times Duck saw her niece, Tina never stayed over with her. The last time she remembered seeing the schoolgirl was the night after the family gathering when Tina walked by her house in the dark but didn't stop to say hello.

Detectives were keen to speak to Valentina, hoping to understand what had gone on between her and Tina that had led to the fight and beating. But when they arrived at her house, they found Tina's biological mother intoxicated and insensible, broken with guilt and grief. She was unable to give a clear account of what had happened, except to say that after their first encounter, she and her daughter had not spent much time together that summer.

Officers had more luck with Valentina's part-time boyfriend, Joseph Nanacowap. The Ojibway-speaking man from the remote reserve of Lake St. Martin remembered seeing Tina four or five times, often with the boy she had introduced as Cody. The last meeting was in late July or early August. Tina and Cody turned up at his place in the North End saying they had nowhere to go, so he allowed them to spend the night on his couch. By early the next morning, the couple was gone. Nanacowap said he hadn't been concerned about the teenager, who appeared happy and in control of her life. "She never seemed under the influence of alcohol and drugs," he later said.

The presence of Cody was mentioned by another witness, a family friend Tina had known since she was a baby. Steve Whitehurst, or Uncle Steve, had been a long-time friend of Tina's father. He said Tina and Cody visited his house in the North End and left behind several shopping bags full of clothes for him to look after. A few days later, at the end of July, Tina returned and asked to use Whitehurst's phone to contact a youth shelter where she had been sleeping. She confessed that she didn't like it there and would prefer to stay with him. But Whitehurst had been wary. Cody seemed always to be at Tina's side, and Whitehurst felt that the boy had a controlling influence. "You can stay at my place, but there are two rules. You can't have your boyfriend over twenty-four seven, and I need to know where you are," he told the girl. Not liking these restrictions, Tina had left. Shortly after, still in late July, Whitehurst took his family on a trip to Sagkeeng. He knew Thelma and Joe were looking for Tina and had spoken to them a couple of times about having seen her. Before he left Winnipeg, his wife messaged the teenager on Facebook to ask if she wanted a lift back home. It was only when they arrived in Sagkeeng that they received Tina's reply saying yes. But by then it was too late and they never heard from her again.

O'Donovan noted that Tina's request for a lift conflicted with her earlier message to her sister saying, "Tell Momma and Papa I love them but I'm not ready to come home." It appeared that within the space of a few weeks, Tina's initial enthusiasm for the city had diminished and she wanted to find her way back to Thelma.

Another relative who had seen Tina in the month before she disappeared was Lana Fontaine, an aunt on Tina's father's side.

Fontaine lived with a brother and sister in Winnipeg's West End, in an apartment complex on Furby Street, close to the faculty buildings of the University of Winnipeg. The Fontaines were the first people the police contacted when they attempted to identify Tina's body. Lana Fontaine told detectives she had seen Tina several times, sometimes with her boyfriend Cody. Once, when it was cold outside, Tina dropped in to borrow a favourite sweater, a "white one with a rope belt," while Cody waited on the street outside. "She looked happy, she always had a bright smile," Fontaine said. The final time they met was the long weekend at the beginning of August, when Tina stayed for two nights, sleeping on a makeshift bed.

Reading through the notes taken by his team, O'Donovan reflected that in the weeks Tina was in the city, her relatives had taken a hands-off approach with the girl. They knew she had "run away from Grandma again" and then fallen out with her biological mother, but none of them tried to make her stay with them or return to Sagkeeng. Nor had any of them kept Thelma regularly informed about her whereabouts. It was clear there had been problems throughout Tina's extended family. Lana's sister Robyn Fontaine later told a CBC reporter that she suspected Valentina and Tina had argued because Valentina tried to push her daughter into sex work, explaining it was something Valentina herself had been forced into doing at a young age. O'Donovan was unable to confirm this. But Valentina was not the only troubled adult in Tina's life. Two years after Tina's death, Lana Fontaine's daughter, Jeanenne Fontaine, was accused of human trafficking for forcing a young woman into prostitution, a charge she denied, saying she had been exploited herself. A year after that, Jeanenne was shot dead in a drug house in the North End, targeted by mistake in a dispute over crystal methamphetamine. Violence, drugs, and instability seemed embedded in Tina's family. In the summer of 2014 her relatives had provided her with shelter, food, and company when she wanted it, but none seemed able to give her a steady home. For their part, they told police that the schoolgirl seemed well and—aside from mentioning that she sometimes smoked weed—sober and happy. They made it clear that they loved Tina very much, but they hadn't thought to curb her independence.

Knowing that women were statistically far more likely to be killed by their intimate partner than by anyone else, detectives turned their attention to Tina's two boyfriends. O'Donovan was already aware of Larry Dumas from Thelma's description of him as a "real gentleman" for bringing Tina home when she had run away. When detectives located Dumas, he confirmed he had known Tina for five or six months and that, for some of that time, they had been a couple. He said they had broken up because Tina wanted them to sell drugs together and he had objected. Later, he found out from Facebook that she had started dating Cody.

Dumas described a normal relationship with Tina despite his deafness, explaining how they communicated by writing messages on his iPad. The last time he had seen Tina was in Portage Place, the glass-roofed shopping mall on Portage Avenue in Winnipeg's downtown. The mall, built in the 1980s, was a popular hangout for Indigenous teenagers, who spent hours in its large food court or by the entrance that led out to Ellice Avenue, a well-known location for drug deals. When Dumas met Tina and Cody there, there was some tension between the three of them, but it had been resolved and they had gone their separate ways. The last Dumas had heard from Tina was a message on Facebook at the beginning of August. He said he could account for his whereabouts for the two weeks after this and was happy to help police in whatever way he could. O'Donovan noted that he seemed an unlikely suspect.

The homicide team quickly established that Tina's second

boyfriend was Cody Mason, an eighteen-year-old Indigenous youth from the northern Manitoba reserve of St. Theresa Point First Nation. A few months before Tina arrived in Winnipeg, Cody had travelled to the city with his father to help him recuperate from a car accident. Searching through airline manifests, detectives were able to verify that Cody checked in for a flight back to the reserve at 6:26 A.M. on August 6. Cody and his father had spent their last two days in Winnipeg in a hotel close to the airport, where staff identified a young girl matching Tina's description as having stayed with them. Because the last confirmed sighting of Tina was after Cody had flown home, he was also not considered a suspect. He was due to return to Sagkeeng to attend Tina's funeral, and O'Donovan made a note to interview him then.

Following up on Steve Whitehurst's recollection that Tina had run away from a youth shelter, detectives visited the Ndinawe group home in the North End. Although Tina had been referred here on July 23 by Southeast Child and Family Services and given a bed for two weeks, the shelter had no authority over the teenager. On July 26, Tina failed to make the curfew of 10:30 P.M. After waiting the better part of a day to see if she would reappear, staff reported her missing. The description they relayed to the police had been taken during Tina's official check-in, and O'Donovan noted that Tina's weight was stated as 45 kilograms (100 pounds), considerably heavier than the 35 kilograms (77 pounds) her body weighed less than a month later. A day after she was reported missing, Tina reappeared at the home. But a day after this, on July 29, she had walked out, saying she was going to stay with her auntie. When she didn't return, Ndinawe staff again reported her missing, this time packing up her clothing and giving away her bed to another vulnerable young person.

At the same time as interviewing witnesses, detectives were also following up on calls that were flooding into a special tip line. Tina's story was still making headlines, and there had been an unprecedented level of public interest in her case, especially from an Indigenous community eager to help. Some leads were clearly mistaken, but others had potential. A fellow resident of Ndinawe contacted the police to say he remembered having a conversation with the teenager in which she said she had been dealing drugs with an ex-boyfriend, who she hadn't named. She said her ex had worked for a man she called "the boss" and owed him $9,000, but he had run away without paying. She said she was continuing to sell on her own to make up the debt.

A woman contacted the detectives to say she was sure she had met Tina one evening in mid-July when she and a friend were sitting outside in the North End. A couple of teenagers had walked by and stopped to pet the woman's dog, and they struck up a conversation. The girl, who matched Tina's description, told them she was from Sagkeeng and had been kicked out of home. The woman remembered the meeting because she had been concerned about the young woman's safety; she had taken her aside to ask her if her boyfriend had been hitting her. The girl said no, but she confided that they were on their way to see their dealer. After an hour of chatting the teenagers left, but fifteen minutes later the women heard screaming coming from the direction in which they had walked. They heard an older woman shout "Why did you bring her here" and "Quit fucking looking at her" before the couple reappeared looking shaken. When the women asked what had happened, the girl replied, "I can't control whether a guy likes looking at me or not."

There were a number of other sightings that placed Tina in the West End, close to the University of Winnipeg, in an area known to be connected to the city's gang scene. One witness came forward to say she had seen Tina with two black males near an address on Spence Street. The district had a large African immigrant population, and this particular house was known to be a drug hangout. Another young woman came forward to report that she had met Tina at Portage Place on Sunday, August 3, and they had gone back to a friend's house on Spence Street to smoke drugs. A few days later, the young woman related, on the morning of August 7, she had gone to a rooming house on Furby Street, three streets over from Spence. The Furby Street house was a well-known crack shack run by a Kenyan and a Nigerian who had connections to the Indian Posse. The woman had seen Tina sleeping in one of the rooms, looking uncomfortable under a dirty white blanket that had a flower design on it. The description triggered O'Donovan's memory of the Chloe Green duvet cover and he made a mental note to have it shown to the witness.

It was still only a few days after Tina's body had been found, and O'Donovan's team held an impromptu briefing in the Homicide Unit to talk through what they knew so far. The strongest theory seemed to be that Tina had been killed because of links to drugs and organized crime. The story that Tina's ex-boyfriend owed a drug boss $9,000 indicated a possible motive. But to the experienced detectives, the details seemed too sketchy to be believed. When they interviewed Larry Dumas he had insisted that he had no knowledge of Tina owing money, and if she did, he said, it hadn't been connected to him. Detectives had collected several reports of Tina selling small amounts of marijuana on the streets, but there was nothing to confirm that she had been involved in moving thousands of dollars' worth of drugs. O'Donovan knew it would be unusual for a dealer to entrust such a young-looking girl with so much, especially one who hadn't been in the city for long. He suspected the story of the $9,000 debt was just Tina talking herself up.

The Kenyan and Nigerian men connected to the gang scene appeared a more promising lead. Detectives had been able to confirm that Tina visited their rooming house on Furby Street and that she met them in person. O'Donovan considered it was possible that the men either had a sexual interest in Tina or had fallen into an argument with her and that this had given them a motive for murder. He issued an alert to all police cruisers to be on the lookout for them.

For the moment, the two men remained the main persons of interest in the investigation. O'Donovan was frustrated not to have made more progress, but with an absence of evidence it was impossible to identify an official suspect. Meanwhile, he asked for a media release to be circulated urging the public to come forward with information regarding Tina's whereabouts specifically on August 8 and 9. From what he had learned from the forensic investigation, O'Donovan believed that these were the teenager's last days alive and he knew that they would be the key to identifying her killer.

6.

TESSA TWOHEARTS

The Thursday after Tina's body was found, O'Donovan treated his team to their customary weekly breakfast. It was a practice he'd instigated when he'd become the head of the Homicide unit, and it had become a sacred moment of levity in the otherwise intense work week. O'Donovan favoured a café on Portage and Memorial where his group of thirteen mostly male detectives were less conspicuous in their plainclothes conformity of buzz cuts, pale shirts, and suit pants. As they walked to their table diners pointed them out, whispering that they recognized O'Donovan from his press conference. It was a new experience for the detective, and he felt awkwardly self-conscious. Ignoring the attention, he turned the conversation to Tina's case. It wasn't the only killing his team were working on, and he was mindful that they needed to stay focused. This morning he wanted to review the information they had been given from the Missing Persons Unit about Tina's movements on August 8 and 9, a crucial piece of the jigsaw of her final days they were desperately trying to construct.

The detective began by running through the list of the times Tina was recorded as missing. The first was on July 10, when Thelma alerted the police and Southeast Child and Family Services to the fact that the teenager had disappeared into the city. From the start, the Missing Persons Unit had marked Tina at risk of sexual exploitation, especially because of her known marijuana use at school. A week later, on July 17, patrol officers responded to a report from the North End that a girl was being dragged down a street by her arm and screaming for help. They arrived to find both Tina and Cody intoxicated. Tina was placed in a short-term detox facility and then given a room at the Capri Hotel on the Pembina Highway, to the south of the city.

At the time, because of the scarcity of foster homes and shelters, it was common practice for CFS to use hotels to house at-risk youth. Hotels were meant to be a temporary solution before more suitable arrangements could be found, but stays often ran into weeks and even months. The hotel environment provided little protection against exploitation, drug use, and problems arising from mental health issues. CFS had contracted out the supervision of their charges to private agencies whose staff were unqualified to provide the one-to-one support often needed. In the year after Tina's death, a CBC investigation found that the hotels had become magnets for drugs and sex work and that the contracted staff were failing to shield young people from illegal activities. That same year, the Manitoba government said it was committed to stopping the practice. In Tina's case, her stay at the Capri Hotel was brief. She ran away almost immediately, prompting the agency to file a second missing persons report with the police.

For a week, the teenager remained off-radar in the North End before CFS found her a bed in the Ndinawe shelter. When Tina left, returned to, and then left the shelter again, the next two missing persons reports were issued. But it was the last report that O'Donovan wanted to discuss. It had been made on August 9, a day after Tina had once more been placed back into CFS care, and he wanted to reconstruct the events that had led up to it.

Detectives were already aware of a sighting of Tina the morning before, on Friday, August 8, next to a property owned by the University of Winnipeg in the inner-city West End. There had been a summer storm that morning and the rain was falling hard. The property, named the Helen Betty Osborne Building after the teenage Indigenous girl beaten to death in 1971, had a parking lot tucked behind it. At around 10 A.M. a security guard received reports of a woman passed out under the overhang at the back of the building. Heading out to investigate, the guard found a young girl asleep behind a car. She was dressed in a green zip-up sweater, pink high-top running shoes, and a white skirt that had been pulled down to her ankles to reveal she wasn't wearing underwear. There were marks on the girl's legs that looked like mosquito bites or cigarette burns, and the guard was concerned that she may have been the victim of a sexual assault. When she couldn't wake her, she called an ambulance.

Later that day, O'Donovan's team identified footage from a nearby security camera that was set to pan across the lot, capturing an image every few seconds. It showed a girl walking in the rain, holding a newspaper above her head and moving with a slight limp. O'Donovan immediately recognized her as Tina and winced at how thin and fragile she appeared. As it panned again, the camera caught an image of Tina sitting down next to the wall where she was found. A while later, it captured the paramedic team arriving and the girl being escorted to an ambulance. Slurring her words and appearing confused, Tina told the paramedics she had been out drinking the night before, smoking marijuana and taking gabbies, the street name for the epilepsy drug gabapentin.

When Tina arrived at the Emergency Room of the Children's Hospital, she refused to respond to the male doctor on duty, so Dr. Andrea Wilkie-Gilmore was called to examine her. Wilkie-Gilmore noted that Tina was not answering questions and avoiding eye contact. There was a smell of alcohol around her and a small blister burn on her lip, but otherwise the teenager seemed healthy. Wilkie-Gilmore ordered blood work and a toxicology screen and planned to return later in the afternoon. Tina fell asleep, waking only when a nurse came to draw blood and replace her soiled skirt with blue hospital pants.

At 3:30 P.M., with some of the test results in hand, Dr. Wilkie-Gilmore returned for a second examination. The blood test confirmed that the teenager had been drinking, but the level of alcohol in her blood was low. The results of the toxicology screen had yet to arrive, so Wilkie-Gilmore asked Tina what drugs she had taken. The teenager wasn't showing the tremors and jerky eye movements of a gabbie overdose, but it was clear she had ingested something. Tina now insisted she had only drunk alcohol and smoked weed. Because she had been found without underwear, Wilkie-Gilmore asked about voluntary or non-voluntary sexual activity. Tina didn't answer. When Wilkie-Gilmore asked if she could conduct a gynecological exam, Tina refused. When she asked about the blister on Tina's lip, the teenager replied that she "fell a few days earlier." The doctor recognized it as the type of blister caused by smoking crack or meth through a plastic pen.

"I tried to counsel her, to get her to open up to me. I told her about the dangers she could be in. I told her not to run from CFS," Wilkie-Gilmore later said. But Tina remained impassive. With no medical reason to hold the teenager, Wilkie-Gilmore discharged her. Earlier in the day the hospital had contacted CFS, and a care worker had been sitting by Tina's bed since the morning. Security camera footage recorded the moment the pair left the hospital building, the teenager trailing after the worker, still wearing blue hospital pants and carrying her skirt in a plastic bag. A few hours later, the toxicology results confirmed that Tina had tested positive for amphetamines, marijuana, and cocaine use. The hospital did not contact CFS to inform them, and CFS did not call back to find out the results.

Kimberly Chute, the CFS worker called to the hospital, was not Tina's primary case worker but a staff member who had been on the intake desk when the news had come in that the teenager was in the Emergency Room. Chute, who had a degree in social work, made sure she was up to date with Tina's file before leaving. She was aware that CFS had registered the girl as someone at high risk of sexual exploitation. The file noted that Tina had been hanging out at Portage Place, which was likely to bring her into contact with pimps and drug pushers. It also indicated that although Tina did have a mother and relatives in the city, they were not able to provide her with a stable home and that Tina herself wouldn't know what care was available to her through the government system.

Chute had actually met Tina three times before. The first was at the Capri Hotel on July 17, when Tina had raised her concerns because she admitted to smoking crack. The second time was on July 23, when Chute saw Tina walking along the street. She had called out to the teenager and tried to persuade her to join her for lunch, but Tina said she was on her way to see her boyfriend. Chute had seen Tina once more, this time in her office at the end of July. CFS had passed on a message through Tina's family that they were looking for her and could give her free bus tickets, so Tina had arrived with Cody and had stayed for a while to chat.

On August 8, after picking her up from the hospital, Chute drove Tina to a McDonald's while she waited for her colleagues to secure a placement for the night. She was conscious that the teenager looked thin and hadn't eaten that day; she also knew that taking kids for a drive and buying them a burger was a good way to get them to open up. As they sat in the drive-through their conversation drifted to the subject of bicycles, a necessity in the city because of the large distances between neighbourhoods. Tina told Chute that she had owned a bike but had lost it and wanted to get a new one. Seeing an opportunity to persuade her to stay in social care, Chute suggested that if Tina remained in her placement, the agency could find the money to buy her one. Tina shook her head. "My friend Sebastian is going to find me a bike," she said.

Chute was not familiar with the name. "Who is Sebastian?" she asked, trying to sound casual.

Tina shrugged her shoulders. "He's a sixty-two-year-old meth user."

Concerned, Chute asked what Tina liked to do with Sebastian.

"Just chill," she replied.

"Have you used crystal meth with Sebastian?"

Tina just shook her head.

Chute asked a few more questions, attempting to sound as relaxed as possible. But the teenager withdrew and the social worker did not want to alienate her. That evening she made notes on the troubling conversation, according to CFS practice. Later, when she heard that Tina's body had been found in the river, she immediately turned them over to the police.

By late afternoon, Chute's fellow staff members had found a bed for Tina in the Best Western Charterhouse hotel in downtown Winnipeg. Once there, the social worker handed responsibility for the teenager over to a member of Complete Care, a private agency contracted by the welfare agency. On duty that day was Ngozi Ikeh, a single mother putting herself through college by working shifts. Ikeh had already prepared Tina's room and began the process of checking her in, noting how tired she looked and that she was still wearing hospital clothes beneath her sweater. They chatted for a while and Tina seemed calm and quiet. Ikeh suggested she get some rest and remain in her room, but Tina said no, she had friends to meet at Portage Place. "That's not a great idea," Ikeh warned, pointing out that Tina's hospital pants were flimsy and the night was cool. But Tina said she would change back into her skirt. Within thirty minutes of arriving the teenager was walking out the door, promising to return by the curfew of 11 P.M. As a contracted care worker, Ikeh had no power to stop her, but she did record what she was wearing—the same clothes she would be found in two weeks later. That night Tina failed to return to the hotel, and at 2 P.M. the following afternoon, CFS registered her as missing to the police for the final time.

O'Donovan instructed his team to search for security camera footage to confirm that Tina had gone to Portage Place after leaving the Best Western. Detectives found that the drive in the shopping mall camera had been overwritten, but they were able to locate pictures of Tina, dressed in her white skirt, outside a restaurant in the nearby West End. "I think she meant to go back to the hotel," O'Donovan told his detectives, pointing out that Tina had not packed her belongings to take with her that night. He believed she had gone to find Sebastian to pick up a new bike. "We've got to find him," he said, noting that Sebastian was an unusual name, so it shouldn't be too hard. "If he met her, we need to see where she went afterwards."

Meanwhile, the Missing Persons Unit had passed on another lead. After Tina was reported missing on August 9, the unit had released a series of media alerts asking for information. On August 11, they received an anonymous text saying that Tina had been seen at 4 A.M. on August 9. This was followed by more texts from the same number saying that Tina had been seen with a black man. O'Donovan passed them to his team to verify.

They discovered that the number belonged to an eighteen-year-old Indigenous girl living in the North End. "Katrina," as she liked to be called, told detectives she often spent time on the streets. She had grown up in CFS care herself, and looking out for street girls had become her way of making a difference. It was because of this that she had encountered Tina.

The first time they had met was on August 7, when the girls struck up a conversation on the West End corner of Langside and Ellice. Tina said she was sixteen and working the streets, a fact that alarmed the older girl. Pretending to walk away to buy cigarettes, Katrina made her way to a nearby police cruiser to tell the officers there was "a little girl out selling her body." When she returned, Tina had disappeared. But within the hour she was back, announcing she had finished with a customer and now had cash to buy drugs.

Tina led Katrina to a house on Furby Street and told her to wait outside while she went in. A few minutes later she appeared with a small plastic bag of marijuana, which she started to smoke, saying she thought it was laced with crack. The pair sat for a while in front of a pizza restaurant and Tina confided that she'd been taking drugs for a while, experimenting with meth, crack, and weed. She described herself as officially missing from CFS care with family living nearby. In return, Katrina shared her own CFS story, later telling a CBC reporter that she "knew the feeling of being alone both emotionally and mentally when you have nobody, and I guess that's why we connected."

The girls hung out until around 2 A.M., when Katrina suggested they make their way to the Macdonald Youth Services shelter a short walk away. The plan was to use the bathroom and grab a bite to eat, but secretly Katrina wanted to force Tina to stay overnight. However, Tina was harder and more streetwise than Katrina had assumed. She checked in using a false name, Tessa Guimond, and refused to answer questions when the desk worker noticed she seemed drunk and had a swollen lip and scratches on her knees. While Tina was using the bathroom, Katrina gave the worker her real name, pleading with her to force Tina to stay. The care worker called the CFS after-hours unit, but they were unaware that the teenager was the subject of a missing persons report. Unable to stop her from walking off into the night, all the worker could do was offer Tina a sweater to keep warm.

The girls headed back to the corner of Langside and Ellice. Tina told Katrina the drugs were kicking in and she was hallucinating, so the older girl stayed close by her side, watching over her as the sun began to lighten the horizon. Suddenly a black truck pulled over and its driver waved at Tina, prompting the teenager to walk over and get into the passenger seat. At first Katrina assumed Tina must have known the driver, but then she realized that the man was cruising the neighbourhood for sex. Panicked, she waved to another police cruiser in the distance to try to alert the officers. She saw the police car follow the truck, and she later found out that officers had arrested the man but let Tina walk away.

When O'Donovan heard this part of Katrina's story, he was confused. Looking back through police records, he could find no reports of an arrest after a vehicle stop on the morning of August 8. The detective sent out an internal appeal to all staff, asking if anyone had had contact that day with his homicide victim. Tina's name and face had been widely publicized, so it would have been impossible not to know her death was under investigation. With rising frustration, the detective requested an internal investigation to check the computer database for a record of anyone running Tina's name. After several days with no answer, he was finally contacted by two patrol officers who admitted it was they who had crossed paths with the teenager that morning.

Constables Brock Jansen and Craig Houle told O'Donovan they had been at the end of a night shift when they started to follow the black truck Tina had got into. Jansen had been the more senior of the pair, experienced in dealing with sexually exploited women and the johns who frequented the area. By contrast, his partner, Constable Houle, was a recent graduate from the academy with only weeks of experience. They described how they became aware of the truck, not because they had seen Katrina waving, but because it had stopped near a group of people. As Jansen drove towards it, it had moved slowly southwards, taking a route that was almost a loop. Suspicious of the driver's intentions, Jansen had turned on his blue lights and pulled him over. Houle ran the licence plate through the police computer while Jansen got out to speak to the driver. The officer found him evasive, turning his head away as if he didn't want to be recognized before reluctantly giving his name as Richard Mohammed. Houle informed Jansen that Mohammed had been flagged for a suspended licence, so Jansen cuffed him and locked him in the back of the patrol car while he went to deal with the passenger.

The girl in the passenger seat initially gave her name as Tessa Twohearts and her date of birth as 1994, facts Jansen relayed to Houle to check. When Houle's computer search drew a blank, Jansen walked back to ask again. Tina gave another fake name that Houle was not able to match. In the patrol car, Mohammed was becoming violent, smashing the back seat with his head and arms and threatening to fight the officers. Once again Jansen asked for

Tina's name, and this time she gave it correctly. Houle checked Tina's information and told Jansen there were no warrants or orders out against her.

"Why did you lie?" Jansen asked when he was back at the passenger window. Tina replied that she thought she would be in trouble. "Not with the police," Jansen told her, and offered to give her a ride home. Tina told him she was staying at the nearby Quest Inn and wanted to walk there herself. It was now 6 A.M. and light. Believing she was in no danger, Jansen let her go.

Later, with the benefit of hindsight, Jansen said he should have paid more attention to Tina's date of birth. To him, the girl had seemed to be dressed maturely and he felt she could easily have passed for eighteen. She also seemed calm and hadn't broken any laws. For his part, Houle admitted that he had failed to notice there was a previous missing persons alert against Tina's name, a detail he said he missed because of his inexperience.

O'Donovan was furious. Not only had the constables withheld vital information from his investigation, their mistake had threatened to destroy the goodwill he was building with the Indigenous community. "Her name was clearly flagged and she looked like she was twelve," he muttered with exasperation to his team. His chief of police, Devon Clunis, considered the matter so serious that he briefed the press himself, telling them the officers had been "assigned to non-operational duties" while an investigation was pending. "For anyone to see a young woman in that condition and to say, 'We've seen so much of that, we're just going to let it go,' is not acceptable," he later said. When journalists contacted Thelma Favel for her reaction, she told them she was still coping with being slammed with a $500 bill for Tina's ambulance ride only days before. "I just can't describe it, how I am still feeling, knowing that if they did their job, my baby might still be here," she told reporters. "It's just another Aboriginal who fell through the cracks."

For a brief moment, O'Donovan worried that the Winnipeg Police might be dealing with a situation similar to the one in which a US cop infamously escorted a victim back into the care of serial killer Jeffrey Dahmer. But his detectives were quickly able to rule Mohammed out as a suspect. The night the officers had picked him up, Mohammed was taken to the drunk tank to sober up. They had decided not to press charges and Mohammed insisted that he'd never see Tina again. O'Donovan's team were able to confirm his alibi. It was later that morning that Tina had been found in the parking lot and taken first to hospital and then put into CFS care at the Best Western hotel, so O'Donovan knew for certain that Mohammed had not been the last person to see her alive.

The detective turned back to Katrina's story. The eighteen-year-old told him she had seen Tina again shortly after the teenager had walked out of the Best Western on August 8. That evening, they met around 8 P.M. Tina was with a young Indigenous man and the girls quickly parted company. Around midnight, they bumped into each other on the corner of Langside and Ellice. Tina made it clear she was working, but they chatted for a while until a sex worker shouted at them to get out of her area. As the girls walked away, Tina told Katrina about the previous night, describing how the cops had let her go and she had hooked up with another customer, got drunk, passed out, and ended up in hospital. She related how CFS had checked her into a hotel and she had been allowed to leave, though she knew that if she didn't get back soon they were going to report her missing again. "I want to go home to Sagkeeng, where I'm loved," Tina told her new friend.

It was now around 4 A.M. on Saturday, August 9. The girls had stopped to sit down on Ellice Avenue to share cigarettes and chat. A skinny young black man walked past, clearly on drugs, and offered twenty dollars for oral sex. Tina agreed to the transaction, telling Katrina to wait for her and she would be back in twenty minutes. Concerned for Tina's safety, Katrina followed the pair as they walked across the street and into an alley, but she lost them in the darkness. After waiting an hour or so for Tina to return, she finally approached two sex workers and asked them to help her look for the teenager. The group searched for over an hour, but Tina did not reappear. It was two days after this that Katrina sent the anonymous text messages to the Missing Persons Unit.

With Katrina's statement, O'Donovan's team now had a potential suspect. His detectives tracked down the sex workers, who confirmed the story of the search. O'Donovan presented Katrina with a photo lineup that included headshots of the Kenyan and Nigerian men from the Furby Street rooming house. When Katrina recognized one of them as the person who had walked off with Tina, O'Donovan instructed his team to put the man under surveillance. As far as he knew, he was the last person to have seen Tina alive. O'Donovan wanted to know who they were dealing with before they brought him in.

But then more information came into the police tip line that questioned this theory. A woman reported seeing a girl fitting Tina's description at the bus stop outside the downtown Millennium Library at lunchtime on Saturday, August 9, hours after Katrina had last seen her. She told detectives that it was the second time she'd seen the teenager. The first had been in the same place a week earlier when she had noticed the girl because she looked thin, and because her hair had been pulled back into a ponytail but was falling out because one side of her head had been shaved. The second time she saw her, the girl had approached her and asked for a cigarette. The woman told the teenager she was too young to be out on the streets, to which the girl had replied that she wanted to go home with the woman and be looked after by her. The request had seemed odd. The girl appeared fragile and vulnerable, but she was a stranger, and the woman said she couldn't help. Instead she gave her a bus ticket, saying she hoped the girl would use it to get somewhere safe.

Now it appeared that the black man was not the last person to have seen Tina alive. Once again O'Donovan gathered his team around him to review the timeline of her final week. They knew that Tina had stayed in the hotel near the airport with her boyfriend, Cody Mason, until the morning of Wednesday, August 6. The following day, on August 7, a witnessed had placed Tina in the Furby Street rooming house under the blanket with a flower pattern. That same evening, Katrina had met Tina for the first time and stayed with her overnight until Tina got into Mohammed's truck and was stopped by the patrol officers. Hours after this, Tina had passed out under the building overhang in the university parking lot. She had been taken to hospital, then for a burger, and then dropped off at the Best Western Charterhouse. From there, she had gone back onto the streets, met Katrina again, and walked off with the black man. A few hours later, she had been outside the library asking for a cigarette.

As O'Donovan's team tried to confirm this last sighting with security camera footage, another promising call came into the police tip line. It was a message from an inmate of a halfway house located on Main Street in the North End. The man said he wanted detectives to visit him in person, as he had something important to say. O'Donovan dispatched a team to take his statement, not knowing that the information he would give would change the entire course of his investigation.

———

Robert Sango was a sixty-year-old former bank robber who had been convicted of a series of offences in the 1980s. He told detectives that while on day parole at the halfway house that August he had got into the habit of sitting outside at a bus stop for one last smoke before curfew at 11 P.M.

On the night of Wednesday, August 6, Sango had been sitting alone on the bus stop bench at around 10 P.M. when a young girl came running around the street corner and headed straight to a pay phone nearby. She made a quick call, slamming down the receiver when she was finished, then turned to walk towards him. Seeing that he was smoking, she asked if she could bum a cigarette. Sango said yes, teasing the girl for being too young to smoke. In response she started to cry, so he patted the bench beside him to indicate she should sit and tell him what was wrong.

In between sobs, the girl began to tell her story. She said she had been hanging out with a girlfriend and her boyfriend at their house earlier that evening when the couple had gone upstairs, leaving her alone with another friend, an older man. He had started to put moves on her and became aggressive when she said she didn't want anything to do with him. "He called her a tramp and a whore," Sango said, and described how the girl had cried even more when she told him this. Sango had tried to cheer her up, telling her not to take the names to heart, as people often said cruel things that weren't true. The girl nodded and told him that the older man had stolen a truck, and that she had run to the pay phone to report him to the police.

Frightened that the man might be following her, the girl asked Sango if he knew a place where she could stay. "Why can't you go to your mother's or father's?" he asked, and she admitted she was a runaway. Sango advised her not to go around telling people this, especially in the North End, where someone might take advantage of her vulnerability.

At this point, a friend of Sango's appeared and joined in the conversation. The men discussed giving the girl money for a bus ticket, but neither had change in their pockets. Instead, they told her they could watch over her as she walked down Main Street to make sure no one was following her. Just before leaving, the girl stood up and held out her hand for Sango to shake, saying, "You are a gentleman, thank you for being honest." Sango remembered how tiny her hand was. She introduced herself as Tina, to which he joked "Just like Tina Turner," but she just looked puzzled. Sango thought how young and sweet she was, but also naïve, certainly too naïve to be out on the streets. True to their promise, the men kept their eyes on her small frame as she walked away down Main Street until she was nothing more than a distant dot. Twelve days later, Sango's friend pointed out a newspaper picture of the girl found in the Red River and asked if that was the same girl they had been speaking to. Tina's hair was different in that photo, so he wasn't sure. But a few hours later, he saw another picture in a different paper and recognized her immediately. That's when he called the police.

O'Donovan immediately deployed a team of detectives to the pay phone to find the number and relay it to the city's emergency communications centre. He wanted to know if there had been any 911 calls made on the night of Wednesday, August 6. The centre confirmed that there had been one, logged at 22:18:41, and emailed a recording of it to him. It was the end of a busy day when the file pinged into O'Donovan's inbox. The detective leaned out of his office to summon his colleagues inside to listen. When they'd squeezed themselves around his desk, he clicked play, and the voice of a female dispatch worker started to speak.

"Nine-one-one, what's your address and emergency?"

There was a pause, and then a thin, young female voice could be heard saying, "Hey, I'd like to report a blue truck that was stolen earlier today."

"Okay, and do you know who stole it?" came the question, to which the girl replied, "This guy named Sebastian."

"Is it your truck?"

"No, he's my friend and he stole it earlier today."

The worker read out a direct phone number for the police and explained that they were the people to deal with this sort of complaint. Then the call ended.

There was silence for a moment as the detectives took in what they'd just heard. It was as if a ghost had come to life. The female voice was very young and high-pitched and had a faint trace of a rural accent. Later, O'Donovan's team played the recording to Tina's aunt Lana Fontaine, who recognized her niece immediately, adding that it sounded as if she was slightly high. But even without this confirmation, there was no question in the office that the voice they were listening to belonged to Tina.

After the frustrations of the forensic investigation and the painstaking effort of piecing together Tina's last movements, the team finally had the break they'd been hoping for. Here was their victim, speaking directly to them, telling them a story they needed to hear. They were back with Sebastian, the "sixty-two-year-old meth user" Tina had liked to chill with, and the man who was supposedly getting her a bike. Not only had Sebastian allegedly stolen a truck, he seemed to have had an aggressive sexual interest in the dead girl.

"Looks like we have a new person of interest," said O'Donovan, as a jolt of energy pulsed through the huddle of tired detectives.

7.

LIFE ON THE
INSTALMENT PLAN

rom the air, the reserve of St. Theresa Point is a tidy collection of houses and open ground tucked into the vast stretch of wilderness that is the Canadian Shield. It's a barely noticeable interruption in an endless mosaic of treetops, rocky islands, and ink-dark lakes. This is the sort of landscape a hunter would prize as an untouched paradise, accessed only by small plane or, during the coldest months, an ice road laid out across the frozen land and water.

Once on the ground, an altogether different picture emerges. After landing on a small, rocky airstrip and crossing the lake by boat, the reserve, so orderly and neat from above, displays multiple wounds of neglect. Houses, squashed up together as if huddled for warmth, are not much more than makeshift trailers. There are stores, schools, and community centres, but hardly anything for sale and very little to do. Five hundred kilometres northeast of

Winnipeg, St. Theresa Point is not an easy place to supply. Bulky or heavy items can only be trucked in when the winter ice road is open, and everything costs three or four times more than it would in the city. It is a close-knit community, but one burdened by isolation and poverty. There are problems with unemployment, alcoholism, drug addiction, and suicide. For decades, residents have had to manage without clean drinking water in their homes or indoor toilets. "We live in Third World conditions," reserve leaders have said repeatedly, angry that their voices are hardly being heard.

This isolated reserve was home to Cody Mason, Tina's boyfriend in the summer of 2014 and the witness O'Donovan regarded as key to understanding her movements in the days leading up to her death. Cody grew up in St. Theresa Point in a tiny, cramped trailer with his parents and siblings. In phone calls to the police that summer, he showed an eagerness to help.

Later, when O'Donovan finally met Cody face to face, he suspected the boy suffered from fetal alcohol syndrome because of his pinched facial features and slowness of thinking. Certainly, the teenager was not an academic kid; he had dropped out of school around the age of twelve, before finishing Grade 6. His ability to speak and read English was limited, and he preferred to use his mother tongue of Oji-Cree. Like most of the kids on his reserve, Cody had a longing to escape the smallness of rural life. At the age of fifteen, during a trip to Winnipeg, he had disappeared from his guardians. The police were informed and a missing persons alert issued before the teenager was found and safely returned home. Two years later, just before his eighteenth birthday, Cody was given another chance to spend time in the city. His father, who'd been injured in a vehicle accident and needed to be evacuated to Winnipeg for treatment, elected to take Cody with him. The pair flew south in May 2014 and remained in Winnipeg until the St. Theresa Point administrative band council said they could no longer finance the trip and insisted they return home.

In their interviews with detectives, Tina's family remembered Cody as quiet and uncommunicative but always physically close to the teenager. To Tina's Uncle Steve, his presence had been menacing, and he believed Cody was a controlling influence. Over time, though, O'Donovan came to regard Tina's boyfriend as having been both fond and protective of her. Cody told O'Donovan that he and Tina had promised never to leave each other, and the detective felt the behaviour that Uncle Steve interpreted as overbearing was just Cody's way of showing loyalty. And it was true that as long as Cody remained by Tina's side, she had stayed alive.

When Cody flew home, the young couple promised to keep in touch by Facebook, but he told police he hadn't heard anything from Tina after leaving Winnipeg on August 6. Later, he read the same Facebook post that Thelma saw on August 17, describing how a body the police had pulled from the Red River had been identified as Tina. This was followed by more posts by Tina's family and friends, some of whom pointed a finger of suspicion at Cody, asking if he was the one who had dumped her body in the water. That had frightened him. Cody planned to return to Sagkeeng to attend Tina's funeral, but was apprehensive about the welcome he would receive and scared he might be attacked.

After his team had ruled Cody out as a suspect, O'Donovan demanded that he be handled with care, cultivated for information rather than interrogated harshly. He deliberately picked the pair of detectives assigned to interview him, choosing the senior and sympathetic officer Esther Schmieder and her partner, Rob Stephanson, whom he trusted to keep the conversation relaxed. Their task was to find out everything Cody and Tina had done in the weeks prior to the discovery of her body and, now that the Homicide Unit was aware of the 911 call, if Cody could shed any light on Tina's relationship with the mysterious older Sebastian.

Cody and his accompanying child welfare officer had checked into an airport hotel in Winnipeg two days before the funeral in Sagkeeng. The detectives chose this as their venue to talk, hoping the more relaxed atmosphere would encourage the teenager to open up. Over a soft drink, Cody said he would answer their questions as best as he could.

He described how, after arriving in Winnipeg that summer, he had been walking through the North End by the Salter Street Bridge when he caught sight of a pretty girl. She introduced herself as Tina, told him she was sixteen, and said that she had run away from home and had nowhere to go. Finding her attractive, Cody invited her to stay with him and his father in the apartment they were renting on nearby Selkirk Avenue. She agreed and spent the next few days sleeping on the couch.

"Do you want to be my boyfriend?" Tina had asked one night as the two of them sat elbow to elbow, sharing a beer.

"I said yes," Cody said. He described their relationship as being close, but not sexual. Later, reading through the notes of the interview, O'Donovan wondered if Cody had said this to protect himself now that he knew Tina was fifteen and under the age of consent.

On O'Donovan's instructions, Stephanson and Schmieder took their time with their subject, making the effort to appear gentle, modulating their voices to suppress any hint of urgency or frustration. After a while Cody began to open up, describing the weeks he had spent with Tina. From what the detectives could understand, the couple's time together had been erratic and nomadic. Cody's father had objected to Tina staying too long, so they had moved around, exploiting whatever opportunities that came their way.

Cody said Tina hated the Ndinawe group home she had been placed in by Child and Family Services, so the couple would alternate between Cody's father's apartment, Joseph Nanacowap's place, her Auntie Angie's house, Cody's grandma's home, and the rooming house on Furby Street. They would stay long enough to sleep, be fed, and use Facebook before moving on again. By day, they would hang out in the Portage Place mall, the place known to child welfare officers as a mecca for underage drug transactions and sexual exploitation. Sometimes they would take a bus ride to the more upmarket Polo Park mall, where they would sit in the food court or check messages from friends on the free-to-use laptops in the Apple Store.

Cody described meeting Tina's ex-boyfriend Larry Dumas, the deaf boy who had brought Tina home when she had run away in May and who communicated by writing messages on his tablet or pieces of paper. Because of their shared interest in Tina, the meetings had sometimes been tense. He recalled a time in Portage Place when Larry had bumped into them and become annoyed because he noticed love bites on Tina's neck. When the police checked this story with Larry, he accused Cody of getting Tina into drugs. But Cody told detectives it had been the other way around. He said he didn't take drugs, but he had seen Larry selling crack cocaine and pushing Tina into doing it as well, though Larry did not confirm these allegations. Cody said this had made him feel uncomfortable, so he would walk away whenever it was happening. Later, Cody admitted he had tried marijuana, crack, and pills himself, but in his initial police interview he was careful to stress that it wasn't his idea to sell drugs for money.

Tina had got to know another dealer for whom she would sell small baggies of weed. Her method was to wander around the North and West End with Cody by her side and strike up conversations with strangers on the streets. "Do you want to get high?" she would ask with a disarmingly impish smile.

Whereas Cody was shy, Tina had been confident and unafraid of approaching people, even the older tattooed men obviously in gangs. But selling drugs on the streets was a risky business. Cody told the officers that at one point, Tina owed a small amount of money to her dealer. She was a tough kid who seemed not to care about the consequences, but Cody was more easily scared, so he stepped in to pay off her debt. In that way, he said they had been good for each other. He knew he wasn't as bright or as spirited as his girlfriend, but his silent presence grounded her and helped steer her away from trouble.

The couple often came across the same people hanging out, including two black men who would sell car rides for money. One was skinny and short and drove a large grey SUV. Cody remembered him because he had once picked them up for free and returned them safely to Cody's father's apartment. That man had a friend, another African immigrant, who had a dark four-door car in which he also used to give people rides. When the detectives relayed these details to O'Donovan, he asked his team to check if these were the same men as the ones from Furby Street already under suspicion.

The question Schmieder and Stephanson were keen to ask was whether Cody knew someone named Sebastian.

Cody recognized the name immediately. Yes, he had known Sebastian. The first time they met was sometime in mid-July, in the early hours of the morning. Cody had been holding a can of Budweiser as he and Tina walked down Charles Street, in the North End. Suddenly, an older guy with long salt-and-pepper hair cycled past, which caught their eye because he was balancing the large bulk of a car muffler on his shoulder.

"Hey, we've got nowhere to go," Cody shouted on impulse, and the man braked and came to a stop beside them.

The teenagers said they were lost and asked for directions to Selkirk Avenue. Cody remembered how the man's accent sounded strange and unfamiliar.

"Call me Sebastian," he said and explained that he was a scrap metal collector who was going to sell the muffler for cash. He told them he knew a place where they could stay for the night: an empty basement in an apartment building a few blocks away.

"I have the keys to the city," he said when they arrived, taking out a screwdriver and using it to pry open a door. Downstairs were old blankets lying on the floor, where, he gestured, they could sleep. Early the next morning he returned to let them out, handing them a twenty-dollar bill to buy breakfast.

After that, the three of them had hung out several times over the summer. Once, Sebastian called out to Cody from across the street, asking for help in breaking into a small yard of junk metal. Another time they met up on Selkirk Avenue. Sebastian always seemed to be on the lookout for metal and copper wire, which he would pile up on his bike or in a stolen shopping cart and wheel to scrap merchants for cash.

On one occasion, the pair followed Sebastian into the yard of a house on Alexander Avenue, a street that led down to the dock on the Red River, close to where Tina's body was later found. He showed them a small tent pitched in the yard, which he explained was his home. Peering through the tent flap, Cody could see he had stored the muffler inside, along with some red-and-black striped blankets and a bunch of pills in bottles. As they chatted, Sebastian picked up one of the bottles and tipped out four or five pills, which he handed to Tina. They were gabbies. He showed her how to snap open the capsules and snort up the powder inside. Tina devoured them in seconds. Sebastian didn't take any himself, preferring to inject crystal meth into his arm.

Cody remembered another time when the three of them left the North End and crossed an old steel bridge over the Red River into the quieter, more affluent suburb of Glenelm. Here, late one evening, Sebastian took them to meet friends of his who lived in the last in a row of plain-looking townhouses, conspicuous in the leafy old neighbourhood. The friends were a couple in their late twenties or early thirties. The woman, who introduced herself as Sarah, appeared part Indigenous, with long dark hair dyed with pink streaks and shaved short over her left ear. Tina liked this, because it mirrored how her own hair was shaved. Sarah's boyfriend, who was also Indigenous, was introduced as Tyrell. Cody related to the detectives how they had sat around drinking Budweiser until Sarah and Tyrell went upstairs to bed. Sebastian left, and Cody and Tina crashed on a bed in the living room. The next morning, Sebastian returned to take them away.

Excited by the insight Cody was giving them into Sebastian's world, Schmieder and Stephanson asked if they could drive him around to point out the places he'd mentioned. But first they stopped by McDonald's for a burger, a treat for the boy from the remote reserve, where fast food was a luxury. When they reached Glenelm, Cody wasn't able to recognize Sarah and Tyrell's townhouse, so the detectives turned to Alexander Avenue, driving slowly to let Cody study each house in turn, hoping he could remember the one with the tent in its backyard. When they reached a house with a chain slung across its entrance, he told them to stop. "This is it," he said, and the detectives noted down the number: 686. Through the car windows, they could see the dome of a small camping tent pitched in the yard behind.

After dropping Cody back at his hotel, Schmieder and Stephanson returned to the Public Safety Building to brief O'Donovan about what they had learned. When their boss heard Cody's testimony, he decided not to bring the teenager straight in to the station. In his view, Cody's statement could wait, but 686 Alexander couldn't. It was possible Sebastian was still there. O'Donovan signalled to Detective Sergeants Jeff Stalker and Myles Riddell to go immediately. Both were experienced officers with a solid background in the case, having already taken part in the duvet cover canvass and interviewed several of the witnesses.

"Do you live here?" Jeff Stalker asked the young woman who appeared when he knocked on the door of 686 Alexander. He and Riddell had already noted that the backyard was open to the street, meaning anyone could come and go from the tent without disturbing the occupants of the house.

The woman identified herself as twenty-year-old Tracey Beardy. At first, she looked puzzled when Stalker asked whether an older man named Sebastian was living in the tent, but then her expression opened up. "Oh, you mean Frenchie?" she said, and gave a perfect description of the man Cody had spoken about: white, in his early fifties, with long, greying hair that he liked to wear in a little ponytail.

Tracey told the detectives she had met Frenchie a year or two earlier, when she had been working in a doughnut shop in the North End. It was open twenty-four hours, the sort of place where cops on the night shift would stop by for coffee. Frenchie would come in because he had nowhere else to go, and she would watch him sit for hours, nursing one cup of coffee. Sometimes she would sell him a day-old doughnut for cheap, letting him stay because he wasn't doing any harm. He could be useful helping to load the shelves when a new batch of doughnuts was ready.

Tracey said her fifteen-year-old sister, Chantelle, had come into the shop a few times and chatted to Frenchie, as had her mom, Ida. Back then he seemed like a cool guy, and they had invited him to their house to hang out. He brought beers and a little weed, which he shared with the girls. Tracey said he hinted that if she let him stay in the house he would have sex with her in return, an idea she described as "a bit gross." But her mom, who had a soft heart for hopeless cases, had taken pity on him. She had found out he was sleeping rough down by the river, and she offered to let the man stay in the family's tent, which she allowed him to pitch in the yard.

By this point, the other occupants of 686 Alexander had gathered around to find out who Tracey was speaking to. Stalker explained they were there to ask about Frenchie and that he and Riddell would interview them in turn, noting down their names and ages.

Chantelle spoke first, confirming she had often hung out with Frenchie and knew he was also called Sebastian. Ida was initially less willing to talk. The forty-six-year-old was the family's matriarch, a battle-hardened, plain-speaking woman with a voice made coarse by years of drinking and smoking. She had had her own trouble with the police and didn't seem pleased to see the officers in her kitchen. But when she realized none of her children were under suspicion, she relaxed and began to open up.

"I feel sorry for people who are homeless, so I let him stay in my backyard," she explained. Frenchie had been there since July, but Ida said she hadn't seen him since somebody had stolen his bike and Frenchie had smashed up her barbecue with a hammer. In the summer they had lit a fire pit outside and, even with the vicious mosquitos, enjoyed sitting around it in the evenings, drinking beer and roasting hot dogs and s'mores. "Frenchie would be there drinking strawberry margaritas," she told the detectives. She seemed as disapproving of his taste in alcohol as she was of his taste in women. She had not liked the way he stared at fifteen-year-old Chantelle when she wore her summer shorts. "It was creepy," she said, adding that Frenchie always seemed to want to get her daughter drunk or high.

Most of the time, Frenchie had been high himself on crystal meth. Once, she found him doing the drug inside her house and kicked him out, only for him to come back a few days later. She would sometimes take pity on him and allow him to use the shower or wash his clothes in the bathroom sink. He had a collection of blankets and bedding that she believed were stolen from the thrift store, Value Village, because she had seen their tags still on them. She described how he would fold these up inside the tent away from summer bugs or hang them out to air on the fence. She had seen them so many times that she could easily recall their patterns and colours.

"Did you ever see Frenchie bring guests back to the tent?" asked Stalker, knowing that Cody had said he and Tina had visited. Although the detectives had not explained why they were there, the family had already guessed they were asking about the famous murder: the girl in the river, Tina Fontaine.

"There was one time he came back with a white couple, and I got mad and threw them out," Tracey told them, adding she had seen the pictures of Tina in the news and was pretty sure she had never visited the house. Chantelle said she had met Tina with friends several times in late July. Once had been outside the Best Western Charterhouse hotel, when Tina had been really drunk and vomited on the pavement. Another time was in Portage Place. But she told the police she was pretty sure she had never seen Frenchie with Tina in the yard.

When Stalker called O'Donovan to update him, the head of the Homicide Unit found Frenchie's interest in fifteen-year-old Chantelle highly suspicious, signalling an unhealthy preoccupation with underage girls. He told his detectives it was urgent they find Sebastian's full name.

Following up on information given by Ida, Stalker and Riddell headed to a nearby scrapyard and gave the woman at the front desk a detailed description of the man they were looking for. She nodded her head in recognition.

"He's called Raymond Cormier," she said, adding that people who worked there were well aware of his identity because he had stolen from them a few weeks before.

Stalker relayed the name straight back to O'Donovan, who ran it through the police database. Seconds later, he was looking at a police headshot of Raymond Joseph Cormier. The photo showed a middle-aged man with messy, shoulder-length greying hair, a moustache, and a goatee. His head was slightly tilted to one side, his eyebrows raised as if caught by surprise, and his eyes dull and unfocused. O'Donovan guessed he had been high on drugs when the photo was taken.

"That's the man who ripped us off," the woman at the desk said when Stalker showed her the mug shot on his phone.

In the Public Safety Building, O'Donovan found himself exhaling a long sigh of relief.

Raymond Joseph Cormier was born on June 2, 1962, and was of no fixed abode. O'Donovan read that he had been convicted and imprisoned multiple times, often for violent offences, including theft, robbery, breaking and entering, and assault with a weapon, along with numerous failures to comply with court orders, probations, and paroles. Cormier was not a native of Winnipeg. He had been born out east, in Moncton, New Brunswick, the youngest of thirteen children in a French-Canadian family. He had first come to the attention of the police as a teenager and had moved around the country, amassing ninety-two convictions in what had become a predictable pattern of offending and incarceration. *You're a man doing life on the instalment plan*, thought the detective when he calculated that Cormier had totalled more than twenty years in jail.

Cormier had been convicted in Ontario, Quebec, Saskatchewan, and finally Alberta, where, a few years before, he had been found guilty of car-jacking and aggravated assault in Calgary. That had led to a spell in the federal Stony Mountain Institution, just outside Winnipeg, and then, in 2012, time in a halfway house located in the North End. From there, as far as O'Donovan could see, he had disappeared into the city until May that year, when he had been picked up for drug possession. He had been released on the condition that he stay out of trouble and turn up for his court appearance. But in early July he had broken that promise when he was found in possession of a vehicle with stolen plates. With warrants out for his arrest, he had disappeared.

To make absolutely sure Raymond Cormier was the same man known as Frenchie or Sebastian, O'Donovan instructed Stalker and Riddell to return to 686 Alexander Avenue to show the occupants a photo lineup in which Cormier was included. When the detectives arrived, only Ida was there. She had no problem picking him out, writing "that's Frenchie" on the back of the photo.

Satisfied, Stalker and Riddell left the house and headed to another local scrapyard, where the employees were also able to verify that the man in the photo was the man they knew as Frenchie. Back at the Public Safety Building, O'Donovan asked the Surveillance Unit to stake out the backyard on Alexander Avenue for the next three days. If Cormier returned, their instructions were to follow him, note his habits and where he lived, but not to apprehend him. For the moment, O'Donovan wanted to watch and wait.

But Cormier remained elusive. A week later, O'Donovan sent Constable Susan Roy-Hageman's forensic team to Alexander to impound the tent to test it for evidence. He was sure Cormier would show up soon, and he wanted to know as much as he could before that happened.

By now it was the end of August, and a sticky prairie heat was hanging over the city, burning up the sidewalks and showing no sign of lifting. Inside the Public Safety Building, O'Donovan's team was struggling to stay focused in the sporadic bursts of cool air pumped out by the ailing air-conditioning system. As usual, the summer homicide rate was high, and they found themselves juggling several cases at once, painfully aware of how they seemed to be failing in the eyes of the press.

In his early-morning briefings, O'Donovan attempted to boost morale. Drawing on his days long ago as a jockey, he told his detectives to view their work as a four-horse race. There were the two black men on Furby, who still needed to be located and put under surveillance. There was Raymond Cormier, who was also at large somewhere in the city. And there was the fourth possibility of a still-unknown suspect. O'Donovan stressed that there was much they didn't yet know. Not one of these suspects was to be given prominence over the others until a clear front-runner emerged.

As the hot days dragged on, calls continued to come in to the Tina Fontaine tip line. One witness reported having seen Tina asking to bum a cigarette on a street corner in the West End. Another said the teenager had been among some street girls who were given bad drugs. There was a report that Tina had been killed by a drug dealer, another that she had been raped and suffocated by two Filipinos and an Indigenous man, who had wrapped her in plastic and thrown her in the Red. O'Donovan was grateful he had held back information about the duvet cover, making it easier to sift the fantastical from the useful.

There were other tips that seemed to give matching details. A witness called in to say she had overheard two black men talking about how they had killed a girl and needed to be careful not to say anything about it. An anonymous email told a similar story. But detectives couldn't confirm either account. O'Donovan added them to his growing file on the Kenyan and Nigerian, judging it was time to send the forensic team to their rooming house to search for traces of Tina's DNA.

Then, suddenly, there was a breakthrough. In the very early days of the investigation, O'Donovan had given a junior constable the task of scrutinizing the security camera footage from the Mere Hotel. From everything he had learned about body float times and river currents, O'Donovan was convinced that Tina's body had been dumped into the water at the dock and that some sort of transport would have been needed to bring her there. The discovery of Tina's 911 phone call about Sebastian having stolen a truck "earlier today" had imbued this idea with extra significance.

After weeks of spooling through the grainy pictures of cars entering and leaving the hotel parking lot, the constable announced he had found something of interest. The footage was of poor quality, but he pointed out what appeared to be a dark four-wheel-drive truck driving into the lot and parking. Its lights were turned off and the driver appeared to sit in the dark for some time. O'Donovan thought he could make out a faint light inside the truck, as if a flashlight was being waved around. For thirty minutes nothing happened, then there was movement around the front passenger side. After this, the truck's headlights came on and the truck accelerated away at speed, ploughing straight over the sidewalk and the grass verge that separated the lot from the road. It seemed that whoever was driving wanted to get out of there as quickly as possible.

O'Donovan calculated the timing. The footage had been recorded in the early hours of August 10. Tina had been seen regularly around the North End and West End up to midday on Saturday, August 9. The fact that no one had seen her after that time, and that she was found wearing the same clothes, indicated that Saturday was her last day alive. Being dumped in the river in the early hours of Sunday, August 10, would match with the pathologist's and search-and-recovery team's estimations of time of death.

A few weeks earlier, after hearing Tina's 911 call, O'Donovan had put out an alert for blue trucks stolen in the city. A landscape gardener had contacted police to say his dark blue 2008 Ford F-150 truck had been stolen on August 6 with gardening equipment in the back. Believing this was the truck stolen by Sebastian, O'Donovan had asked to be personally notified if it was located. He didn't have to wait long. On September 17, the detective received a call from a patrol officer who said the stolen truck had been found abandoned near Portage Avenue. The driver's window had been smashed in, and a man with blood on his hands was seen wandering near it. O'Donovan instructed his team to interview the man and ordered the truck to be towed to the Public Safety Building for forensic analysis. If it was the same one mentioned by Tina, he wanted to know if any trace of her could be found inside.

Meanwhile, Raymond Cormier was still at large. O'Donovan, convinced he was still in Winnipeg, added Cormier's name to a "Crime Stoppers' Most Wanted" feature that the police sent regularly to the *Winnipeg Sun* newspaper. He was vague about why Cormier was wanted, mentioning only that the man had breached the conditions of his parole. Not wanting his suspect to go to ground, O'Donovan was careful not to connect Cormier's name with Tina Fontaine. The detective knew the chances were slim that the notice would help, but he was willing to try anything.

8.

22 CARMEN

As the warm weather continued into the end of September, the impromptu memorial to Tina that had sprung up at the Alexander Docks continued to grow in size. Well-wishers left flowers and soft toys and pebbles painted with the words *love* and *strength*. Tina's death had triggered nationwide anger, amplifying the calls for a government inquiry into murdered and missing Indigenous women. Among those was the Canadian Human Rights Commission, which urged that Tina's case not disappear into the statistics. "We have a duty to ensure she leaves a legacy, and that her legacy is to bring an end to the chronic cycle of violence that rips Aboriginal women and girls from the fabric of family and community at this alarming rate," it said in a statement. "This is not acceptable in a country like Canada."

In the Homicide Unit office, O'Donovan checked the unit's answering machine, realizing no one had done so for a while. He discovered that for several days a message had been sitting there from a guard at the Milner Ridge Correctional Centre, a prison to the northeast of the city. "There's an inmate here who says he has details of a homicide. He's requested to talk to an officer face to face," the voice said.

O'Donovan guessed at once that the call was about Tina Fontaine. His natural inclination was to be wary; in high-profile cases, it wasn't unusual for inmates to come forward with "crucial" information. Mostly, these jailhouse informants wanted something in return: a reduction of their sentence, a cash reward, a special favour, or something that would look good on their record. And their testimony, sometimes convincing and sensational, had been known to contribute to miscarriages of justice.

But the guard assured the unit that this prisoner wanted nothing more than to help and to get his information "off his chest." So, shortly after 9 A.M. on October 1, O'Donovan assigned the team of Detective Sergeants Jeff Stalker and Myles Riddell to make the hour's drive to speak to him in person.

Ernest DeWolfe, or Ernie, was a tall, slim man with a face lined and hardened by alcohol and drugs. His deep, thick voice betrayed a lifelong habit of chain smoking. The forty-eight-year-old had been in Milner Ridge since August on a charge for theft. Over the years he had served time for a string of offences, including sexual assault, assault causing bodily harm, and armed robbery. When he wasn't in prison, he made a living working on construction sites as a carpenter, bricklayer, or general labourer.

Without knowing Raymond Cormier was already a suspect, DeWolfe told the detectives that his information was about Cormier. DeWolfe was also a native of New Brunswick, and it was this shared background that had brought the two convicts together when they were both serving time in Stony Mountain prison. They had struck up an uneasy friendship that had continued into their release to the same halfway house in Winnipeg. DeWolfe had once considered Cormier a potential business partner until Cormier had failed to pay back a loan and the pair had fallen out and drifted apart. They had reconnected earlier that summer, before Tina was killed.

"What makes you think he's connected to Tina's murder?" Riddell asked, impatient to get to the point.

"He told me he had sex with her," DeWolfe replied.

The detectives looked at each other.

"And you think this was true?"

DeWolfe explained that he had seen Cormier and Tina together several times at an address in the Winnipeg suburb of Glenelm where Cormier used to hang out with his friends Sarah Holland and Tyrell Morrison. He knew Cormier was sexually interested in Tina and found out that the two of them had got into a fight over a stolen truck. Shortly after that, he heard that Tina's body had been pulled from the river. The coincidence of the events had worried him.

"I'm not a shining example of a pillar of the community, but I do have morals," he told the detectives. "I've never ratted on anyone before, but it's been on my mind that I needed to tell someone." Once again, he stressed he didn't want anything in return.

It was shortly after 1 P.M. when Riddell and Stalker radioed their boss to relay DeWolfe's information. As O'Donovan listened, he felt his pulse begin to quicken. Everything DeWolfe said seemed to fit the investigation. Glenelm was the suburb Cody had visited with Tina and Cormier to meet the older couple. The stolen truck could be the same one taken from the gardener on August 6, the one Tina called police about later that evening. It might even be the truck seen in the grainy Mere Hotel security camera footage. And DeWolfe's reference to the fight between Tina and Cormier matched the story told by the former bank robber Robert Sango about meeting a distraught-looking Tina at the bus stop.

O'Donovan instructed the detectives to bring DeWolfe to Winnipeg, where he could personally monitor his statement as he gave it. Then he walked into the unit office and motioned to two of his most senior team members, Detective Sergeants Wade McDonald and Scott Taylor, and told them to head to the Glenelm address DeWolfe had given to pick up Sarah Holland and Tyrell Morrison.

Twenty-two Carmen Avenue was exactly as Cody had described: the last in a row of four plain-looking townhouses, each with a slightly raised front and back door reached by sets of wooden steps. The detectives parked their unmarked SUV slightly out of sight in a laneway and walked up to the front door.

A slim woman in her thirties answered and confirmed she was Sarah Holland. She looked tired and pale and was dressed in pyjamas even though it was now the afternoon. When the detectives informed her they were from the city's Homicide Unit and were investigating the murder of Tina Fontaine, she nodded calmly. She didn't seem surprised to see them.

"I need a few minutes to get dressed," she said, indicating that she would be happy to go to the station. The detectives asked if Tyrell Morrison was at home, but Holland told them he no longer lived there.

McDonald and Taylor headed back to their car to wait for Holland to join them. A few minutes later, she emerged and mentioned that she had left a friend inside the house. It was a detail the detectives did not at first register as significant. But as Holland was getting into the car, they noticed a man opening the back door to put out bags of garbage. He looked straight at them, making eye contact for a moment, and as he did they both realized they were looking directly into the face of their chief suspect, Raymond Cormier.

"Oh my God, that's him!" shouted Taylor.

It took Cormier a split second to register that the well-built men with buzz cuts were police officers in an unmarked car. He hurried back inside the house, and the detectives radioed O'Donovan for instructions.

"Bring him in," came the order.

McDonald ran to the back of the house and Taylor to the front, where he collided with Cormier, who was trying to escape on a bicycle. Cormier threw the bike straight at him and headed back into the house.

"You won't get me on any chickenshit charges," he yelled as the detective struggled to follow him through the hallway.

At the rear of the house, McDonald had reached the steps to the back door when it burst open and Cormier made a flying leap from the top. He began sprinting down an alley with McDonald and Taylor both in pursuit, yelling for him to stop. With the detectives closing in, Cormier lunged for the top of a six-foot-tall backyard fence. As he tried to pull himself over, McDonald made a grab for his ankle and the two men fell down hard, one on top of the other.

"What are you arresting me for?" Cormier shouted when McDonald had pinned him to the ground.

McDonald realized that he wasn't sure, so Taylor radioed O'Donovan for clarity, asking whether they should reference Cormier s outstanding warrants or Tina Fontaine.

"Tell him you're arresting him on the warrants, but caution him he may be charged with the murder of Tina Fontaine," O'Donovan replied.

Hearing this, Cormier shouted that he had important information about Tina and would tell them if they let him go. McDonald told him to save it. As Cormier lay in the dirt, McDonald read him his rights. Once Cormier had been subdued and handcuffed, the detectives put him in the back of their SUV, transferring Holland to a patrol car, which had arrived on the scene to help.

With his prime suspect on the way to the Public Safety Building, O'Donovan considered his next move. From the moment he had heard DeWolfe's story, the detective knew he needed to interview everyone who'd been identified as spending time at 22 Carmen. His initial objective had been to build up a comprehensive picture of what had happened at the house before bringing Cormier in. But as Cormier had run from his officers, he felt it was the right decision to arrest him. He hoped the outstanding warrants would be enough to keep him while they built up their case.

O'Donovan began to map out his new strategy. He gave orders for Holland, DeWolfe, and Morrison to be questioned that afternoon. The witnesses were to be separated and kept out of sight of each other to make sure they couldn't confer. The detective planned to watch their testimonies in the video monitoring room and decide how to confront Cormier when he had heard what they had to say. Until then, his prime suspect was to be detained in Interview Room 1. It was the closest secure room to his office, and O'Donovan felt comfortable knowing that Cormier would be sweating it out barely thirty metres away.

Farther along the corridor, in Interview Room 7, Ernest DeWolfe was already being interviewed by Stalker and Riddell, who were attempting to establish how well the group knew each other. The convict relayed how he had become involved with Morrison and Holland after meeting Morrison buying crack cocaine. He said he had become fond of the couple, especially Holland, whom he felt both protective of and attracted to, even though he was living with his girlfriend at the time. By day, he had worked on a construction site, but at night he would head to their place to spend time listening to music and getting high.

Cormier had been introduced into this friendship after DeWolfe had bumped into him and invited him over. The older man had been a reliable source of drugs, and they'd got used to having him around. Early one morning in July, DeWolfe related, he arrived at the house to find two Indigenous teenagers waking up on the futon in the living room. It was where Cormier often slept, using his own bedding, which he would store away in backpacks. DeWolfe had never seen the kids before and thought the girl looked very young, maybe thirteen or fourteen.

"Cormier told me he'd slept with her," DeWolfe told the detectives. Cormier had confided this to him a few hours after the teenagers left.

DeWolfe was shocked. "I was like, 'Isn't she a bit young?'" he said.

Cormier replied that Tina was actually eighteen. DeWolfe didn't believe him, and the conversation had stuck in his mind.

A few weeks later, Holland and Morrison told him about an explosive fight Cormier had had with Tina, which led to her storming out of the house. It had something to do with a truck, which DeWolfe remembered seeing, a dark Ford F-150, which had been parked at the back of the house for several days. The next time DeWolfe saw him, Cormier admitted stealing it and said that was why Tina had been shouting. But the argument had also been about something else.

"Cormier told me that she'd run out of the house because he was creeping her out. He was coming on to her," DeWolfe told the detectives. "He'd followed her out of the back door and she'd run away down an alley, shouting she was going to call the cops and rat him out."

When Cormier told him this story, DeWolfe had become worried. With the amount of drugs being used at the house, he didn't want the cops anywhere near. Cormier reassured him that it was okay. He had taken care of the problem and sold the truck.

"He'd said he'd talked to Tina and taken care of her as well, just the day before," DeWolfe said. Knowing what had happened to the teenager, he now believed Cormier was admitting to having killed her.

"What date did you have this conversation?" Stalker asked.

DeWolfe hesitated. The days of getting high at 22 Carmen had run into each other that summer. But there were a few dates that stuck in his mind. One was his birthday, on August 19. A few days before, on August 16, he and Sarah Holland had left to party in a cheap hotel. Cormier had initially gone with them but had got into an argument with the taxi driver, accusing him of taking a roundabout route, and had suddenly jumped out of the car. DeWolfe remembered that the conversation about Tina having been "taken care of" happened just before they had left for the hotel, on Friday, August 15.

If this was true, the detectives noted, it meant that Cormier had talked to Tina on August 14—days after the last sighting of her outside the Millennium Library on August 9. It was also days after O'Donovan believed her body had been driven to the Alexander Docks and dumped in the river.

"Could you be mistaken?" they asked DeWolfe.

He replied that he was pretty sure he was right, though admitted that drugs had affected his memory.

———

While DeWolfe was being questioned in one room, Sarah Holland was being led into another by Detective Sergeants Cory Francis and Marc Philippot, who had experience working with vulnerable women. In the harsh light of the interview room, Holland appeared much older than her thirty-two years. From the moment she began to speak, in a gentle but articulate voice, the detectives placed her as someone who had had a good upbringing. Holland was from Winnipeg's Métis population. She had attended college and flitted between jobs before claiming disability benefits because of fibromyalgia. By the time she met Tina, she had two young kids who were living with their father. The detectives noted she had a conviction for assault, but otherwise her record was clean.

Holland said she had met Tyrell Morrison in 2013, when she was living in the North End, close to where her children were going to school. Morrison was a little younger than her, Indigenous, and strikingly good-looking, with an angular, handsome face. From the moment they got together, the couple had been heavily into partying with alcohol and drugs. In June 2014 they had become engaged and taken a lease on the house at 22 Carmen. By then DeWolfe was becoming a regular part of their circle and came over most nights to smoke crack. But Holland's relationship with Morrison was beginning to unravel. Her fibromyalgia had flared up, and she would often spend all day upstairs in her bedroom, too ill to get dressed. Morrison was becoming abusive and would sometimes hit her. She said it was good that DeWolfe had been there to defuse the tension.

She remembered it was July when DeWolfe introduced his old friend Raymond Cormier—"Frenchie," as he liked to be known— into this mix. As far as Holland knew, he was living in a tent by the river and making his money by rifling through dumpsters for anything he could sell.

"Frenchie was as normal as you can be when you're on drugs," she told the detectives.

At first, Cormier had seemed like a nice guy who was down on his luck, constantly on the move and looking for ways to make money, carrying his belongings around in backpacks. Holland remembered seeing that he had blankets and a duvet cover with flowers on it, a radio, and a bag full of drug paraphernalia that he would some-times leave out on the floor. She told him she didn't mind if he stayed from time to time, and he would sleep on the futon in the downstairs room. But within a few weeks, Cormier had become a constant presence and was beginning to irritate her. He used to let himself in by a broken window, coming and going from the house as he pleased. Holland said it had been on her mind to fix it.

It was Cormier, she said, who'd introduced them to "banging," or injecting, crystal meth. "He showed us how you didn't need to heat it up, because you could dissolve the crystals in water," she told the detectives. "He showed us how to fill the syringe, find a vein, stick the needle in, and pull the plunger out a little so some blood came back into the needle. That meant you had the right spot."

Holland explained that sometimes finding a vein took several goes. And the needle could get clogged, so you needed to flush it out. Cormier had demonstrated how to do this, by drawing water into the needle, then pointing it upwards and quickly forcing the plunger back in. You knew it was clear when the water sprayed out over the walls and ceiling, leaving behind a satisfying arc of tiny droplets that would glisten pink with blood before fading away.

Although Cormier had established himself as the procurer of drugs for 22 Carmen, his friendship with Holland blew hot and cold. Holland felt an ambivalence towards the older man. On the one hand, Cormier was resourceful and could be fun to hang out with. On the other, he annoyed her by making lewd comments when Morrison wasn't around. A few times, he let her know he wanted to have sex with her. One afternoon he stumbled in on Morrison trying to rape her in her bedroom. Cormier reacted by smacking her boyfriend on the leg with a metal pipe and holding a screwdriver to his throat. She was grateful he had stepped in but was shocked by the violence of his temper.

"Tell us about the first time you met Tina Fontaine," prompted Philippot, gently steering her towards the subject of the teenager.

"I didn't know her as Tina," said Holland. "She said her name was Nicole."

Holland described how Cormier had brought a young Indigenous couple around one evening, possibly in late July, but she wasn't sure. Tina had introduced herself as eighteen-year-old Nicole and her boyfriend as nineteen-year-old Cody. Holland didn't believe her.

"I wasn't born yesterday," she told the detectives. "She looked younger, and I assumed she was a runaway, but I'd rather she was in my home than out on the streets."

Holland said she offered the kids a beer but was adamant that she and Morrison had not offered them drugs, because it was clear they were underage. She said it had been a relaxing evening. The group chatted for a while until Holland went upstairs to bed. As far as she knew, the others had left around the same time.

"Did you see Tina again?" asked Philippot.

Holland said yes, and this time she could remember the exact date. It was August 6, her son's birthday. Her ex-partner had refused to let her see him, and this left her feeling "broken." Around lunchtime, Tina appeared at the house on her bicycle. It was Cormier who opened the door to her.

"She was really upset and crying and wanted to see her mom," said Holland. "Her boyfriend had left and had gone back to his reserve, so I told her if she kept out of my way, she could stay."

Morrison and Cormier chatted to Tina downstairs, but Holland, still upset, retreated to her bedroom. For a while, Tina stayed with the men. But then she knocked on Holland's door and asked to come in.

"She told me Frenchie was creeping her out—grabbing at her, groping her, and making inappropriate comments," said Holland.

Holland told Tina she could stay with her as long as she was quiet. The day was hot and muggy, and the house had no air-conditioning so Holland had opened the bedroom window to let in a breeze. She lay on her bed, thumbing through magazines, while Tina settled into a comfortable old chair in a corner of the room. It had been a pleasant way to spend the afternoon, until Morrison and Cormier suddenly barged in and demanded that the women talk to them. Holland said Morrison seemed drunk. She thought Cormier was being predatory.

"He tried to make it sound like a joke," she said, "but I saw him try to go for Tina's boobs and say, 'Just do me.' Tina moved out of his way, shouting, 'Fuck off, you know I'm sixteen.' But he just laughed. We all said, 'Hey, she's just a baby, leave her alone!'"

When she first told the story to the detectives, Holland said she recalled the atmosphere that afternoon as being fairly lighthearted. Later, after she had time to think about the exchange, she changed her statement to say the mood had been hostile and aggressive. She said that Tina accused Cormier of being a "skinner," the street word for a sexual predator, commonly used for convicted pedophiles and rapists. After the women shouted at him, Cormier retreated downstairs.

Holland said she and Tina remained in the bedroom, reading and drinking beer into the early evening. Then Morrison came running up the stairs shouting for her to come to the kitchen. Once there, Holland found that every surface had been covered with

greasy power tools and gardening equipment. Cormier was bringing more stuff in from outside, and Holland assumed it was all stolen. She yelled at Cormier to get it out of her house.

A while later, Tina told her she was going downstairs for a glass
of water. Within minutes, Holland heard the sound of screaming
coming in through her open window. Morrison ran upstairs to tell
her that Cormier and Tina were getting into a big fight in the back
alley. He went into another bedroom to get a better view.

"I heard Tina yelling she would be calling the cops right away,"
said Holland. "I didn't really hear what Frenchie said—only the
word *river.*"

The screaming lasted several minutes until it seemed Tina had
run away. It was, Holland told the detectives, the last time she saw
or heard from the teenager. After the fight was over, Cormier came
back into the house looking angry and asked if Holland thought the
teenager would really call the police.

"I said no. It's my house, not yours, and I don't think she wants
to get me into trouble," said Holland.

Later that evening, the argument forgotten, Cormier went out
to buy drugs and they all got high.

"At any point, did you see a truck parked near 22 Carmen?"
asked Philippot.

Holland said no, she did not remember actually seeing a truck,
only the tools that Cormier had brought into the kitchen.

"When did you realize the girl in your house was Tina Fontaine?"
Philippot asked.

It was a while afterwards, Holland told him. She confirmed
DeWolfe's account of how they had caught a taxi to a hotel and
Cormier had jumped out on the way. Holland and DeWolfe contin-
ued on and stayed in the hotel until DeWolfe's birthday, on August 19.
That morning he gave her some money to buy food, and she was on

her way out when she caught sight of a newspaper lying in the lobby. On the front page was a story about how two bodies had been pulled from the Red River on the same day: the homeless hero and Tina Fontaine. She looked at the picture but did not recognize the girl. Hours later she saw another newspaper, and this time recognized the picture. It was the girl she knew as Nicole, and she was wearing exactly the same clothes she'd been wearing when Holland first met her.

Holland and DeWolfe returned to 22 Carmen, arriving to find Morrison, his cousin, and Cormier at the house. Holland said she waved the paper in front of the group, wanting to gauge their reactions, especially Cormier's.

"I asked Frenchie if he did it," she told Philippot.

He told her no. "He said the girl was exploited, murdered, and thrown in the river, and that was sad because she was just a kid," she said.

"Did he seem surprised?" asked Philippot.

Initially Holland said yes, though later she said he didn't seem too concerned. They didn't spend much time talking about the subject, as someone had brought meth and they wanted to get high. It was the last time the whole group was together at 22 Carmen. Two days later Morrison assaulted her again, this time injuring her badly enough to send her to hospital. He was arrested, released on bail, and moved back in with his mother while he waited for his trial. A week later, DeWolfe was arrested for stealing. By October 1, only Holland and Cormier were left in the house.

The detectives asked Holland to sign her statement and arranged for a car to take her back to 22 Carmen. They told her that a forensic team would be over in the next few hours, so she should keep everything as she had left it that morning. As Holland was preparing to leave, her now ex-boyfriend, Tyrell Morrison, was being settled into another interview room farther down the corridor. Earlier that day, Detective Sergeants Tracy Oliver and Doug Bailey had arrived at Morrison's mother's house unannounced and asked the twenty-six-year-old to accompany them back to the station to answer questions about Tina Fontaine. Morrison had been cooperative.

In a matter-of-fact manner, Morrison corroborated Holland and DeWolfe's version of what had happened that summer. When Oliver asked when he'd first met Tina, Morrison told him he had seen the teenager only twice. The first time was when Tina and Cody arrived at 22 Carmen one evening in July. He took a liking to the young girl, who had seemed spirited and talkative, while her boyfriend remained silently by her side. They drank beer and chatted, and Morrison was adamant that he and Holland hadn't given Tina anything stronger than that.

"We were kind of greedy with our drugs, so we didn't share," he explained. "But I did see Frenchie giving her a crack pipe to smoke."

The detectives found Morrison's next statement shocking.

"I remember she said it was better than the stuff her mom had given her," he said.

The last time Morrison saw Tina was on August 6, without Cody, when she knocked on the front door and walked into the house, crying, holding on to her bike. He recounted how Tina asked to stay and cleaned up the kitchen as a goodwill gesture. In return, he offered to make her lunch. At some point she went into the main room where Cormier was staying, and a while later Morrison walked in to see her sitting on the couch with Cormier's head in her lap. When Cormier spotted Morrison, he sat up quickly.

"What happened next?" asked Oliver.

Morrison said he had been taking so many drugs at the time that he struggled to remember. But Cormier must have left the house, because the next time he saw him was a few hours later, when he pulled up in a dark four-by-four and started unloading gardening equipment. After Holland got angry, Cormier sped out of the house on Tina's bike. While he was away, Morrison told Tina to throw the truck keys into the garden in case the cops came. When Cormier returned a short while later, he demanded that Tina find them, yelling at her that she was a bitch.

O'Donovan, watching the interview from the monitoring room, suddenly thought of a question that none of the witnesses had answered. If Tina had arrived on her bike, why didn't she also leave on it? Something had clearly happened, because two days later she told her CFS worker she no longer had a bike but that her meth-user friend Sebastian was going to get her a new one.

In the interview room, Detective Sergeant Oliver picked up on the same train of thought.

"If Tina was angry and wanted to get out of the house quickly, why didn't she use her bike?" he asked.

"Because by then her bike was only two wheels," explained Morrison.

It seemed that after Cormier had left the house on Tina's bike, he sold its frame for a bag of weed. When Tina asked for it back, Cormier pointed to the wheels and said, "There it is." It was another reason why she had stormed out in a rage.

Morrison said his last view of Tina was of her running off down the alley, still screaming at Cormier. The truck remained outside the house for a couple of days, but then it disappeared. Much later, Holland and DeWolfe showed him the newspaper with Tina's picture on the front page. Morrison remembered reading out loud that she was only fifteen and wanting to see what Cormier's reaction would be.

"Frenchie said, 'Holy shit, no wonder she didn't put out,'" Morrison told the detectives.

With all three interviews concluded, O'Donovan pondered what to do next. It had been a phenomenally good day for his investigation, and he was pleased with how the questioning had gone. Despite their drug-fuelled lifestyles, the witnesses had been consistent. O'Donovan had been particularly impressed with DeWolfe, who would likely face a hostile reception back in prison for talking. Morrison had seemed reliable too. He had not given a lot of detail, but neither did he seem to be holding anything back.

The only reservation O'Donovan had was about Sarah Holland's interview. She had confirmed Cormier's predatory sexual interest in Tina but had not remembered the stolen truck. After Philippot and Francis had finished their interview, O'Donovan sent them back in twice more to ask her about it. Each time, she kept to her story and insisted that she had never seen it. This detail annoyed the detective, who would have preferred that all the accounts of what had happened at 22 Carmen tie up neatly together.

Still, there was enough to start building a case against Raymond Cormier. The next step would be to interview him and record his statement on video. O'Donovan was struck with an uncomfortable sense of both hope and worry: hope that he would get a confession, or at least a story, which would resolve the case, alleviate the crushing public pressure on his team, and fulfill his own desire to find out the truth; worry that Cormier would sit in silence and give them nothing. The detective had known cases where this had happened, and it had been impossible to move them forward. He glanced at the clock. By now it was late afternoon, and Cormier had been sitting alone for nearly two hours. It was time for his detectives to pay him a visit.

9.

"I DID NOT KILL THAT GIRL"

nterview Room 1 was approximately thirteen square metres in size, lit by a fluorescent light, and bare except for a metal chair and table bolted to the floor. Since 2:47 P.M. on October 1, Raymond Cormier had been locked inside this secure, windowless box. Detectives had checked in on him from time to time, either by sliding open a small window in the steel door or by watching the video feed displayed in the monitoring room. Despite having run from the detectives who arrested him, Cormier now maintained he had important information about Tina's murder. But he had been told to sit tight until the detectives were ready, so had lain down on the floor and tried to fall asleep. He was coming down from crystal meth and feeling the withdrawal. "My hands are swollen, my body's sore, and I'm hungry and tired," he said.

At 4:16 P.M., Detective Sergeants Wade McDonald and Scott Taylor entered the room carrying two chairs, a cup of coffee, and a cup of water. As the senior of the two detectives, McDonald had been instructed to take the lead in the interview. He knew this might be the first of several rounds of questioning, and so he planned to proceed slowly.

Addressing Cormier in a friendly tone, he asked him to sit up. Cormier complied, slowly pulling himself to his feet and slumping down on his chair so that his head rested against the side wall. He was wearing a black long-sleeved T-shirt, and his shoulder-length hair was tied back in a ponytail. When McDonald offered him coffee, he refused it.

"You can call me Wade, and you can call him Scott," began McDonald. "Can I call you Ray?"

"Doesn't matter what you call me," Cormier replied, turning his face to the wall so that it was difficult to hear what he was saying.

McDonald told Cormier that he wanted to make sure he understood what was going on, to which Cormier nodded that he did. He sat with his head bowed and his arms crossed in front of him.

"We're arresting you for the murder of Tina Fontaine," said McDonald.

"I don't understand how you can arrest someone and not charge them," Cormier snapped back. McDonald didn't think it necessary to explain that this was normal practice.

"Don't focus on me as the guy that did this, 'cause I didn't do it, right?" Cormier mumbled.

McDonald didn't respond to this statement and instead asked Cormier if he would like to call a lawyer. Cormier replied that he would, but only if he was being charged. McDonald made it clear that he was free to call one at any time.

"You knew Tina Fontaine for how long?" the detective asked.

"Two weeks, maybe a month?" Cormier replied, adding that he had hardly known her at all and that she didn't deserve what had happened to her.

McDonald wanted to know how they met. In a series of rambling answers, Cormier described how he had been cycling in
the North End at around 4 A.M., heading towards the downtown
area, when he first saw Tina and Cody. They had been walking in
the other direction and had waved to him. He couldn't remember
who had shouted first, and he replied that if they wanted to get
him to stop they better have something to get him high. They said
they had a little weed to share.

When Cormier found out they were homeless, he took them to
the basement of an apartment block for the night. After that, they
bumped into each other five or six times. The teenagers bragged
about dealing weed at Portage Place. Cormier said he thought Tina
had had some sort of argument with her welfare workers, because
she was sleeping on couches or in stairwells. By way of explanation
of his own lifestyle, he told the detectives he was addicted to crystal
meth, which he took nearly every day. It meant he hardly ever slept.

McDonald nodded slowly, taking in the details. The first interview with a suspect was about establishing a version of events and
recognizing weaknesses that could be challenged later. He turned
the conversation to 22 Carmen Avenue, in particular the events of
August 6, when Tina arrived at the house on her own. He wanted
to know what Cormier was thinking when he saw her.

"She was crying," Cormier told him. "She was distraught. Cody
had gone back to the reserve."

After Tina had cycled there on her mountain bike, Cormier said
they sat around drinking and smoking pot. The pot had run out
and so he'd borrowed her bike to get more. Tina mentioned she
was planning to sell the bike, so he felt she'd given him the green
light to take it himself and sell it for dope. The money he got was
enough for almost two grams of weed.

But when he returned, Tina demanded to know where her bike was. Cormier told her it was gone, and they got into a fight. She stormed out and he followed.

"She's just yelling and screaming and I'm yelling and screaming, and she said something and I got pissed off and threw her weed at her feet," he said. "And she's gone. See you later." Days later, he read in the newspaper she had been murdered.

As Cormier spoke, he kept his arms wrapped around him and his head close to the wall. His hair, some of which had worked free from his ponytail, had started to hang down over his forehead, obscuring his eyes and mouth. His speech was slurred and sometimes difficult to understand. But watching in the video monitoring room, O'Donovan noted that Cormier was quite coherent for a junkie coming down from a high. He seemed to be choosing his words carefully, and it was notable that he had not mentioned the stolen truck or the gardening tools the other witnesses remembered.

Cormier continued with his story. When Tina turned up at 22 Carmen, she confessed to him that she'd just stolen $250 from an unnamed guy. "She's kind of crazy a little bit, you know," he said. "Like lost. Her mom and dad hurt her and everything like that."

He said the man she'd ripped off wasn't the only suspicious guy hanging around. When he and Tina were arguing outside, he noticed that there was a stranger with long dirty-blond hair walking on the sidewalk just behind her.

"What the fuck, man? Did she get murdered right after she left me, or did it happen the next day?" he asked. "After I left and you've got a pretty young girl, distraught and crying and screaming, hysterical a little bit. Is that person the one who went up to her and said, 'Hey are you okay?'"

Cormier explained that what he was trying to do was think like a cop and attempt to figure out what had happened. The man on the street had raised his suspicions. And he had a third possible lead. This one concerned the apartment block where Cody's dad had been living. He said there had been a crystal meth shooting gallery—a "jib house"—on the ground floor where sex workers would go to get high, and he had heard there was a murder there.

"What does Sarah think happened to her?" asked McDonald, his tone calm and level.

"She knows what happened to her. She got murdered. She got fucking skinned on and fucking murdered," Cormier replied, his voice now animated, referring to his theory that Tina had been killed by a pedophile.

McDonald asked him about Holland. "Did you have a relationship with her?"

Cormier raised his head a little. "Oh, believe me, I wanted it so badly," he said.

Now, seemingly warmed up, Cormier started to blurt out more information, flitting quickly between random thoughts. Tina had made him think of his own daughter, who had been given up for adoption. He had two sons as well. One of them was an auto body technician, living in Montreal with a wife and kids. Cormier said he had come to Winnipeg only because he'd been locked up in Stony Mountain prison, which was close to the city. He didn't like it here because he had no friends, though there was a time when he thought he'd had a chance with Sarah. The last time he had seen Tina was the only time her boyfriend hadn't been with her, her "royal guard," as he liked to call Cody.

"Have you been with Tina intimately?" asked McDonald, his voice still calm and friendly.

"No, I never went there," Cormier answered firmly, adding that he now knew Tina had been only sixteen.

McDonald raised his eyebrows. "She looked eighteen," the detective said. He was challenging Cormier, wondering if he was deliberately recalling Tina's age as sixteen rather than fifteen because he didn't want to admit she was under the age of consent.

Cormier shrugged. "That's what I thought too, and then I found out she was fifteen or sixteen," he said, correcting himself. "And, fuck, if she was fifteen, that would have made me a pedophile. But I'm not a skinner or anything."

McDonald wanted to go back over the events of the summer. Cormier told him he first met Ernest DeWolfe in Stony Mountain prison and described him as a "bad junkie." He admitted he'd fallen in love with Sarah and called Tyrell Morrison "a piece of shit" for treating her badly. He said the first night he'd gone over to 22 Carmen, he had stopped Morrison from trying to rape her.

"I came close to committing the first murder of my life that night," he said. "I still don't know why I didn't drive that screwdriver through his fucking heart."

Cormier said he made a living from scrap metal, explaining how he would take the cords from abandoned TVs and electrical appliances and burn off the plastic to expose the copper wiring inside. The money from this and from collecting empty bottles was enough to fund his dope habit. McDonald asked if he'd ever stolen bicycles or vehicles. Cormier nodded yes, in the winter, when it was freezing, when he could find a car with the keys still in it. But, he stressed, the last vehicle he had stolen was in Calgary. He had never stolen one in Winnipeg.

"I believe one of the charges that they have on me now is for possession of a stolen vehicle," he said, fishing for information. "Like, how do you know that's not my vehicle?"

McDonald ignored the question and steered the conversation

back to Tina and the last time Cormier had seen her. "Did you say it was a few days before she was found? How come you never called us?" he asked.

"Well, buddy, they got warrants out for my arrest and I knew that," Cormier replied. He said he talked to Holland about going to the police a couple of times. But the combination of the outstanding warrants and his meth addiction meant he had done nothing about it.

Conscious that Cormier's timeline of events did not match the account given by the other witnesses, McDonald asked again if the last time Cormier saw Tina was a couple of days before she was found. Again Cormier said that it was, or at least that's what he remembered. He said it could have been a Friday night, but he wasn't sure.

"So when you saw her walking and you threw dope at her, where did you go?" asked the detective. "Why didn't you continue to follow her?"

His head still against the wall, Cormier seemed irritated.

"She's hysterical, she's yelling and screaming in the middle of the road, and I knew that person was over there, and I just . . . I had enough, I just threw it," he explained, once again mentioning the stranger he'd seen on the street. "I walk away from people all the time that are homeless and distraught," he said.

But the argument had forced him to see Tina in a different light, he continued. He now thought of her as being like his daughter, and his real daughter had once been homeless too. Though he admitted that when he'd first seen the teenager, he thought she was a "nice little tight . . ." His voice trailed off.

"First you admitted what?" asked McDonald, struggling to understand.

"Nice little tightie. A nice hot chickie. You know what I mean," replied Cormier. "And then her age came, oh, no. That's when I started to . . ." The rest of what he said was inaudible.

For the first time in the interview, Detective Sergeant Taylor spoke up. They were having a hard time hearing him, Taylor said, because his hair was hanging over his mouth. Cormier responded by saying that he knew he was a mess. He was sore and he wanted to leave. The detectives ignored his request.

Cormier continued to speak. "Sarah knew that she was just too young. Sarah's like a straight-up mother . . . she's like a hundred percent mother material."

McDonald again asked Cormier what happened after the argument. Cormier explained that after he threw the bag of weed at her feet, Tina bent down to pick it up as he turned to walk away.

"Did she threaten you, to call the cops?" asked the detective.

"She said . . . She was going to . . . Like I said, there we were, yelling and screaming at each other." Cormier was hesitating.

"Did she assault you?" asked McDonald.

"No." Now his voice was firm. "She's a fucking kid, man. She was angry 'cause I just sold her bike."

"When did she change from a hot ticket to a daughter?" McDonald asked.

Cormier said nothing for a few seconds. "I think it was that first night. And I might have said something derogatory about banging her."

"You were going to bang her?" asked McDonald.

"Not that I was going to bang her. That I . . . It would be nice to get a b-job or whatever . . . Something sexual in nature or whatever. And then Sarah kind of said, 'She's kind of young, you know.'"

"Did you ever tell anyone you slept with Tina?"

"No."

Feeling that he was beginning to get a clearer picture of Cormier's relationship with Tina, McDonald asked him to describe exactly how close he had been to her. Cormier replied that Tina had shown him the tattoo on her back with her father's name on it. If his own daughter had done that, he would be proud of her. His tone became avuncular. It would have been nice to be in a position to help Tina and Cody, he said. If anyone had hurt his daughter like Tina had been hurt, he would have killed him.

"How could I forgive a pedophile for being a pedophile?" he explained, adding that he didn't think there were any excuses for behaving that way. "I had a couple of bad things happen to me as a kid, but I don't go around fucking skinning and fucking raping and killing," he said, his voice thick with emotion. "I can see fucking maybe escaping into drugs or medicating myself . . . It doesn't change the fact that a sixteen-year-old was fucking butchered and fucking dumped."

He said he hoped McDonald and Taylor found the stranger who'd been walking on the other side of the street when he and Tina were arguing. He described him as looking like Robert Plant, the lead singer from the rock band Led Zeppelin. Cormier noticed the guy because he was high at the time. The crystal meth did that, he explained; it heightened his awareness, made him notice every little detail.

"Some of her last words to me were 'I'm homeless,' and she's crying and yelling and screaming," he continued. "And I think she did threaten to call the cops that night. I think."

McDonald's response was quick. "On what?"

"I don't know. It was something, stealing a bike or whatever. I don't know," replied Cormier, sidestepping any mention of a stolen truck.

"I'm not blind. I saw. She was a very beautiful young girl," Cormier admitted. "It would be nice to get a blow job from her was the thought in the back of my head. You know. It's the way it is. The truth."

McDonald asked if Tina had ever shown him any affection in return.

"Not sexual affection, if that's what you mean, no," said Cormier, though he added that when Tina had knocked on the door of 22 Carmen, alone and in tears, he wondered what he would get out of it. "When a woman is crying, you know how they . . . I don't know, hug you or . . ." he said, hinting that Tina may have wanted something more than just fatherly reassurance.

The interview had now been running for well over an hour. Cormier was sounding increasingly frustrated and was trying to steer the conversation away from his own relationship with Tina. He accused Tyrell Morrison of being the person who killed her, saying he knew that Morrison was a violent man who had assaulted Sarah several times.

"There must be some kind of DNA or fucking something like that," he demanded.

McDonald reassured him that DNA would be part of the investigation. It was now 5:43 P.M., and the detective suggested a break. Cormier told them he wanted a blanket but nothing to eat. As the detectives left the room, he once again settled down on the floor.

McDonald and Taylor headed straight to the video monitoring room, where O'Donovan had been watching the entire interview. Over coffee, the men discussed how struck they were by Cormier's lack of emotion. O'Donovan's impression was that Cormier had protested his innocence too much. He had seen many drug addicts in his career, and, once in a police interview room, most tended to become tearful and remorseful. Cormier was different. He had seemed in control and defensive, carefully deflecting the questions and trying to change the course of the conversation. Although he had admitted he wanted to have sex with Tina, he had also been keen to paint himself as a fatherly figure who wanted to look after her. O'Donovan said he didn't believe that for a second. It troubled him that Cormier mentioned seeing Tina's tattoo. It was in the middle of her back, between her shoulder blades, and it wouldn't be visible if she was wearing clothes. This suggested that Cormier might have got further with Tina than he was admitting.

Then there was the matter of the stolen truck. Cormier had avoided mentioning it even when the questions were clearly pointing that way. Instead, he had suggested other suspects. The detectives counted them up. There was the crystal meth house beneath Cody's father's apartment, where Cormier said a murder had taken place. There was the man who Tina had allegedly stolen $250 from before arriving at 22 Carmen on the day of the argument. There was the Robert Plant lookalike who'd heard the argument on the street and perhaps used it as an excuse to approach Tina. And there was Tyrell Morrison, who Cormier said had the temperament to commit sex crimes.

"He's bullshitting," said McDonald.

O'Donovan nodded his head slowly. Not for the first time, he thought of Cormier as the arch survivor. He decided they would leave their suspect to sleep for several hours while they planned the next phase of their interview. He needed time to give the detectives a detailed briefing of what had been said by DeWolfe, Holland, and Morrison so that they could use the information to challenge Cormier's version of events.

———

At 9:40 P.M., four hours after the first interview, the detectives returned to Interview Room 1. Taylor carried with him a cup of water. Cormier appeared to be asleep on the floor under the blanket they had given him. McDonald pulled it away from him. "Hey, I was going to put that round me," protested Cormier, sitting up, with his head bowed and his hair hanging over his face.

McDonald had made the gesture to demonstrate that from now on Cormier would not be getting an easy ride. "We work with truths," he said sternly. He told Cormier he wanted to go back to the night he had argued with Tina. Other witnesses had given their side of the story. "You had tools at Sarah's, power tools?" McDonald asked.

Cormier kept his head bowed and his arms crossed and took his time to respond. He appeared sleepy, and when he finally spoke, his voice was more hostile than it had been earlier. "I'm baffled here. What have power tools to do with Tina being murdered?" he asked.

"What vehicle did you have with you that night?" McDonald said.

At first, Cormier was unresponsive. He asked again what any of this had to do with Tina's murder. For the first time, he wondered aloud whether he should call a lawyer.

"I'm telling you guys, you've got the fucking wrong guy . . . I never killed Tina, okay? She was just a fucking little girl!" he shouted.

McDonald tried to reassure him, telling him repeatedly that they were not going to charge him for stealing the truck. But Cormier, his head still down and against the wall, said he didn't want to talk about it.

"You're one of the last people to see her alive," Taylor said.

"We want you to be honest about the last time you saw her," McDonald added. "What type of vehicle was it?"

"A truck, black . . . that's too much info . . ." The words were slurred.

"Where did you get it?" asked McDonald.

"It doesn't matter. It had nothing to do with the fucking murder."

Cormier was angry now. He stood up for a few seconds, then lay down in the fetal position, demanding to speak to a lawyer. McDonald left the room and came back a few minutes later with a cell phone in his hand. He told Cormier he had the duty lawyer on the line. Cormier was still on the floor, saying he was sleepy, but he took the phone and the detectives turned off the video and audio monitoring so he could speak to the lawyer privately.

Ten minutes later, the phone call over, the detectives returned to the room. By now Cormier was sitting up on the floor, still with his head bowed, saying he wasn't going to get up.

"We have to search you," McDonald said.

Cormier stayed where he was, refusing to move. The detectives told him that they needed him to remove his hair tie. Cormier still refused to move.

"I don't know why you're so angry," said McDonald.

"You're investigating the wrong person!" Cormier shouted.

Suddenly he pulled his hair tie out with such force that a clump of hair came out with it.

"Here, you want to fucking search? Pat it all down!"

He stood up and began ripping the clothes off his body. "Here!" he yelled as he threw them to the floor.

He was now standing in front of them totally naked, his arms and legs outstretched like a star. The detectives could see tattoos on his forearms and torso and noted that, although thin and badly nourished, he still looked strong and muscular.

"You go find the person who fucking did it!" Cormier screamed, the veins in his neck bulging as his fists clenched with anger.

The detectives sat still on their chairs, staring up at him impassively. Privately, McDonald was shocked by the level of rage in the man in front of him, who seemed to have escalated from docile to "complete animal" within a matter of seconds. After a minute or so, Cormier appeared to calm down. Taylor picked up his clothes and began to list them as evidence, bagging them to be processed for DNA. One black hair tie, a pair of white and grey Asics runners, a pair of black and orange gloves, a black long-sleeved T-shirt, jeans, a black wallet, a cigarette lighter, some ID and bank cards. McDonald passed Cormier some white paper disposable pants and a top to put on. Cormier pulled on the pants but left the top on the table and went back to lying in the fetal position on the floor, facing the back wall with his head underneath his chair.

McDonald addressed Cormier's motionless back. "Have I been an asshole to you today?" he asked.

"My lawyer says you're charging me for this murder. Are you fucking serious?" replied Cormier, his voice muffled.

"We're not going to charge an innocent person," McDonald reassured him, explaining that it would be the Crown prosecutor who would decide whether to authorize the charge. Both detectives were now firing questions at Cormier, ordering him to sit up and respond properly. But their suspect was refusing to move. Finally, he said he wanted his lawyer present.

"I did not kill that girl. I didn't kill fucking nobody. I don't know what happened to that fucking little girl!" he shouted.

He turned his back to the detectives again, but McDonald and Taylor kept going.

"Tina Fontaine has a family who are crying every day, wondering what happened to her," said McDonald. By now, he and Taylor had moved their chairs closer to Cormier's prone body and were leaning over him.

"Ray, come on, that fifteen-year-old girl hasn't had the privilege or pleasure of getting married, having kids, going to school, getting a job." McDonald's tactics had turned to the emotional. "The rage in you, Ray, is unbelievable. Why are you such an angry person? Why did you run away from the police?"

Cormier remained silent on the floor. Eventually, after twenty minutes with no response, the detectives gave up. They noted the time as 10:58 P.M. Telling Cormier the interview was over, they helped him to his feet and walked him into the corridor.

O'Donovan appeared outside the room to conduct the necessary official review of the interview and to sign the log sheet.

He looked at Cormier. "Were you mistreated?" It was a question he was required to ask.

Cormier shook his head. His hair was hanging over this face and he was still naked from the waist up.

"Put on your shirt," said O'Donovan.

Cormier looked at him and grunted but did nothing.

O'Donovan felt his anger rising. "If you have no respect for us, at least have some self-respect!" he shouted. "Put on your shirt!"

Cormier reacted immediately, pulling on the paper top without looking up. Out of the corner of his eye O'Donovan could sense Taylor staring at him, his eyebrows arched in surprise. His team was not used to hearing him raise his voice. There was an awkward silence as the detectives turned their suspect around to take him to be fingerprinted.

"Get that child-killer out of my station," O'Donovan hissed, loud enough for Cormier to hear as he was walked away. O'Donovan watched the trio disappear down the corridor then stormed back into his office. "Fuck!" he shouted and slammed his door.

For a moment he stood still, paralyzed with frustration. It was unusual for him to become so personally invested and betray his emotions, but he'd never been more convinced that he had the right man. O'Donovan knew his conviction was anchored in instinct, not evidence, but he saw too many red flags to dismiss it. Cormier's skilful deflection of McDonald's questions about the stolen truck suggested the vehicle was significant. His obvious sexual interest in the teenager combined with his explosive temper implied a motive. And although he'd said the last time he saw her was the day of their argument, Tina had told her social worker two days later that her friend Sebastian would be getting her a bike. When had he promised this? He hadn't admitted to saying it during the argument. Had she made another arrangement to go back to see him? Was this when she was killed? Before he got rid of the stolen truck, had he used it to transport her body to the river?

It's going to be a long night, O'Donovan thought, sitting down at his computer to download the recording of the interview. He was determined to watch it over and over again until he knew it by heart. He told himself that there must be something in Cormier's words that would betray his guilt.

10.

THE CHLOE GREEN
DUVET COVER

The next few days presented a logistical challenge for O'Donovan. He didn't have the confession he needed to charge Cormier with Tina's murder, but he wanted to keep him in custody for as long as he could. The detective knew that if he released Cormier back onto the streets, it would be difficult to keep him under surveillance. He was also genuinely concerned that Cormier might attack another young woman. For the moment, his suspect was being held under the two warrants issued for past minor offences, the "chickenshit charges" Cormier had referred to when resisting arrest. O'Donovan sought the advice of a senior prosecutor to find out how long these would keep him detained, and the reply was disheartening: only a week to ten days at the most. The problem was keeping the detective awake at night.

But then he had a stroke of luck. Investigators from other departments regularly sent out email bulletins with security camera images of theft suspects. One of these showed a robbery at a Winnipeg supermarket in which a man had stolen a large quantity of meat and threatened the security guard with a screwdriver. Detective Sergeant Taylor was able to identify Cormier as the perpetrator because of the tattoos he'd seen when Cormier had stripped down. O'Donovan immediately contacted the department and instructed them to arrest Cormier themselves. The new charge was serious enough for him to be locked up for several months until his case was heard.

Although O'Donovan was excited to be finally moving ahead with the case, it was frustrating that he couldn't share his prog-ress with the wider community. The press was still demanding to know why no one had been charged for killing Tina. Most diffi-cult of all was not being able to update Tina's guardian, Thelma Favel. Thelma had rung him repeatedly, usually after hearing about arrests in other homicide cases. She was always friendly, inquiring after O'Donovan's health and family before tentatively asking whether he'd made any headway with Tina.

"We're still working on it and making progress, but I can't give you specifics," O'Donovan would say, stressing it was a difficult case that relied on the evidence of transient people, making his job harder.

Thelma would listen politely and thank him for his work, but O'Donovan was left with the impression that she didn't quite believe him. He felt as if he was failing her, but it was better to say nothing than to give false hope.

At the end of October, happy in the knowledge that he'd bought himself some time with Cormier, O'Donovan gathered his team to assess where they stood. Cormier was their prime suspect, but other leads needed to be followed up on, not least the two men from the Furby Street rooming house. Detectives were still tracking down security camera footage that might have recorded Tina during her last few days. Calls to the tip line continued to flood in, and each one needed to be meticulously examined and crossed off the list. It was unusual, O'Donovan reflected, that a homicide investigation should demand so many personnel hours so far in. But this case was unprecedented in so many ways.

The key task for O'Donovan remained unravelling Cormier's interview. The detective felt he was clearly hiding something and needed to know whether this was just the theft of the truck or something more sinister. The team gathered to discuss ways Cormier might be encouraged to talk. It was unlikely he would open up to a police officer, but he might confess to another prisoner. So, on November 3, O'Donovan asked Detective Sergeants Stalker and Riddell to travel to Milner Ridge Correctional Centre to speak to Ernest DeWolfe. With Cormier scheduled to be moved there soon, O'Donovan wanted his men to ask DeWolfe if he would become a police informant.

When Stalker and Riddell arrived, they found that DeWolfe had already asked the prison authorities for a separation order so that he and Cormier would be kept apart.

"I thought he might be sent here," DeWolfe explained. "I don't know what the police told him about my statement, but if he knows I've ratted on him, he'll come after me."

DeWolfe said he was disgusted by Cormier, who he now firmly believed had killed Tina. Given the strength of his feelings, he felt he wouldn't be able to pull off the role of confidant. Prison wasn't the place to put yourself in that sort of danger, he said, though he'd be happy to help after he was released.

O'Donovan hesitated when he heard the offer, knowing DeWolfe's drug habit meant he could be unpredictable. He decided to decline. A few days later, Cormier was sent to Milner Ridge. As he had chosen not to apply for bail, he would be held there until his trial. O'Donovan obtained a warrant to obtain a sample of his DNA.

"Mr. Cormier, if you had nothing to do with Miss Fontaine's death, this will prove it," Detective Sergeant Doug Bailey said when he arrived to collect it, holding the DNA pack up for Cormier to see.

Cormier nodded. He seemed in a surprisingly cooperative mood and was open to chatting, particularly about how the detectives worked and any evidence they might have gathered. He had shaved his long hair down to a buzz cut, and as he spoke he ran his hand over his now exposed scalp.

"You know, if you find any of my hairs on Tina, it's because my hair used to be long—it fell out everywhere," he said. He and Tina often spent time in the same room and sat on the same chairs and couches, he explained. "But you won't find any of my sperm on her," he added confidently.

Bailey pricked Cormier's fingertip with a sterile lancet and squeezed a single drop of blood onto the collection card. As Bailey went about his work, Cormier changed the conversation to the subject of the stolen truck.

"Let's just say I was driving it," he said. "Would that mean I'd be charged with stealing it?"

Bailey's reply was noncommittal. Throughout the conversation, the detective tried to appear open to Cormier's suggestions without giving too much away. Back at the Public Safety Building, he told O'Donovan that he thought Cormier had been fishing for information and was clearly worried about his DNA. O'Donovan agreed. But Cormier's comment about not finding his semen bothered him. He steadfastly believed that Cormier had had a sexual relationship with Tina, so this confidence was perplexing.

O'Donovan pondered the issue as he headed home that Friday night. Early the next morning, he received a surprise phone call from the duty inspector at work. "Prepare yourself for a long day," his colleague warned.

Another young woman had been found by the river. This time it was the Assiniboine, the wide tributary that fed into the Red in central Winnipeg. She was still alive and had been taken to hospital, but she was in critical condition and not expected to survive beyond a few hours. The duty inspector said it was likely that the case would become a homicide.

Oh, God, not again, O'Donovan thought as he wolfed down his breakfast before heading to his car.

The victim was identified as a sixteen-year-old Indigenous schoolgirl who had been found earlier that morning, semi-clothed and unconscious, on the riverbank close to the water's edge. It appeared that she had lain there for several hours before being noticed by a passerby on an early-morning walk. The girl had been badly beaten and sexually assaulted, and she was suffering from such severe hypothermia that her family had been told to prepare for the worst.

But miraculously, by late afternoon the girl was showing signs of recovery. When O'Donovan announced the good news in his office, a loud cheer erupted. It had been a tense few months. Although morale remained high within the unit, many officers had daughters of their own, and the strain of working on Tina's case had taken its toll. Now, at last, they had something rare to celebrate: a victim clawed back from the brink of death. But as good as this news was, the mood soon sobered when the details of what had happened emerged.

The previous evening, the girl had been out with friends on what was a typical Friday night for the teenager. It appeared that two strangers had enticed her to walk away from her group and follow them down a secluded path underneath the Midtown Bridge. Here, she had been violently sexually assaulted. It was not clear whether she had waded into the river to escape, or her attackers had thrown her in, but she had ended up flailing in the freezing water. She had managed to get herself back to the bank, scrabbling over jagged rocks a few metres upstream, only to be confronted by her attackers again, who viciously beat her for a second time. The men left her on the riverbank to die, soaking wet and half-naked. O'Donovan noted that the overnight temperature had been −5°C, but the wind chill was far colder.

On Monday morning, with Tina's case in mind, O'Donovan's boss, Superintendent Danny Smyth, decided the Homicide Unit would make a public appeal for information and took the unusual step of releasing the girl's name to the press. Even though she was a minor and entitled to anonymity, emphasizing the victim's identity had provoked such a strong public response in Tina's case that Smyth decided it was a practice worth repeating.

His instincts were correct. Within hours, the unit's phone line was inundated with calls. Crucially, information came in about a similar incident with a different woman that had happened on the same night. Putting the two together, detectives were able to identify a young Indigenous man and a teenager as responsible for both attacks.

"I think their crimes and the viciousness of them speak for themselves," Smyth told a crowded press conference after the arrests were announced.

Although the speed at which they had solved the investigation and the teenager's eventual recovery was a well-publicized victory for the Winnipeg Police Service, it also refocused attention back onto their lack of progress in Tina's case. Tina was now firmly the national face of the disproportionately high number of missing and murdered Indigenous women in Canada, which was now a regular headline issue. Two months earlier, an Indigenous woman, Holly Jarrett, had posted a selfie on social media holding up a sign on which she had written "#AmINext?" Her protest came after her cousin Loretta Saunders, who had been working on a thesis on violence against Indigenous women, was herself murdered. Jarrett asked other Indigenous women to post their own pictures, and the campaign took off, gaining international coverage. The women added their voices to the growing number of people demanding a national inquiry into the root causes of the violence. The result was that the Homicide Unit felt under mounting pressure to announce an arrest for Tina's murder and was facing public criticism for dragging its feet.

But O'Donovan refused to be distracted. His customary style was to work slowly and methodically, and he was determined to stick to his plan. His officers were well aware of the media scrutiny and were working far harder than he could remember. All they could do was keep moving forward and trust that results would eventually appear.

A week later, at the end of November, Detective Sergeant Doug Bailey knocked on O'Donovan's office door.

"Cormier's just called me to say he knows who killed Tina," Bailey told his boss.

O'Donovan paused for a second to digest the information. His immediate thought was to assume that Cormier was sending them on a wild goose chase or was fishing for information. But it was possible he might have something valuable to say.

"Well, we'd better hear him out," he replied.

A couple of days later, on December 1, 2014, Cormier arrived at police headquarters for an interview. He was informed that he was still a suspect in the Tina Fontaine case and could call a lawyer anytime, but Cormier declined, saying he was impatient to talk. He told detectives that for the last few days he'd been sharing his cell with a biker who was deeply entrenched in Winnipeg's crystal meth subculture.

"This guy told me he knows who the real killer is," Cormier said, revealing it was the leader of a biker gang.

Cormier elaborated, saying his cellmate had been too scared to give him the guy's real name, but he knew who he was and was sure DNA evidence would link him to the murder. He said he had found out that Tina was killed because she had ripped the gang leader off on a bad coke deal. He knew that she had ripped others off before, reminding the detectives that he already told them about how Tina owed a man $250. He said he was so sure about the strength of his information that he was prepared to wear a wire to record his cellmate's conversation.

Bailey and Oliver listened patiently, nodding their heads as Cormier gave details. They did not recognize the name of Cormier's cellmate and had no prior knowledge of the gang leader he had accused. Nor had they found any evidence that corroborated Cormier's claim that Tina had owed $250.

From the lengths he was going to, Bailey told Cormier, it was clear that he must really care about Tina.

"I was attracted to her," Cormier admitted. "You know, the first time I met her, when I was cycling down the street, she flashed her titties at me." He stole a look at the detectives to see how they would react. Though when he'd found out she was fifteen, he added, he was no longer interested in having sex with her.

Watching from the monitoring room, O'Donovan noted this detail. It was unlikely that Tina had lifted her top to show her breasts, but it wasn't impossible. Cody hadn't mentioned it, but then again, he hadn't been asked the question specifically. If true, it might help explain Cormier's fixation on the teenager.

Cormier now started to ask his own questions, trying to gauge how the investigation was going. He was most interested in the DNA, in particular whether his sample had matched anything gathered from Tina's body. "Everyone but Tina was using needles in 22 Carmen and there was blood all over the place," he said. "Tina could easily have got some of that on her, or maybe borrowed clothes from Sarah that had my blood on them."

When he could see that the detectives weren't going to be drawn into speculating, Cormier became hostile. He brought up a well-known case of a wrongful conviction in which a man had been found guilty of a more serious crime because he hadn't wanted to admit to a lesser one. The detectives understood that Cormier was hinting that, for him, the theft of the truck was the lesser crime. But he still stopped short of admitting he'd stolen it.

Later that day, O'Donovan received news that Cormier's DNA did not match anything found on Tina or on the duvet cover. Disappointed, he told detectives it was time to move to the next logical line of questioning. A number of witnesses had mentioned that they had seen Cormier using his own bedding, describing how he had packed and unpacked it as he moved about. Now O'Donovan wanted each of these witnesses to be shown a photo of the same cover pattern as the one Tina was found in to find out if any of them could connect it to Cormier.

Detectives were still managing to keep details of the duvet cover out of the press. No one outside of the unit knew the cover was a Costco brand and the pattern was called Chloe Green, with brown, red, russet, and green leaves embroidered on an off-white background. Even during the months-long canvass that had started in August, when officers tried to track all four duvet cover patterns sold under the same Costco barcode, they did not explain why they were conducting the search. O'Donovan felt it was time to capitalize on this information.

Exactly how he would go about asking the witnesses to identify the cover had been a complicated decision. Under Canadian case law, when witnesses were asked to identify a suspect, the police were required to show a photo lineup of people of a similar race, age, and physical build to ensure that the identification was fair. But there were no such guidelines when it came to identifying a piece of property.

O'Donovan carefully weighed up the benefits of showing either just one picture of a duvet cover pattern or a lineup of ten similar ones. If he showed only the one, he could be accused of not providing a choice and leading witnesses on. But if he showed an array of them, they might be so similar that witnesses ended up guessing between them. It was a difficult call, and O'Donovan realized that he also had to consider future cases that might be affected by his choice. In the end, he decided that the detectives would show only one photo of the Chloe Green pattern. It would get definite yes or no answers on which they could build their case. He thought it best not to select a catalogue photo, which might look too pristine, and instead chose one of the more amateur-looking photos sent in during the canvass that showed a Chloe Green cover draped over a chair. If you didn't know it was a duvet cover, you could easily mistake it for a bedspread, a curtain, or a tablecloth.

The first witnesses on the list were Ida and Chantelle Beardy. O'Donovan once again assigned Detective Sergeants Jeff Stalker and Myles Riddell to visit them at the house where Cormier had lived in a tent during the summer. The last time they'd been there, Ida Beardy had mentioned how Cormier would fold up his blankets and stack them into a neat pile or hang them out to air on the fence.

When they arrived at 686 Alexander Avenue, the detectives found Ida and Chantelle sitting separately in the kitchen and living room, out of earshot of each other. Despite nearly twenty years' experience, it was the first time Stalker had asked a witness to identify an object, and he and O'Donovan had spent considerable time discussing how to go about it. They knew they had to be careful not to lead the witnesses, so Stalker did not refer to his previous visits, fearing it might prompt the women to connect his presence with Raymond Cormier. Instead, he approached Ida saying he had something to show her and immediately handed her the single photo of the duvet cover. "What does this mean to you?" he asked, taking out his notebook to record exactly what she said.

Ida's eyes widened. "That's Frenchie's blanket," she said loudly.

Stalker was taken aback by the passion of her response. He hadn't expected such a strong reaction.

"That's the blanket Frenchie brought over, and we had it here, in the back room," Ida explained. "He also had a red blanket in the tent. This one is the sort of blanket you open up and put another blanket inside," she added, pointing at the picture.

For a moment Stalker was confused, until Ida patiently explained what a duvet cover was. He didn't have any at home and had not been sure how they were used.

"Frenchie got his blankets from Value Village," Ida continued. "I didn't see it after the summer. Frenchie must have taken it with him."

Stalker asked Ida to initial the back of the photo to confirm that she had definitely recognized it. The conversation over, she made it clear that she had given him enough time and had other things to do. Ida left the kitchen, to be replaced by Chantelle. Once again, Stalker took out a fresh copy of the duvet cover photo and started the process of identification.

"What does this mean to you?" he asked.

"That's Sebastian's blanket!" Chantelle said, with even more conviction than her mother. "He had it here at the house."

Chantelle told Stalker that Cormier's duvet cover had been slightly darker than the one in the photo and had possibly been stained. But the pattern of leaves was exactly as she remembered. Like Ida, she hadn't seen it in the house after Cormier left in the summer. Stalker noted down her response and again handed over the photo for her to sign. To be helpful, Chantelle also wrote down her cell number in case they had further questions.

"This is it!" O'Donovan shouted when Stalker later relayed what had happened.

Finally, after months of searching, his detectives had found a concrete link between Cormier and Tina's body. O'Donovan was confident of the interviews, even though he knew they were circumstantial and not conclusive. Ida Beardy was a complicated character, and her alcohol and drug habit meant she would likely be seen as an unreliable witness in court. But she was also a straight talker, and the conviction behind her recognition had made a powerful impression on Stalker. Moreover, Chantelle had corroborated her statement. This was the most progress the team had made since they had begun investigating Cormier, and now more than ever O'Donovan was convinced they had the right man. But the detective knew they would need stronger evidence linking Cormier with Tina's death if they were to have any chance of seeing him convicted.

A day later, Stalker and Riddell showed the Chloe Green duvet cover picture to Ernest DeWolfe. Cormier's former friend had been eager to help.

"I remember a blanket with a fall scene, brown leaves," he told them when they asked him to describe Cormier's bedding.

Riddell placed a picture of the Chloe Green cover in front of him. "Do you recognize this?" he asked.

"That looks like Ray's blanket," said DeWolfe. "I can't say one hundred percent that's the one, but it looks like it."

Once again, O'Donovan let himself feel a mild beat of excitement. Now he had two separate sets of witnesses confirming that the duvet cover had belonged to Cormier. But he realized that DeWolfe, like Ida Beardy, would not be considered a star witness. A self-confessed drug addict and a convicted thief, DeWolfe would likely be pulled apart on the stand, his character and motivation questioned at every turn. And it didn't help that a few days later, Sarah Holland was shown the picture of the duvet cover but failed to recognize it.

O'Donovan was still pinning his hopes on forensic evidence to provide the smoking gun he needed. But as the results from the tests on 22 Carmen and the stolen truck trickled in, there was nothing to lift his spirits. The team had found areas of blood splatter on the walls and ceilings of 22 Carmen which they were able to match to the known drug users in the house. But they could find no connection between Cormier and Tina's body or the duvet cover. They had got no further with the truck. Although it appeared to have been wiped down both inside and out, analysts had found hairs and fibres which they sent to be tested. But again, the results revealed there was nothing that pointed to either Cormier or Tina having been inside the vehicle.

Christmas was now approaching, and the prairies were shrouded in a deep blanket of snow. Soon the ice on the Red and Assiniboine Rivers would be thick enough to carve out a skating trail. Along with his team, in between time off to enjoy the holidays, O'Donovan was still spending hours working on Tina's case. With no new leads to pursue on Cormier, the detectives had turned their attention back to the other suspects. O'Donovan still believed that Cormier should be persecuted, but he wanted to make sure that every lead was properly pursued.

For a while, Tyrell Morrison was placed under investigation. In the summer of 2014, Morrison had been arrested for assaulting Sarah Holland, though the charges were later stayed. A witness had come forward to say that Holland had told her Morrison stabbed Tina in the vagina before killing her. The detectives tried to verify this account, rechecking the pathologist's report for anything that indicated such an injury. But they could find nothing to support the story. Holland was given a polygraph test and denied making the allegation. She did remember something else of significance, however: a small detail from the argument Cormier had with Tina outside 22 Carmen on August 6. She recalled him shouting at the teenager, "You're going to end up in the river."

Another tip came in about the low-budget Windsor Hotel, in the downtown district. Long-time residents described how, a few days before Tina was found, they saw a girl matching her description in a hotel room across the hallway. She had arrived with a bicycle and a backpack, and two weeks later they saw the people in the room trying to push the bike and backpack out through a window. O'Donovan's team tried to verify the story but found that the witnesses were too high on alcohol and crystal meth to be coherent. Even if the story were true, the timeline did not match. O'Donovan told his team to disregard the information and move on.

Detectives were still receiving information from the public connecting Tina with the Kenyan and Nigerian from the Furby Street rooming house. O'Donovan told his team that it was time to either eliminate the men from the investigation or bring them in for questioning. The first step would be to see if they could be connected to the Chloe Green duvet cover. O'Donovan asked for it to be shown to the witness from the rooming house who had reported seeing Tina lying under a pale-coloured blanket with flowers on it. She was happy to help but was unable to recognize the pattern.

Still, O'Donovan felt he had enough circumstantial evidence to arrest the men on suspicion of murder. But once they had been interviewed, his opinion changed. He could see that both men were genuinely shocked to be charged. Whereas Cormier had been aggressive and defensive, trying to deflect blame by mentioning other potential suspects and refusing to cooperate, the men held nothing back about their drug-and-sex-fuelled lives. Though they had the right to remain silent, they tried to be as helpful as they could, even volunteering their DNA. The results from the forensic tests backed up their story: they were not a match for anything the police had collected. The men also lacked access to a vehicle in which to have transported Tina's body. Finally, the gang leader who employed the men to run the Furby Street crack house came forward to corroborate their version of events. O'Donovan concluded there was no truth to the rumours that they had killed Tina. This left Cormier as the sole suspect in his investigation.

Just at that point, in late January, the national news magazine *Maclean's* published a story under the headline "Welcome to Winnipeg: Where Canada's Racism Problem Is at Its Worst." The main image was of Thelma holding a picture of Tina while wiping away her tears. The writer, Nancy Macdonald, herself Winnipeg-born and raised, had been spurred to write the article because of the horror she felt at Tina's killing and the second Indigenous schoolgirl's attack. Macdonald described the city as having a festering race problem, one that had recently become obvious during the mayoral campaign when some candidates had made public derogatory comments about the Indigenous community. She cited studies showing that racist attitudes and a lack of inclusion were worse in Manitoba than in any other Canadian province, despite its having the highest per capita Indigenous population.

The article prompted an immediate reaction from the city's mayor, Brian Bowman, himself Métis, who held an emotional press conference in which he tearfully admitted that it had highlighted a truth. He promised to do better. "We're not going to end racism tomorrow, but we're sure as hell going to try," he said, flanked by chiefs and leaders from the Indigenous community.

It was clear that the apparent lack of progress in Tina's case was becoming a nationwide public relations problem for Winnipeg. This was especially true for the city police, who were still reeling from Constables Houle and Jansen's failure to protect Tina when they had stopped her on the street. Reflecting on the article, the police chief, Devon Clunis, said he wasn't surprised by its contents and felt the city needed to have a "meaningful conversation" about racism. But, he said, it was unfair to put responsibility for eliminating the appalling chasm between Indigenous and mainstream society solely on the shoulders of his service. "Far too many social issues are left to the police to rectify," he said, urging a more holistic approach to the problem. Meanwhile, O'Donovan was angry, feeling the article ignored the hard work being done by many officers.

In March, when the temperatures had finally started to rise and the ice on the river was beginning to break up, Cormier was convicted on his earlier charge and given a ten-month sentence. Because of time already served, his release date was set for mid-June. In court, he told the sentencing judge that once out, his plan was to leave Winnipeg and return to Calgary, where he had lived a few years before.

With the frustrating absence of forensic evidence, O'Donovan was desperate to find ways to move Tina's investigation forward. Officers at the Milner Ridge Correctional Centre told him that Cormier was keeping himself to himself, refusing to mingle with the other prisoners or even go out into the exercise yard. Throughout his accumulated years of jail time, Cormier had never isolated himself like this. O'Donovan saw it as a deliberate strategy to avoid being informed on, and it quashed any idea of being able to get a confession out of him through another inmate.

It was now more than six months since Tina's body had been pulled from the Red River. On a bright, clear Sunday at the end of March, John and Mary O'Donovan treated themselves to brunch at one of the many restaurants at the Forks, at the confluence of the Red and Assiniboine. Afterwards, as they strolled along the river trail, O'Donovan's eye was drawn to a group of Indigenous teenagers dressed in hoodies, smoking cigarettes by the waterside. They were chatting and laughing, caught up in their own world and oblivious to the families and couples walking cautiously around them. O'Donovan registered their separateness, noting how they seemed to exist on the fringes of society, and was reminded of how Tina had lived in the weeks before her death.

His thoughts wandered back to another homicide earlier in his career. Like Tina, the victim had been thrown into the Red River in a brutal killing. O'Donovan had identified a prime suspect, a woman, but could find nothing more than circumstantial evidence against her. To solve the case, he had set up his first undercover operation. He had a fondness for Greek mythology and named his plan Project Echidna after a terrifying creature, half-woman, half-snake, who was said to have consumed raw flesh. His officers had done the best they could, but after months of ingratiating themselves with their target and offering her incentives to talk, they could not get a confession. Eventually, prosecutors ruled that the evidence they collected was too weak to go to court. It had been a failure. With the benefit of hindsight, O'Donovan felt Echidna had been too small to bring a prosecution. He had promised himself that if he had the chance to launch such an investigation again, he would be far more ambitious.

As he walked along the river, the detective's gaze drifted down to the dark pools of water that were beginning to appear in the ice. A small number of geese had already returned for the spring and were squawking loudly on the bank. Turning to Mary, he began to describe how he had set up Project Echidna, suggesting that a similar operation might be the key to cracking Tina's case. Mary listened as he ran through the idea and weighed up its chances of success. It would be a difficult feat to pull off, O'Donovan said, and Cormier had already proven himself a cunning and vigilant opponent. But with the right resources, he was confident he could make it work. And this time, he would make sure his project was too big to fail.

As the plan began to crystallize, O'Donovan realized it was possibly his only chance to bring Cormier to trial before he likely returned to his itinerant criminal existence. That was not an option the detective was willing to accept, feeling he would be letting down not only Tina and her family, but his entire profession as well. Although it had been months since he'd first seen the autopsy pictures, the images still haunted him. Every homicide was wrong, but this one felt especially cruel and O'Donovan knew he wouldn't stop searching until he had all the answers. An undercover operation would be a high-risk strategy, but given the intense public interest in Tina's killing, the detective felt it was more than justified.

Looking down at the Red, O'Donovan suddenly knew what he would call his operation. He would name it after another river, the one from Greek mythology that separated the living from the underworld. The final push to try to solve Tina's case would be called Project Styx.

11.

PROJECT STYX

A week later, O'Donovan's superior, Staff Sergeant Dale McMillan, was thumbing through the document the detective had handed him outlining an elaborate plan to determine whether Raymond Cormier was responsible for Tina Fontaine's death.

"It's a Mr. Big," explained O'Donovan.

Mr. Big was the name of an undercover strategy pioneered by the RCMP in British Columbia in the early 1990s. It was a technique employed for investigations that had gone cold, or where a suspect had been identified but there was not enough evidence to convict. O'Donovan told McMillan it was the perfect tool with which to solve Tina's killing.

All Mr. Big stings followed a similar script, he explained, and Project Styx would be no different. Cormier would be profiled to understand his habits and personality, and this information would be used to identify an undercover officer with whom he was likely to bond. A seemingly chance meeting would be engineered between them. The officer would ask Cormier for a favour—a light for a cigarette, help moving a heavy bag—and this small, ingratiating task would mark the beginning of a friendship.

Eventually, the undercover officer would confide in Cormier that he was a member of an organized criminal gang and tell him he was welcome to join. He would ensure that Cormier was well paid for carrying out small errands and made to feel included. Then, when trust had been built and Cormier was on his way to becoming a fully fledged gang member, another meeting would be arranged, this time with the gang boss, their "Mr. Big." This boss would confront Cormier with details of Tina's murder and tell him that if he confessed to it, the gang might be able to protect him from the police. If Cormier didn't speak up, his status in the gang would be threatened. In this way, if Cormier was guilty, the undercover cops would get their confession.

McMillan had concerns. Although O'Donovan was confident he had the experience to oversee the plan, it would be the most elaborate and ambitious undercover operation the Winnipeg Police Service had ever attempted. More to the point, Mr. Big stings weren't without controversy. They had been widely criticized for preying on the vulnerability of suspects, pressuring them into making false confessions with offers of money, friendship, and a sense of belonging. Although the RCMP cited an impressively high success rate of at least 75 percent, a number of Mr. Big convictions had been overturned.

Both O'Donovan and McMillan were well aware of the Canadian Supreme Court ruling of the previous year that had laid down guidelines for Mr. Bigs after a particularly controversial operation. The Hart ruling was named after a case in which the Crown withdrew charges against the suspect due to insufficient evidence. It stipulated that the value of any evidence collected from a Mr. Big operation had to outweigh the harm it might cause. Mr. Bigs were outlawed in the United States, the United Kingdom, and Europe, where they were viewed as coercion, and the Supreme Court wanted to make sure that if the police used them in Canada, they would be conducted fairly. Ideally, the confession they secured would be beyond doubt, containing information only the guilty would know.

O'Donovan reassured his boss that Project Styx took these guidelines into account. He wouldn't do anything to push Cormier into a more serious criminal lifestyle than the one he was already leading or put him in harm's way. If anything, O'Donovan said, the Supreme Court ruling had made his job easier, giving him strict parameters within which to work.

McMillan's next question was predictable. "And the cost?"

O'Donovan's calculations hinged on whether Cormier moved to Calgary or remained in Winnipeg. The scenarios the detective had in mind for either city were similar, but an operation in Calgary would require expensive long-distance logistics.

"I'm thinking at least $120,000 for Winnipeg and double that for Calgary," O'Donovan said, explaining he would need a staff of at least a dozen full-time officers. The estimate did not factor in over-time costs and the thousands of dollars that might be paid directly to Cormier to entice him into the gang.

"And it's a risk," O'Donovan added. "We may invest a load of time and money and we're not guaranteed a result."

McMillan nodded in acknowledgment. The scale of O'Donovan's plan was unprecedented and would need to be referred up the Winnipeg Police Service chain of command for approval. But they both knew that the likelihood of being granted approval was strong. The Tina Fontaine case was the most high-profile homicide any of them could remember, and there was a force-wide commitment to do whatever it took to deliver justice.

By mid-afternoon, McMillan was back in O'Donovan's office. "You're on," he told him. "Do everything you can."

O'Donovan set about assembling his core team, drawing up a shortlist of candidates he considered experienced and enthusiastic. He wanted people who wouldn't be afraid to voice their opinions but who also wouldn't run away with their own ideas. He would need a coordinator, senior investigators, surveillance supervisors, and an officer dedicated to writing affidavits for the necessary court orders and warrants. Central to his operation would be the undercover officers, in particular Cormier's main confidant. O'Donovan contacted the police psychologist to discuss what sort of person Cormier would most easily bond with. She advised him to choose a man who would not threaten Cormier's self-image as an alpha male, someone who would appear impressed by his criminal exploits and sexual conquests.

O'Donovan's undercover coordinator pointed him towards one of their most experienced operatives, a man in his late fifties who had immigrated to Winnipeg from the Middle East. At first, O'Donovan worried that Cormier might respond negatively to someone from a minority. But Mohammad, as the man's character was known—or Mo—was so easygoing and affable that O'Donovan felt he would have no problem winning Cormier over.

"I'm honoured," the officer said when O'Donovan approached him about the project. He had worked undercover for most of his twenty-year police career, masquerading variously as a drug dealer, a hit man, and a cellmate who would befriend prisoners for information. He had quickly realized he'd found his niche and loved the process of embodying the physical appearance and mindset of his characters. It gave him a rush to pretend to be someone else, and an even bigger rush to arrest and prosecute dangerous criminals.

It had taken a while, but Mo's family had finally accepted the dangers of his work. He had a slight build, making him far smaller than many of the gang members he associated with, and his wife had been petrified when he first found himself trapped in volatile situations with knives and guns. But he had assured her that he was well protected by colleagues, who were never far away. To everyone outside his family, the operative seemed a mild-mannered, middle-aged white-collar worker who led an uneventful suburban life.

Mo's developing friendship with Cormier would be the focal point around which Project Styx unfolded. But O'Donovan felt they needed to deploy a second character who could be physically close to Mo and act as backup if needed. Providing Mo with a part-time girlfriend would be an excellent cover, and it had the additional benefit of letting them observe how Cormier acted around women. The girlfriend would have a backstory of working as a cleaner and living in an apartment across the city with a cat that needed feeding. That would explain why she could only be with Mo some of the time.

This role was harder to cast. O'Donovan needed an experienced officer who could hold her own if threatened but who would also be seen as feminine, vulnerable, and submissive. He chose an attractive blond officer in her early forties who had worked for the Vice Unit, now named Counter Exploitation. Her undercover name was Candace.

Candace's first taste of undercover work had been to pose as a sex worker soliciting for clients. She remembered being so nervous that she had smoked cigarette after cigarette as she stood exposed on one of Winnipeg's well-known red-light streets. But by the time O'Donovan sounded her out, she had developed a passion for her work. Like Mo, she loved the challenge of having to think on her feet while making sure the invented scenario was played out. And, like Mo, she felt she was making a difference. One of her most successful roles had been to target a man who'd moved to Winnipeg after serving a sentence for stalking and killing a female jogger. The police found out that he was picking up sex workers, so Candace posed as one to ensnare him.

"You know you're doing a good job especially when you can see who the next victim would have been," the officer confided to O'Donovan when he outlined what she would be doing for Project Styx.

Happy with the casting of his two key roles, O'Donovan moved ahead with planning the details of the operation. His major concern was that Cormier would slip town and disappear back into his shadow world of sleeping rough and drifting from city to city, making it almost impossible for the police to keep track of him. To prevent this, the detective hatched a plan to keep Cormier in Winnipeg by offering him free accommodation. He sent an officer to the Manitoba office for subsidized housing, which agreed to lend the police two furnished apartments on the top floor of a small, nondescript block on a busy North End street. One of these apartments would be offered to Cormier as part of a fabricated government initiative for older recently released offenders. The other apartment would become a home for Mo.

Cormier's release was scheduled for Saturday, June 13, 2015. The day before, O'Donovan gathered his team together for one final briefing. Looking around the room, the detective felt a sudden rush of apprehension. He knew how hard his officers would need to work, the long hours ahead of them, and the personal sacrifices they would be making. And there was no guarantee of success.

"At seven-thirty tomorrow morning, he'll be out," he told the group assembled around him. "We need to take it carefully. What we want to do at this stage is just watch and learn."

He explained that Cormier would be put under surveillance until Monday morning, when he was scheduled to attend an appointment at the city's Employment and Income Assistance office. The employees there had been instructed to refer him to Manitoba Housing, which would offer him the free accommodation at 400 Logan Avenue, apartment 502.

O'Donovan had already obtained a warrant to place surveillance and recording devices inside and outside the apartment on Logan Avenue. He described how a camera in the fifth-floor hallway would transmit a live feed to the intercept office at the Public Safety Building. When the civilian monitoring staff, who were based in a covert location near police headquarters, saw Cormier enter his apartment, they would turn on the audio recording devices inside the apartment. The staff would listen to the recordings live and make notes, which they would then pass to O'Donovan. The detective said he planned to listen to as many of the conversations as he could himself and would decide which ones were worth transcribing in full. They were expecting a huge volume of information, so the lead investigators volunteered to listen as well. There would also be recordings to analyze from the wires worn by each undercover officer.

As the meeting ended, O'Donovan took Mo to one side to ask him how he was planning to develop his character. Mo told him that he had been thinking through a number of cover stories but had decided to keep it simple. "I'll just bump into him and start chatting," he said. He would let Cormier dictate the pace of their friendship. He had been told the suspect was a narcissist, so his plan was to appear submissive and compliant around him.

Candace had also been preparing her approach, in particular her appearance. She wanted to look convincing as a woman without much money but still appear attractive to Cormier, who she had been told was a ladies' man. It was almost summer and already warm, so she had assembled a wardrobe of leggings, flip-flops, and tight vest tops that would show cleavage but not reveal the mic taped to the centre of her bra. Her eyes would be lined with heavy black eyeliner, but she would leave her hair curly and unbrushed and was letting its dark roots grow out. The only problem with this look was that it was quite similar to her real appearance, and she worried that Cormier might chance on her travelling to or from her home, where she lived with her husband and children. So she had come up with another disguise to wear into work: a dark wig and a false pregnant belly, which was so convincing that it fooled her co-workers.

For a final touch of authenticity, Candace asked Mo to pose for a selfie with her outside. The picture showed Mo wearing a red T-shirt and mirrored sunglasses, his hair slicked back and his arm around Candace, also in dark glasses. Candace printed it out and put it into a cheap photo frame decorated with the words "A friend is one of life's greatest gifts," which she gave to Mo to display in his apartment.

At 7:30 A.M. on Saturday, June 13, Cormier was released from Milner Ridge Correctional Centre. A surveillance unit followed the correctional van that took him from the prison to a bus station on the eastern fringe of the city. From here, they followed him on and off several buses until he reached McPhillips Street, at the edge of the North End. Officers observed Cormier rifling through dumpsters and filling up a white plastic grocery bag with the items he found. Later, they saw him meet up with friends, one of whom passed him a pair of wire cutters and pliers. They watched as Cormier used these to strip down some wires he had picked up. Then he made calls on a pay phone. To O'Donovan's relief, it did not look like he was making plans to leave the city.

On Monday morning, Cormier showed up early for his meeting at the employment assistance office. When his case worker told him he might be eligible for free accommodation, Cormier seemed excited. He was in a chatty mood, telling the worker that he had thought about leaving Winnipeg but had decided to stay to clear his name, because the police believed he was the person who had killed Tina Fontaine. He said he might have been the last person to see her alive.

On Tuesday morning, at 7:30 A.M., Detective Sergeant Doug Bailey received a call from Cormier on his cell phone.

"I want to t-t-t-talk about Tina," Cormier said, stuttering badly.

He told Bailey that he hadn't slept since his release on Saturday morning, because he had nowhere to go.

"I went down to Alexander Docks. I thought it was closed, but I got in," Cormier said. "I sat by Tina's memorial." He was referring to the collection of painted rocks, flowers, and soft toys that had been placed there.

Cormier told Bailey that he couldn't leave Winnipeg until he cleared his name and that he would be asking other street people to help find out information on Tina. He said he wanted to meet to talk about the case and that he was willing to undergo hypnosis to see if he could remember any new details about the Robert Plant lookalike he'd seen on the other side of the street when he'd argued with Tina.

O'Donovan listened to Bailey's account of the conversation with interest, thinking back to the beginning of the investigation the previous August, when he had scoured the video footage from Tina's vigil to look for anyone acting suspiciously. Here was Cormier admitting that he spent time at Tina's memorial, offering to insert himself into the police investigation, and highlighting a different suspect who looked rather like himself. O'Donovan knew these were all details a criminal profiler would focus on, and they all made Cormier look guilty.

Later that day, Cormier obtained the keys to his new apartment on Logan Avenue. Cormier called Bailey again the next morning, this time to update him with his new address. Once more, he wanted to talk about the Tina Fontaine investigation, asking if any arrests had been made. He said he would be going to the library to research any unsolved deaths in Winnipeg over the last fifteen years and suggested that the police use him as bait for the real killer. And to Bailey's surprise, he suggested they bug his apartment.

O'Donovan called a briefing. "I think we can all agree he's obsessed with Tina," he told his team.

Now that they had succeeded in settling Cormier into 400 Logan, the detective was impatient to move forward with the next stage of the plan. It was time for Mo to be introduced.

The following day at Logan, Cormier found himself riding the elevator with a man who introduced himself as a tenant.

"Hi, I'm Mohammad, but call me Mo," the man said, extending his hand to shake Cormier's.

"I'm Sebastian," came the reply.

Cormier said he'd just moved in, and the two men chatted briefly about what it was like to live in the apartment block before going their separate ways. Listening to Mo's recording in the monitoring room, O'Donovan concluded that the first encounter had been a success.

In Cormier's apartment, the installed mics were beginning to pick up conversations between him and his guests, friends he'd met on the streets or in the hotels and crack houses that dominated the landscape of the North End. The monitoring staff alerted O'Donovan to a suspicious exchange between Cormier and an unknown female that had occurred a few days after he'd bumped into Mo. From the sound of her voice, the female was young. The detective put on headphones to listen to the recording. He heard the girl speak first.

"Swear to me that . . . you've never done it before. Have you ever hit a woman before . . . ever?" she asked.

"I've done it before, but it was a drunken . . . blackout rage," Cormier replied, before admitting that he had hit a woman twice.

"You felt remorse?" asked the girl.

"Never do it again," he replied.

The conversation drifted a little, then Cormier's voice became serious. "There's something you need to know about me," he said, and he described how he had been investigated for the Tina Fontaine murder.

"Okay," said the girl, slowly and deliberately, taking in the seriousness of the statement. "Why do they think it was you?"

Cormier mumbled that the cops hadn't come up with his name out of the blue and there must be something going on. He said he had been taking too many drugs at the time.

"I just wanted to . . . tell you this because it's . . . it's . . ."—he paused and cleared his throat—"it's something difficult."

Perhaps in sympathy, the girl began to tell her own story of how one night she had taken too many drugs herself and had been grabbed by a group of men on the street. They had dragged her into a nearby housing complex.

"All I remember is being underneath the stairwell and having my underwear . . . being ripped off . . . and . . . me . . . making it home," she said. "The cops . . . they didn't take my fricking rape report, they didn't take anything. They made me feel like I was the one who did something wrong. Just because I was a fuckin' crackhead." Her voice had become tense and angry.

Listening, O'Donovan shifted uncomfortably in his chair.

"And that's part of the problem with the city police," agreed Cormier.

After a pause, the conversation returned to Tina. Cormier described how he first met the teenager as he was cycling down a street in the middle of the night with a car muffler balanced on his shoulder.

"I always said that 'all the gold in Babylon is mine, and I want it all.' I remember saying that to her, and she misunderstood. She flashed me her tits, eh. And whoa . . . nice little titties, eh?"

Cormier said he could see that Tina was young but wasn't sure how young.

"She's gonna tell you of course she's old enough," said the girl.

"Exactly, and that's what happened, eh. And, uh, uh, four, five times, five, six times I . . ." Cormier's voice trailed away, and the rest of the sentence was inaudible.

O'Donovan wondered if Cormier was referring to how many times he'd had sex with the teenager, but the meaning wasn't clear.

Cormier continued to talk, describing the night Tina had arrived at 22 Carmen after Cody had left for his reserve. He said she had been annoyed because she couldn't manipulate him anymore.

"What are you feeling guilty about?" his young friend asked when he had finished his story.

"My last words to her were 'Go jump off a bridge,'" said Cormier.

The conversation ended with Cormier's friend telling him he should ask God for forgiveness, and Cormier saying he was determined to find out who had killed Tina. As the recording clicked off O'Donovan remained in his chair, trying to grasp its significance. He agreed with the girl that Cormier sounded guilty. But what, exactly, was he guilty of?

Meanwhile, Mo's relationship with Cormier was developing. The men had crossed paths several times and had smoked cigarettes together outside by the bins. Mo told Cormier that he ran a small removal company with his girlfriend and casually asked if Cormier would help him move boxes from his van to his apartment. Cormier agreed, and Mo gave him ten dollars for his trouble.

Small as the amount was, O'Donovan felt Cormier was probably grateful for the easy cash. From the surveillance reports, he could see that Cormier had gone back to supporting himself by scavenging through dumpsters, collecting cans, and stealing. He would spend all night out, searching for scrap and breaking into poorly secured basements with his screwdriver, his "keys to the city." His apartment was beginning to fill up with the bicycles he and his crew had lifted around town. Cormier would dismantle them, swapping one part with another so their owners wouldn't recognize them back on the streets. His place was a hive of activity, with people coming and going at all hours and a growing collection of bicycle parts and wires scattered over the floor.

Cormier's energy came from crystal meth, or "jib," which, at ten dollars a hit, was easy to score and fast becoming the drug of choice in the city. He confided to Mo how he had been introduced to the drug while staying in Winnipeg's Salvation Army hostel, as he wandered outside one morning in the early hours. He had been surprised to see two men injecting it. Cormier hadn't realized you could do that, and asked to try it himself. As soon as the needle was in his arm, he had felt the rush.

But now he had quit injecting. He still smoked meth, and it kept him wide awake, paranoid, and constantly on the move. If he wasn't out scavenging, he would throw his energy into cleaning: bleaching the bathroom or mopping the hallway. He confided that meth intensified his sexual pleasure, and he liked to share his drugs with teenage Indigenous girls from the streets, who he would invite over to hang out on his sofa. Often, in exchange for a fix, they'd have sex with him. When his friends stayed too long, Cormier would lose his temper and scream at them to get out. He would get violent, scattering their belongings out of windows and slamming the door behind them. But they seemed to be used to his mood swings and would never go far, usually drifting back to the apartment within a matter of hours.

A few days after Cormier first helped him, Mo approached him with another job. He said he was expecting a load of boxes from Calgary and offered to pay Cormier a hundred dollars to help move them. Cormier said he would and, as an aside, told Mo his real name.

"What happened to Sebastian?" Mo joked.

"No, it's Raymond," Cormier said, his voice sounding serious.

Later, over beers and cigarettes in Mo's apartment, Cormier asked Mo about his background. He seemed fascinated to find out that Mohammad was a Shiite Muslim from Iran who had fled the country during the 1979 revolution. Cormier wanted to talk about religion. He had read the Quran and the Bible, which he was fond of quoting. Although he had left school without much of an education, he had used his time in prison to read and was particularly fond of the theological works of the English writer C.S. Lewis. Mo was surprised. He found Cormier to be the most articulate, hard-working, and well-read criminal he had ever worked with.

Soon, the monitoring team brought O'Donovan's attention to another conversation recorded in the apartment in which Cormier was talking to a young woman. He had told her he was being investigated for a murder.

"You would never do something like that, never, ever, ever," the girl said, her voice confident and trusting.

"Fifteen-year-old girl. Fuck. I drew the line and that's why she got killed," Cormier replied. "She got killed because we found out . . . I found out she was fifteen years old," he continued. "And when she found out I knew that, then the jig's up, eh? She don't have her surrogate dad anymore."

The girl guessed he was talking about Tina Fontaine.

"She was fifteen years old. I didn't know that. When I found out, that was it. Said I'm not gonna bang her no more. I don't want nothing to do with you that way," Cormier said.

To O'Donovan, this was a definite confession that Cormier had had a sexual relationship with Tina. Although Ernest DeWolfe had told the police that Cormier said he'd slept with Tina, this was the first time O'Donovan heard Cormier appear to say it himself. After months of dedicated labour and costly financial investment, the detective felt they were finally making progress. But the statement, if true, only confirmed Cormier's sexual relationship with Tina and was far from evidence of guilt in her murder.

At the apartment building, Mo dropped in to visit Cormier.

"Whoa, buddy, what's all this you've got here?" he asked when he saw the piles of wires and scrap metal littered on the floor.

"I can make a fortune from this," Cormier said, waving his arms over the dirty mess, his words jumbling together with excitement.

He had plans to sell the scrap and wanted to know if Mo would go into business with him. But, he warned his new friend, he was a suspect in the Tina Fontaine investigation and Mo might want to consider what that meant before becoming too involved. Mo was ready for the comment having discussed how he would react with the Project Styx team. His strategy was to remain non-judgmental and allow Cormier to talk without leading him on. He shrugged as if to say he didn't care. There might be a point when he would ask Cormier directly about Tina, but, wary of how volatile Cormier could be, Mo knew he would have to choose that moment wisely.

That same day, Cormier attended an appointment at the city employment assistance office in which he appeared paranoid and said he wanted to talk about Tina. He said he was being investigated for her murder and suspected the police had put undercover officers into the employment assistance office to spy on him. He was emotional, at once crying about Tina, his own children whom he hadn't seen since birth, and the sexual abuse he had suffered as a child when he was sent to reform school.

After the meeting was over, the intake officer contacted the Styx team to say she'd gotten the impression that Cormier had been trying to deflect suspicion for Tina's killing away from himself. He had made a series of odd comments. In particular, he said he had only recently found out that the police had chanced on Tina's body when they were searching for Faron Hall, the homeless hero. In Cormier's mind, this was a game changer.

Why do you care how Tina was found? wondered O'Donovan.

Project Styx had been underway for more than a month, and O'Donovan, keen to assess its progress, gathered his team to review what they had achieved. Public interest in Tina's case had not diminished, but the pressure the team was working under was largely self-imposed. They were constantly second-guessing their strategies. Were they setting up the right scenarios? Should they be more daring? For the moment, everyone seemed satisfied with how organically Mo's connection with Cormier was growing. The team discussed deepening it by putting Mo and Cormier into business together. They also felt it was time to introduce Candace, who had been mentioned frequently but had not yet appeared in person. The original idea had been to use Candace to gauge how Cormier behaved around women, but as most of Cormier's girl-friends appeared to be teenagers, O'Donovan suspected he might find Candace too old to relate to as a potential sexual partner. So he discussed introducing another, younger undercover female officer who could act as a second girlfriend to Mo and give him the excuse to bring up the subject of sex with teenagers. Mo was instructed to introduce this idea into his conversations.

A day later, Cormier made another unscheduled visit to the employment assistance office.

"You need to move me," he told the same intake officer he had spoken to before. "There are too many dealers and users in this place." He described how it was hard for him to stay away from drugs at 400 Logan if they were around.

The officer said she would look into it but instead informed the Homicide Unit. Before doing anything, O'Donovan checked with the monitoring team to find out if Cormier had mentioned wanting to move in any of his conversations. They said no, but he did seem to be having trouble with people staying over who did not respect his belongings. O'Donovan thought it might be a good idea to put some distance between Cormier and Mo. Cormier increasingly wanted to spend time with his new friend, and the Styx team was finding it difficult to come up with excuses as to why Mo was so frequently absent. But Manitoba Housing told the detective no other suitable accommodation could be offered to house Cormier at that moment.

A few days later, Mo invited Cormier over for a beer. His guest arrived looking flustered but pleased with himself, saying his own place was a mess because he'd had a girl over the previous night. She was Indigenous, named Danielle, and he really liked her, but at twenty-four, she was half his age. Mo laughed at him for thinking that was a problem.

Mo brought Cormier into the living room, where his own girlfriend, Candace, was watching TV.

"It's a pleasure to meet you," said Cormier when Candace looked up from the sofa. He bowed his head and shook her fingers daintily in an exaggerated imitation of an old-fashioned gentleman. When she smiled back, he offered to sell her a stolen bike and promised to give her an excellent deal.

From the start, it was clear that Cormier warmed to Candace. He was kind to her and always made a point of being polite and respectful in her presence. For her part, Candace played the wide-eyed girlfriend who was slightly in awe of the men's conversation. O'Donovan wanted to try out a scenario in which Mo would assert his dominance over her, signalling to Cormier that he was comfortable using violence against women. A few days later, when Cormier had dropped in for a beer, Candace tapped Mo on his back to get his attention and Mo spun around, raising his hand as if he was going to hit her.

"Don't you ever do that to me again!" he yelled as Candace backed away from him.

Cormier reacted by trying to calm the situation, moving towards Candace with his hands held out to comfort her.

"Don't worry, Candace, I'll get you a bike, I'll get you a bike," he said, his voice dropping to a whisper.

Over the next week, Mo met Cormier several times to talk about the possibility of going into business. Cormier was excited and mentioned other friends who might also get involved. After one meeting, he conspicuously left his wallet on Mo's coffee table before heading back to his own apartment.

"Hey, I think this is yours," Mo said, having immediately walked over to Cormier's place to return it. Cormier checked to make sure no cash was missing, and Mo felt he had passed an important test.

When Candace wasn't around, Mo confided to Cormier that he had recently met another girl at a party. Her name was Jenna, and she was much younger than him, only nineteen, and hot. The two of them had spent the weekend in bed together. Cormier egged Mo on, wanting to hear more details, though at the same time scolding him for cheating on Candace, who he thought was worth hanging on to. He promised Mo that his secret was safe with him.

On another occasion, the mics in Cormier's apartment picked up a conversation in which Cormier and another man were talking to a young girl about drugs. The man said he would give her some as long as she knew when to stop.

Cormier joined in the conversation. "Don't overdose here 'cause then your body's gonna be wrapped up in a fuckin' carpet and thrown in the river."

"Really?" asked the girl.

"I'm just joking," said Cormier.

It was late at night when O'Donovan listened to this exchange. He had got into the habit of shutting himself in the monitoring room twice a day to catch up on the recordings, once in the afternoon and then again after 9 P.M., when everyone had gone home for the night. The evening was his preferred listening time, when the office was empty of distractions and he had the time and mental space to plan his next move. As he listened, he would scribble notes and try to draw connections between any mention of Tina by Cormier and the information he knew about her death. O'Donovan felt his suspect was always skirting around the issue, giving out little hints and details that suggested he knew more than he was willing to admit. It was as if he wanted to unburden his conscience, but every time, at the last second, made sure he held himself back. Project Styx's challenge was how to coax Cormier into letting his guard down so that he would finally confess everything.

The following morning, O'Donovan met Mo to talk through the next stage of the operation. Mo was to take Cormier with him on a moving job and pay him for his help. The locations for the pickup and drop-off were chosen deliberately far apart to give the men time to chat in the relaxed atmosphere of Mo's van. O'Donovan felt it was also time to introduce Mo's gang boss, the "Mr. Big," into the picture and told the undercover officer to engineer a meeting with him after the drop-off was completed.

After Mo had picked him up from their apartment building and they were on their way, Cormier pointed out the rear view of a young girl crossing the road, saying, "Look at the fuckin' mover on that."

The comment gave Mo an excuse to turn the conversation to Jenna.

"You have to see this chick, dude. She's so fuckin' pretty and young," he said. He offered Cormier a smoke and launched into a visceral description of what it was like to have sex with his new teenage girlfriend. Cormier laughed along but seemed concerned about Candace.

"If she ever found out it would crush her, and it would fuckin' fuck you up too, do you know that?" he said.

Mo shrugged and once more attempted to engage Cormier with an even more graphic account of the kinky sex he had enjoyed with Jenna. Cormier seemed to enjoy hearing the details, chipping in to add his own experiences. But he soon changed the topic to his favourite religious conspiracy theory that Jesus and the devil were actually one and the same, and he stayed on this subject until Mo parked the van and asked him for help loading up heavy boxes. When they were back on the road, Mo pointed out a group of young girls walking along the street.

"Now, those were young," he said, turning to Cormier with a sly smile.

"Yeah, but some of them are sooo . . ." Cormier's voice trailed off, and he was silent for a couple of seconds before saying that's what had happened with Tina.

"You old enough or what? Do you draw the line at sixteen or do you draw the line at fifteen? Fifteen is illegal. You are going to go to jail for it," he said.

Mo decided not to push the Tina reference, and Cormier changed the subject to how much he liked taking crystal meth. A few minutes later they pulled up outside a storage unit close to the airport, where an undercover officer posing as a gang member wheeled out a pallet for them to unload the boxes onto. The job done, the men got back in the van.

Once again, Mo steered the conversation to sex.

"Tell me, Raymond, have you fucked a fifteen-year-old?"

"I might have, one or two, yeah," Cormier replied.

"How does it feel?"

"Same as every other one, except that it's stretching the boundaries a bit, you know what I mean."

Mo requested more details, but Cormier wanted to talk about Tina.

"If Sarah wouldn't have found out, I would have fucked Tina," he said. He confided that he was trying to find out who had actually killed her; he had a few good leads to follow up on. But Mo could not get him to admit he'd had sex with the teenager.

The excursion ended with Mo introducing Cormier to his boss, Jay, who was played by a well-built officer dressed casually in jeans and a button-down shirt. Mo introduced Cormier as a neighbour who was helping out from time to time. Jay appeared happy to meet him, paying Cormier for his trouble and hinting that there might be more work in the future. Cormier seemed impressed.

At least that part worked out, thought O'Donovan later as he listened to the recording from Mo's wire. It was frustrating that Mo hadn't been able to get more out of Cormier. O'Donovan couldn't fault Mo for trying, but Cormier seemed too clever to be tripped up that easily.

By now it was late at night. O'Donovan left the monitoring room to walk down the corridor to his office, where he shut the door behind him. The street lights outside cast a faint orange glow across his desk, but otherwise the room was dark, and it was quiet, still enough to focus his mind.

Project Styx had started well, but Cormier was proving himself to be too good at keeping his secrets. Although Mo and Cormier had clearly bonded, it seemed unlikely that they would learn more from their friendship alone. O'Donovan considered introducing an element of stress to provoke his suspect into breaking his silence. Over the past few days the team had been brainstorming ideas about Mo's teenage bit on the side, Jenna, suggesting ways in which she could be brought into the scenarios. The detective wondered if Jenna could be the key to getting Cormier to talk. But first, he needed to find a suitable candidate to play her.

12.

JENNA

A few days later, a twenty-eight-year-old officer who had only just completed the Winnipeg Police Service's undercover training course received a message on her cell phone from Project Styx's undercover coordinator.

"Can you come in? We have a potential role we think you fit, demographically and appearance-wise."

Intrigued, the officer made her way to the Homicide Unit. Like most of the staff working in the Public Safety Building, she had no knowledge of Project Styx and its objectives. When she arrived, O'Donovan steered her towards a meeting room and motioned for his other team members to join them.

"We want to tell you what's going on and see if you're up for what we have in mind," he explained, before giving her a very brief overview of the project and the character of Jenna. "We need you to look young. Could you pull off nineteen?"

The officer nodded. She thought she could. She was a slight, athletic young woman from a small town in the Prairies, where she'd grown up playing hockey and hanging out with boys. People often commented that she looked younger than her age. With the right clothes, she said, becoming Jenna would not be a problem.

"You're going to be a vulnerable girl who we'll put in close proximity to a man we think might be a dangerous sex murderer," said O'Donovan, asking her if she felt okay with that.

"I understand," she said calmly, carefully holding her expression steady so as not to betray a growing sense of excitement.

This was the opportunity she had longed for since qualifying. After graduating with a degree in criminology, she had almost chosen a career in law but had found office work too dull and far removed from the action of real life. She knew how rare it was to be included in a project this important, especially in a city as small as Winnipeg. And this case was personal. Jenna had been deeply shocked by the discovery of Tina's body and, now that she had the opportunity, she was determined to do everything she could to help solve the crime. "Ultimately, Tina deserves justice, so I'm thankful to be part of it," she told O'Donovan.

O'Donovan told Jenna to prepare to be introduced to Cormier by Mo at 400 Logan. Jenna chose a simple outfit of jeans and a low-cut T-shirt. She bought a hat with a small peak, into which she scrunched up her long blond hair, hoping it would take years off her appearance.

Once at the apartment building, she and Mo took the elevator to the fifth floor. Jenna was nervous, but Mo reassured her that it would be a straightforward meeting. When they approached the door to Cormier's apartment, Mo took her hand firmly in his before knocking.

"Hey, bud, how is it?" he asked when Cormier opened the door.

"Who is this?" Cormier replied, looking Jenna up and down.

"This is my young party friend, Jenna," Mo said, and Jenna smiled in acknowledgment.

Cormier smiled back and nudged Mo as if to say well done. He invited them in, but Mo said no, he and Jenna were going to hang out in his apartment. Before they left, Mo asked Cormier to stay on the lookout for Candace in case she turned up by surprise. The meeting was over in a matter of minutes, and O'Donovan considered it a successful start.

While the Styx team planned Jenna's next appearance, O'Donovan instructed Mo to take Cormier on another bag drop and mention that Jenna was beginning to cause him trouble to see how Cormier would react.

Cormier arrived looking distracted. He had been out all night scavenging for wire and had returned home to find too many people crashing at his place and a pair of his shoes missing. He was angry; he wanted a beer; he wanted to tell Mo what he'd picked up last night and show him exactly where to find the best copper wires in the city. His mind was whirring with thoughts about religion, the Illuminati, and the Muslim Brotherhood. Most of all, he was tired and wanted out of his current existence. He was thinking about settling down with his new girl, Danielle.

Mo listened for a while, then casually brought the conversation around to Jenna. She was being a pain by calling and texting him constantly, pestering him to spend more time with her, and he wasn't sure what to do about it.

"She's just a fling, buddy. Candace is the keeper," Cormier said. He told Mo that Jenna was becoming crazy like most of the young girls he knew, and he was stupid for bringing her back to his home.

"Get her to fall in love with another guy," he suggested. "I'll do that for you. Get her to fall in love with me, then I'll tell her to fuck off."

Except, he said, he wouldn't do that, because he was falling in love with Danielle, who reminded him so much of Tina.

Mo nodded in sympathy. Young flesh was the best, and now that he'd slept with Jenna, he was keen to find someone even younger.

Cormier disagreed. Mo was taking too big a risk and should know where to draw the line.

"But you said you fucked Tina," said Mo, sounding surprised.

Cormier's reply was firm. "No, I wanted to fuck Tina, but there was something weird there, man."

Mo changed the subject to Jay and the bags they were picking up for him. Cormier asked what was in them, but Mo said it wasn't necessary to know. They had to remain loyal, and if Cormier wanted to work for Jay, he needed to be prepared to go all the way. If it came to it, he might even have to kill. Mo wanted to know if Cormier would be prepared to do that. Years ago, he said, when he was a teenager fleeing Iran, he had killed a man who threatened to harm his father. It was a confession that Mo had talked through with the Styx team, aimed at deepening the intimacy between the two men.

"You did what you had to do," said Cormier, reassuring Mo that he would keep his secrets.

Just before the men parted, Mo paid Cormier forty dollars and brought up the subject of Jenna again. He wasn't sure what to do.

"You've got a storm coming," laughed Cormier as he climbed out of the van and nodded a goodbye.

As O'Donovan listened in the monitoring room, he felt his ideas about how to use Jenna were taking shape. If Cormier thought she was crazy, they would give him crazy. He had lost his temper when

Tina became emotional, so it would be interesting to see whether a distraught Jenna might provoke the same reaction.

Meanwhile, the Project Styx team had thought of another lead to pursue. Mo was instructed to bring Cormier to a storage locker to help move bags of dry dog food. The cover story was that Jay was heavily involved in dog fighting. One of the bags was fixed so that when Cormier lifted it, it would rip open and spill its contents over the floor. Mo would be distracted by a phone call, leaving Cormier to clean the mess up. O'Donovan procured a duvet cover from the same Chloe Green Costco range that Tina had been found in, though in a different colour and pattern. He arranged for it to be left lying on the floor so that Cormier would think of using it as a makeshift bag. The point was to see if the knot he tied when he gathered up the food was the same as the knot tied in the duvet cover found with Tina.

Everything went according to plan. The bag burst as it was supposed to, and Cormier quickly found the duvet cover. He laid it out on the floor and piled the dog food into the middle, pulling up the corners to tie them together when he'd finished. As soon as he and Mo left, officers from the Forensic Identification Unit arrived to take photographs, which they sent to a forensic knot expert in Ontario.

O'Donovan was hoping for an unequivocal match. But when the expert replied a few days later, the results were disappointing. The corners had been joined together with a combination of commonly used knots, and it was impossible to say with any certainty whether they had been tied by the same hand.

Jenna was called to the Homicide Unit to be briefed for her next appearance. This time, she would be working alone. She was to go to Mo's apartment and knock on his door, screaming at him to answer and threatening to tell Candace about their affair. The point was to remind Cormier that Jenna was still very much in Mo's life and getting angrier by the day. O'Donovan reassured Jenna that although it was possible Cormier might come out of his apartment to see what the noise was about, it was unlikely he would engage with her directly.

When the elevator door opened onto the fifth floor of 400 Logan, Jenna took a deep breath and steadied herself. Her mind was racing. She felt exposed without Mo and was terrified of making a mistake and banging on the wrong door, even though she had rehearsed the scenario over and over in her mind. She had smeared mascara down her cheeks to look like she had been crying. But she had decided not to wear her hat, as she thought it unlikely that Cormier would get close enough to take a good look at her face.

Jenna started to pound on Mo's door. "Mohammad, open up, it's Jenna, open the fuckin' door. Where the fuck are you? Mohammad, what the fuck, you asshole, answer the fuckin' door."

Within a few seconds, Cormier was by her side. "What are you doing?" he asked.

"I'm trying to get a hold of Mohammad. He won't fuckin' call me back," cried Jenna, pounding even harder.

In the Public Safety Building, the Styx team were watching the drama unfold on a live feed from the camera in the apartment hallway. They hadn't expected Cormier to become so involved and were exchanging looks of concern. Each of them silently willed Jenna to hold her nerve.

"I'm gonna fuckin' tell Candace. That's what I'm going to do!" Jenna was screaming. "I'm losing my fuckin' mind. He's not calling me back. Do you know where he is?"

"Can you lower your voice?" asked Cormier, moving in closer so that he could get a good view of her face. "Take a time out just for a second. Take a deep breath in and out."

He put his hands on her shoulders and pulled her towards him, telling her to match her breathing with his.

"Look at me, please look at me. How old are you?" he asked.

"N-n-nineteen," replied Jenna, who was now crying for real as the adrenaline surged through her body.

"Okay, I'm eighteen," said Cormier, and for a second Jenna wondered if he'd seen through her act.

Cormier laughed and told her to chill. "Give me your hand," he said. "I'm going to introduce you to my girlfriend. I'm going to introduce you to my best friend . . . You're going to come over to my place." He pulled her towards his apartment door.

In unison, the Styx team shouted, "Don't go in!" at the monitor screen. O'Donovan radioed a member of his undercover team who was on standby in a vehicle nearby and told her to head straight up to the fifth floor, pretending to be in the apartment building visiting friends. He wanted her to be close enough to intervene if Jenna needed help.

In the hallway, Jenna calculated that it would be better to calm down and try to regain control of the situation. Cormier asked her if she knew his name.

"It's Raymond," she said.

"No, it's not. It's Sebastian," he told her.

O'Donovan thought this was significant. Cormier had been "Sebastian" to Tina. He seemed to prefer to use this name when he was dealing with young women, especially when he was trying to seduce them.

"You're acting like somebody who's lost their sense of reality, Jenna," said Cormier, his voice gentle and coaxing. "There's children downstairs and you're scaring them."

"I'm sorry, I'm sorry," said Jenna. "Can you just get him to call me?"

Cormier said he would but that first he wanted her to give him Mo's phone number. O'Donovan knew that Cormier already had it, so wondered if he was testing the officer. Jenna, who in reality didn't know it, tried to dodge the question. Cormier suggested they sit together at the top of the stairs to the fire exit so that she could calm down. Again, she hesitated.

"I need to breathe and I breathe better standing," she said, adding she would leave right now if he promised to tell Mo to call her. Again, Cormier asked for Mo's phone number, and Jenna replied that she couldn't think straight. For O'Donovan, the scenario had gone on long enough, and he instructed the undercover operator to move in.

"It's okay, she's distraught," said Cormier when he saw the woman approaching.

The officer came close and put her hand on Jenna's arm, asking if she was okay.

"I'm fine, I just want to go home," said Jenna as Cormier stepped back towards his apartment.

The two women waited for the elevator together. Once inside, the undercover officer squeezed Jenna's hand and told her to stay in character outside the building in case Cormier was watching from a window. She was to head west for a couple of blocks until an unmarked car appeared to take her to the Public Safety Building.

When Jenna arrived at headquarters, the team congratulated her on a convincing performance, in particular her surprising ability to cry on cue. Although the scenario had been nail-biting at times, O'Donovan considered it a complete success. On the surface, Cormier had seemed kindly, but his close physical proximity to the officer and his insistence that she follow him into his apartment confirmed the detective's opinion that Cormier was a predator of young women.

The question now was how to build on this. The team had been toying with the idea of putting Cormier into the middle of a domestic assault incident between Mo and Candace to gauge his tolerance for violence. But after the drama in the hallway, O'Donovan thought Jenna would be the better victim.

"Let's beat up Jenna," he suggested to his team, who agreed that Cormier seemed to be more sexually interested in Jenna than the older woman.

It was now September, three months since Project Styx had begun, and Cormier's involvement with Mo's fictional criminal gang was becoming a regular occurrence. The men had met Jay again, who had paid Cormier $200 for his latest job and sounded him out for more complicated work that involved picking up bags from the airport luggage carousel and delivering them to a nearby hotel. Cormier was excited, calculating that the higher the risk, the more chance he had of making good money. He saw a future with the gang, especially after Mo assured him that they looked after their people well.

At the airport hotel, Cormier was introduced to Chris, a tall, well-dressed undercover officer who, like Cormier, had a French-Canadian background. Cormier had walked into the hotel room to find Chris sitting next to a vacuum-sealing machine, which he was using to pack up wads of cash. Cormier seemed in awe of Chris's professional demeanour. When Chris mentioned that he didn't realize there were French Canadians in New Brunswick, Cormier launched into a history lesson about his Acadian ancestors, descendants of French colonists who had settled in Canada's Maritime provinces. In the eighteenth century, he told Chris, they had been expelled by the British, and some had settled in Louisiana, where they had become the Cajuns. One of these had been the pirate Jean Lafitte, who had helped the American colonists against the British. To Cormier, Lafitte was a rebel who had turned his life around to do something righteous—rather like himself, he told Chris, pleased that they had a topic over which they could bond.

The improvement in Cormier's working life was in distinct contrast to the situation in his apartment, which was deteriorating by the day. He confided to Mo that he had started carrying a knife with him for protection. He had thrown out a couple of male friends and even shouted at Danielle, who had walked out in tears. The meth was making him paranoid. He felt as if he were living in a shadow world where nothing was real and no one could be trusted. People were taking advantage of him, and he had a lingering suspicion that he was constantly under some sort of surveillance. Mo listened sympathetically but told him his fears were just in his head. The drugs were making him crazy.

The mics in Cormier's apartment picked up a late-night conversation between him and a young female friend.

"You ever been haunted by something?" asked Cormier. He continued, "I know, I'm really moving into the realm of fucking psychiatry . . . psychology . . . What happened there . . . it's not right. Fuck! It's right on the shore. So what do I do? Threw her in."

O'Donovan pressed pause so he could take in Cormier's words. Was he admitting he had killed Tina on the banks of the Red River and then thrown her in? He noted the time of the statement and turned the recording on again.

"What do you mean?" the girl asked.

"I did Tina, fuckin' supposed to be legal and only fifteen. No going back, too. The cops said if there would have been DNA, then probably they would have had enough evidence to charge me, you know that? For the murder of Tina Fontaine."

Cormier was clearly high. His words were slurring into each other, and O'Donovan was struggling to understand them. Cormier mentioned the truck and that someone had seen it. He said there were things about the police investigation that his friend didn't know.

"You know what MOM means when you're being investigated?" he asked. "The means, the opportunity, and the motive." He explained this was what detectives searched for when they tried to identify a suspect. He said if he could reverse time, he would have had a sexual relationship with Tina, even if it meant going to jail.

The girl asked him what he meant by this, but Cormier changed the subject, suggesting instead they go out and get smashed. There was no more mention of Tina, and the couple remained in the apartment chatting.

Half an hour later, Cormier suddenly said, "I beat two murders."

The girl asked if this meant he had killed his brother. Cormier just laughed, and again O'Donovan had the frustrating sense that his suspect had once more edged close to saying something significant but had been clever enough to pull himself back from the brink.

The Project Styx team were now pinning their hopes for a confession on the domestic violence scenario between Jenna and Mo. They settled on a storyline in which Cormier would walk into the aftermath of a vicious argument between the couple. Mo would tell Cormier that he had knocked Jenna to the floor and she would appear close to death. Mo would then enlist Cormier's help in trying to get rid of her. The hope was that Cormier would give practical advice about how to make Jenna's body disappear and perhaps even confess that he had been through something similar with Tina.

The date was set for the evening of October 1, 2015, exactly one year after Cormier was first arrested and interviewed for Tina's murder. That afternoon, Jenna arrived at work to be met by a professional makeup artist. O'Donovan explained she'd been hired to make it look like Jenna had been violently attacked.

For the next hour, the undercover officer sat patiently as the makeup artist took instruction from the Styx team. They wanted Jenna to have a swollen eye and a cut nose from being punched in the face. The makeup artist carefully applied fake congealed blood to Jenna's hairline to mimic the appearance of the serious injury she would get from falling and smashing her head on Mo's coffee table after he punched her.

Once the monitoring team had confirmed that Cormier was at home, Mo and Jenna installed themselves in Mo's apartment and prepared to start arguing. The idea was that Cormier would hear them and come over to see what the noise was about. Concerned that the fight might appear staged, Mo took a cheese grater from the kitchen and scraped his knuckles until blood dripped down his hand. Jenna looked on in awe at his commitment.

This time, the officers were each wearing two body packs to record audio. They briefly turned away from each other to switch them on, then stood face to face in silence, waiting to begin. In the Public Safety Building, the Styx team had gathered together in the monitoring room to listen to the live audio feed, and O'Donovan had positioned more officers in vehicles close to the apartment building in case backup was needed.

Mo counted them down. "Three . . . two . . . one . . ."

"Fucking why did you come here?" he screamed.

"It doesn't fuckin' matter," Jenna screamed back, and the fight was on.

Jenna grabbed an open beer can and threw it against the wall, splattering beer from floor to ceiling. In return, Mo picked up a framed picture and hurled it across the room, watching with satisfaction as the glass shattered into tiny pieces. A shard caught Jenna on her hand, adding her blood to the growing mess and chaos.

The officers were doing their best to make as much noise as they could, but after five minutes of shouting, it was clear that Cormier wasn't coming.

"I'm going to get him," Mo whispered to Jenna.

After he left, Jenna lay down on the floor with her head next to the coffee table to wait for the men to return. Her instructions were to make faint noises to show she was still conscious, but only just. The main lights in the room were off, and she positioned herself so that her face lay in a long shadow thrown by a lamp in the corner of the room, praying that it was dark enough to make her injuries look real.

In the apartment hallway, Mo was banging on Cormier's door.

"It's Mohammad, Raymond," he shouted. "I need your help for a second, buddy, five minutes."

When Cormier answered the door, Mo could see he was dressed ready for a night out stealing and had collected a group of men to go with him. After a brief discussion, Cormier reluctantly agreed to leave them and followed Mo back to his apartment.

"Hey, look at her fuckin' like this. This is not good," said Mo, dragging Cormier to stand over Jenna's limp body.

Cormier took a flashlight from his backpack and shone it down onto Jenna's face.

"Whoa," he said.

Mo told Cormier to grab a coat to wrap Jenna up in it. He said he had already called Jay, who was out of town but was sending over one of his men to take Jenna away. On the floor, Jenna made a gurgling noise as if she were struggling to breathe.

Cormier snapped into action, kicking off Jenna's sandals and picking her up by her belt buckle. Jenna stayed limp as Cormier secured her onto Mo's shoulders in a piggyback lift. He walked behind them, still holding onto Jenna's belt, as they shuffled out into the hallway. Conscious of the bright lights outside the apartment, Jenna made sure the coat stayed securely over her face as Mo struggled to carry her down the stairs.

"Fucking cameras all over this fucking place," said Cormier, suggesting they should stop to cover them up.

Mo said no, they had to hurry up and get Jenna out to Jay's man, who would be waiting for them by now in his hatchback by the back door. Once there, Cormier helped Mo throw Jenna into the back. He tried to speak to the undercover officer who was masquerading as the driver, but the man gave only a curt reply before driving away at speed.

As they walked back upstairs, Mo asked Cormier if he would come in and sit with him for a while. "Give me five minutes," Mo said. He was acting as if he was in shock, insisting he had only hit Jenna because she had run at him with a knife.

Cormier hesitated, saying that his crew was waiting for him. But Mo kept pressing until Cormier finally relented and followed him inside.

"If she dies and she told somebody about you, they're gonna come here. We have to fucking clean this place up," Cormier said, looking at the mess. He told Mo there was stuff they could buy that would get rid of every drop of blood.

Mo paced up and down, too worried he might be sent to jail to start cleaning. Cormier reassured him, saying it was unlikely the cops would come after him when he didn't have a record for domestic abuse and wasn't a known gang member.

As Mo acted panicked, Cormier remained relaxed. He seemed

to be taking control of the situation and enjoying his role as mentor. He asked if the neighbours had heard anything. Had Mo had sex with Jenna earlier in the evening, which would mean his DNA would be in her body? Mo told him yes, he had, but he was confident that Jay would look after him. He knew Jay had dirty cops on his payroll and this was just the sort of problem they could make go away. Cormier urged him to be careful, telling him to clean the place up and get away as soon as he could. If the cops came by, Cormier would cover for him. If they knew Jenna had been at his place, he would say that she'd been drinking too much and had fallen over. He said he would try to get the tapes from the security camera in the hallway, a detail that amused the team listening in the monitoring room. Cormier was thinking back to a time when security camera footage was recorded on VCR, but now it was digital and stored on a remote server.

Meanwhile, Jenna had returned to the Public Safety Building and was listening to the conversation with the rest of the team. O'Donovan was impressed by Cormier's knowledge of how to clean up a crime scene, but as yet he had said nothing to indicate he had done something similar with Tina.

In the apartment, Cormier told Mo he needed to go back to his own place to check on his crew and take a shower. Half an hour later, he was back at Mo's door holding a gift box of stolen shower goods, which he offered to sell him for forty dollars, saying he was giving Mo a fantastic discount. Mo looked at him in disbelief, then brushed him aside, saying now was not the time to make money. He was still acting as if panicked about what he should do. Just as he said this, the officer playing Jay called Mo's cell to say that his men had told him that Jenna was still alive but was barely clinging to life.

"Dump the body," said Cormier when Mo got off the call.

"What do you mean? How do you fuckin' dump a body?" asked Mo.

"Never to be found," Cormier replied. Jay would know what to do, he said.

Cormier was sure that as long as there wasn't a body, the police would not be able to pin anything on Mo. Once more, he said he would try to get the tapes from the security camera in the hallway to make sure no one could connect Jenna with Mo's apartment. But, he warned, if a forensic team came, they would find blood, no matter how hard he and Mo tried to clean it up.

"But if they don't find a body, then where was she?" he said calmly before helping himself to a can of beer.

Sensing that Cormier was beginning to relax, Mo changed his tactics from appearing panicked to praising Cormier, telling him that Jay knew how much of a help he was being and had been really impressed. Flattered, Cormier continued to give out advice.

"If I found myself in a situation where a body had to disappear, it would disappear, there's no way you're gonna find it," he said, letting out a chuckle.

He advised Mo to keep his mouth shut if the police arrived. He should give only his name and address and ask to speak to a lawyer. Cormier knew how the game worked. They were going to ask questions, but Mo should keep quiet. Mo needed to get his story straight. The only way the police would know what happened was if there was some sort of surveillance in the apartment building.

"I was investigated for the murder of Tina Fontaine, remember?" he said. "I'm still here, y'know what I mean?"

The important thing was, Cormier said, could Mo live with himself if she was dead? Would he be able to look himself in the mirror? Of course he was going to feel shitty, but he had to stay free and stick with the plan. Cormier added that, as for himself, there was no way he was going back to jail. If Jay could keep Mo out of prison, then Mo would owe Jay his life.

Once again, Cormier went over Mo's story to make sure he had it straight. He instructed him to throw away his bloody clothes, but not in the garbage, and burn the coffee table on which Jenna had hit her head. Mo was his friend, so he was giving this advice to look after him. Mo nodded with gratitude, saying that when he had cleaned up he would head to Candace's place and lie low for a while, but he would be in touch soon.

"Don't panic," Cormier advised him before the men parted ways.

To the Project Styx team, the night had been a success. It had given them a chilling insight into Cormier's mind. Although he had not specifically admitted to disposing of Tina's body, he had behaved like a man who knew exactly how to make someone disappear. Cormier's ability to remain calm and take control had been impressive and had confirmed their belief that he was the person responsible for wrapping Tina in a duvet cover and weighting her body down in the river.

You're exactly where we want you, thought O'Donovan, already planning where Styx would go next. Helping dispose of Jenna had cemented Mo, Jay, and Cormier into an alliance that would be very useful for their future plans. From this point on, O'Donovan would work on sucking Cormier further into the criminal organization, deepening his relationship with Mr. Big, and building up to a grand finale in which he would be pressured to tell the truth about Tina. O'Donovan did not yet know exactly how this would happen, but he suspected the end game was not far away. It would be a challenge, but he was confident Styx was moving ever closer to delivering the justice Tina deserved.

13.

WHISTLER

The day after Jenna was attacked, Cormier called Mo's cell to ask how he was doing.

"Everything's fine," said Mo, refusing to be drawn into a conversation. He hinted that he would talk to Cormier when they were face to face.

Later, listening to the audio recording, O'Donovan approved of the conspiratorial tone. The closer the alliance between Mo and Cormier, the more he could exploit it.

For the moment, Cormier was distracted by a visitor. For the first time in a year, his former friend from 22 Carmen, Sarah Holland, appeared on his doorstep and asked if they could talk. Cormier was happy to see her, kicking out another girlfriend so they could spend time alone. Holland wanted him to know that the police had come to her house asking questions about both him and Ernest DeWolfe and that she had been asked to identify an old duvet cover. Listening to her account, Cormier became angry, blaming DeWolfe for bringing the cops to her doorstep and even for murdering Tina.

But Holland disagreed. DeWolfe had been a good friend, she said. The couple debated late into the night, lowering their voices to a whisper when they mentioned Tina's name. When he listened to the conversation, O'Donovan wondered if Holland had gone to the apartment to satisfy her own curiosity about whether Cormier had killed Tina.

A week later, Mo returned to 400 Logan and told Cormier it was time they met with Jay to discuss what had happened to Jenna.

"How is she?" Cormier asked, after he had climbed into Mo's van. They were driving to an agreed meeting point at a secluded sports field.

Mo said he didn't know. He had been instructed that if Cormier pressed for an answer he should tell him that Jenna had died of her injuries and Jay had ordered that her body be burned in the animal incinerator used by his dog-fighting friends. For the moment, though, Mo judged it more effective to keep Cormier in the dark about Jenna's fate.

A chill October wind was stirring up the leaves when the men left Mo's van and walked to where Jay was standing. At first the chat was casual, but then Jay ordered them to turn off their phones.

"Are you in a bit of a jam?" he asked Cormier.

"I don't know what you're talking about," Cormier replied.

"I can deal with issues, but not if you have secrets," said Jay. He told Cormier that he had been in situations far worse than Cormier could imagine. As long as there were no surprises, there was nothing he couldn't handle.

But Cormier remained tight-lipped. "I don't know you from a hole in the ground," he said when Jay insisted on hearing his account of the night Jenna was hurt.

Listening to the recording, O'Donovan was struck by how much of a lone operator Cormier was and how little he trusted other people. Eventually, it was Mo who persuaded him to open up, by telling Jay how grateful he had been that Cormier had helped get Jenna out of the apartment. Mo had learned that flattery was the fastest route to getting his subject to talk.

"We share a bond now," Cormier admitted. "As long as we stay solid, we're good."

Now that he had some leverage with Jay, Cormier asked him to help him out with some crystal meth dealers who were causing problems. Jay let him know he would do his best.

"Your stock is rising," Jay said. He handed Cormier a hundred dollars to spend on smartening himself up, saying he wanted to take him out that weekend.

When Saturday evening rolled around, Cormier had tied back his hair and put on clean clothes in anticipation of an evening out at Jay's expense. He was in a chatty mood as Mo drove him to the upmarket steakhouse the Styx team had chosen to impress him. Jay greeted Cormier warmly and told him to order whatever he wanted, because the night was all about showing his appreciation. Chris, the undercover cop who Cormier had seemed in awe of, chatted to him in French like an old friend. The officers' brief was to give their suspect centre stage and make him feel as if he had been granted access to their inner circle. They listened intently when Cormier confided how he was planning to steal a car, strip it down, and sell it for parts. They smiled when he detailed his sexual conquests and talked at length about his growing attraction to Danielle. When he wanted to know how they managed to stay in shape, they laughed and told him it was stress that was keeping them slim.

Just before paying for the meal in cash, in a gesture that deeply impressed Cormier, Jay took him outside for a cigarette. He whispered that he had a deal coming up in Vancouver that could make them all rich if he managed to pull it off.

On the ride home, Cormier wanted to know if Mo had enjoyed the evening as much as he had. When Mo confessed he had just learnt that Jenna had died from her injuries and he'd been too worried about whether the cops would come after him to relax, Cormier laughed and told him to pray to God to absolve him.

"The only way it isn't over is if you won't let it," he said. He reasoned that if they had taken Jenna to a hospital, there might have been a different outcome. But Jay had dealt with it his way, and if it had been up to Cormier, he would have done the same thing.

The Project Styx team were now firmly focused on drawing Cormier ever closer to Mo and Jay. They wanted to show Cormier how good life could be if he stayed loyal to his Mr. Big believing the tighter the bond between the men, the more chance there was that Cormier would eventually confess. The team discussed scenarios in which Cormier could be paid for carrying out small tasks, knowing these would ingratiate him further with the gang. They could see their target was easily bored, so they tried to inject an element of danger. A few days after the dinner, Mo was instructed to sound Cormier out about a high-risk job that needed to be done under the cover of darkness.

The following evening, Mo drove Cormier one hundred kilometres south to a rural property close to the US border where Jay was waiting with bags of dog food. When Cormier looked confused, Jay opened one up to reveal handguns still in their packaging hidden inside. Cormier wanted to know how they performed, so Jay took him outside, unpacked a gun, and fired rounds into a hay bale fifteen metres away. When the muzzle flashes blazed in the dark, Cormier laughed and rubbed his hands together. He listened intently when Jay instructed him to drive slowly back to the city and stash the bags in a storage locker and was delighted with the $1,000 cash payment he received for his work. The amount marked a financial escalation for the project, but O'Donovan was confident that they could afford it. Even with overtime costs, they were operating within their $120,000 budget, and the detective saw no reason to scale things down.

A more immediate threat to Styx's success came from Cormier's own behaviour. The other tenants of 400 Logan were becoming angry about the constant commotion from his apartment, complaining about noise and what they suspected were drug deals on the premises. Concerned that Cormier might be arrested by local patrol officers, O'Donovan was forced to tell them about the operation and ask them to sign non-disclosure agreements to make sure it remained a secret. The decision worked in his favour. The officers were able to act as extra surveillance, keeping an eye on who was coming and going from the building and turning away some of the more unsavoury characters who tended to drift towards there late at night.

There was also the problem of Cormier's predilection for young women. His fondness for Danielle had not deterred him from having sex with other girls, and the team identified a dozen who would come to his apartment on a regular basis. Cormier seemed to have an insatiable sexual appetite and would confide in Mo about the opportunities he was hoping to exploit. He knew a woman who was pimping out her fourteen-year-old daughter, and though he had not taken up the offer, he had noticed that the girl had a lisp and was "cute." Cormier was aware that the young women he slept with were often frightened of his temper. Having observed Cormier's behaviour close up, O'Donovan was also concerned. Several times he discussed how the team would intervene or halt the project if they sensed a girl was in immediate danger.

On October 19, the federal Liberal Party candidate, Justin Trudeau, was elected Canada's new prime minister. Reacting to the public outrage that had followed Tina Fontaine's death, Trudeau had campaigned on a promise to launch a national public inquiry into missing and murdered Indigenous women as soon as he was in office. In Winnipeg, O'Donovan watched the election results with a sense of detachment. He was relieved to see the problem finally addressed at a national level, but within the intense secretive world of Project Styx, Trudeau's pledge seemed an irrelevant distraction.

That fall, as the temperature dropped and snow began to fall, the detective grew more concerned about keeping Cormier under control. One evening the monitoring staff made a panicked call directly to him to say they had heard Cormier offering chocolate chip cookies to two young Indigenous women in exchange for sex. Because the girls had been wearing thick coats when they passed beneath the hallway surveillance camera, the staff couldn't judge whether they were old enough to consent. O'Donovan immediately dispatched two uniformed officers to knock on Cormier's door and ask for IDs, pretending they were responding to a noise complaint. Satisfied that the girls were over eighteen and not in distress, the officers left. Cormier later told friends he suspected the police had given a bogus excuse to get into his place because they wanted to spy on him.

O'Donovan took the opportunity to exploit Cormier's paranoia to his advantage, sending two officers to his apartment to say they were investigating a missing persons report about Jenna. The first time they knocked on his door, Cormier refused to open it. But they returned the following day and managed to get inside to show

Jenna's photo. Cormier looked at it for several seconds but did not say a word.

The tactic worked. A day later, Cormier arranged to meet Mo at a car wash to tell him that the cops had been sniffing around. He reassured Mo that the chances of him being caught were slight, as Jenna was still listed as a missing person, not as a homicide. When Mo told him Jenna's body would not be found because it had been incinerated, he relaxed even more.

"Get a good lawyer," Cormier advised. "But fucking don't tell him anything either. Your lawyer is obligated to act on what you tell them, so keep your mouth shut."

Towards the end of October, the monitoring staff alerted O'Donovan to a conversation recorded between Cormier and a young female friend who occasionally spent time in the apartment. Cormier was talking about Tina.

"We had sex and we fuck. Sure enough . . . fuck. Tina finds a knife . . . She got angry and . . . get the fuck away from me . . . Blah, blah, blah . . ." he continued.

The mention of the knife was new to O'Donovan, and it sounded like Cormier was talking about a different argument from the one he and Tina had had outside 22 Carmen on August 6. If Tina had been angry and had brandished a knife, it could explain why Cormier might have harmed her. But Cormier's speech was rambling and incoherent, too vague for the detective to be sure of its meaning.

"I'm into this . . . dark side I guess. The dark side starts looking at the dark side," Cormier told his friend. "By sunset she died," he continued. "That's why I don't joke: I've seen a lot of shit."

The Project Styx team could see that Cormier's crystal meth addiction was deepening, and his behaviour becoming more unpredictable. In early November Cormier learned that his older brother had been diagnosed with a brain tumour. He reacted by smashing up his phone and lashing out at the people around him. His initial resolve to keep Jenna's murder a secret was weakening, and he hinted to two friends that someone had been killed in the apartment building and made them promise to keep their mouths shut. He accused other friends of stealing and Danielle of only caring about him because he gave her dope. He continued to talk obsessively about Tina, saying he was conducting his own investigation into her death and he believed that dirty cops had been involved. Between his drug-induced highs Cormier's moods fluctuated. Aggression and mania flooded through him on waves of nervous energy.

The Styx team continued to present Jay as the man who could make Cormier's problems disappear. Mo let Cormier know that business was going so well for his boss that Jay was going to buy him and Candace a new condo, and there was a suggestion that later he might do the same for Cormier. Jay said he was closing in on his big Vancouver deal and there would be more than enough work to go around. Meanwhile, Mo and Cormier were ordered to conduct surveillance on a man who had flown in from the West Coast. Cormier's criminal instinct was so attuned that he quickly picked out the real undercover team that was tailing Mo's van. This impressed O'Donovan but also made him nervous. He knew they had to push on with the project before Cormier realized what was really going on.

Jay told Cormier that his long-term plan was to fly him to Vancouver to work for him there. O'Donovan calculated that this would both impress Cormier and convince him that Jay was a serious player with a criminal network throughout the country. While Cormier waited for a fake ID, Jay introduced him to the "dirty cop" on this team, an undercover officer named Brad. Jay said he had been concerned because Brad had told him that the police were investigating Jenna's disappearance and had security camera footage of the hatchback car that had driven her away. But Brad reassured him that detectives were still searching for answers and definitely did not have any footage from inside the apartment building. Everyone agreed that there was no immediate cause for alarm.

O'Donovan felt it was time to remind Cormier how rewarding life could be if he pledged his full allegiance to Jay. Following a well-honed Mr. Big strategy, he planned an ostentatious party. The location was a newly built luxury penthouse in Winnipeg's fashionable Osborne Village, which Jay would pass off as one of his many properties. The team rented a top-of-the-line Cadillac SUV, packed the fridge full of alcohol, including Cormier's favourite fruit beers, and hired caterers to wander around with trays of canapés. Thirty undercover officers were invited to be guests and told to dress up for a big night out. Most already knew about Styx. The ones who didn't were instructed to drink, look happy, and keep their conversation light. O'Donovan estimated he would be spending more than $5,000 on this one evening, but he calculated it was worth it if it lured Cormier closer.

With the stage set for an exciting event, the only person who seemed unimpressed was Cormier himself. When Jay arrived to pick him up in his Cadillac, he found him in a depressed mood. Cormier said he had just ended his relationship with Danielle and was already regretting his decision. He had made an effort to smarten up, slicking back his hair, pulling on clean jeans, and buying a bottle of whisky so he wouldn't be seen as a "schmuck." But the party wasn't really his scene, and he told Jay he might not last the evening.

His spirits lifted a little when he realized the event was being held in a building from which he'd stolen copper pipes when it was under construction. Reassured to be on somewhat familiar ground, Cormier tried to forget his romantic troubles and socialize with the other guests. Candace made a point of taking him under her wing, introducing him to her friends and praising him as a fantastic guy. Everyone feigned delight to meet him. Jay casually mentioned he had been so impressed with Cormier's work that he was considering buying another penthouse and installing Cormier in it while it was being renovated. He, Cormier, and an undercover officer posing as a corrupt mortgage broker fell into a deep conversation about property fraud while Candace rallied the guests into singing along to "American Pie," which she had turned to full volume in the kitchen. When Mo and Candace offered to drive him home at 4 A.M., Cormier told them he had never had such good friends.

"I love you both," he said from the back seat of their car.

"We love you too," replied Candace.

O'Donovan listened to the exchange with a sense of satisfaction. His goal of switching Cormier's dependence away from his street friends and onto Jay and Mo seemed to be working. As Cormier's life continued to spiral downwards, O'Donovan hoped he would come to rely on them even more. He felt it was only a matter of time before Cormier finally cracked.

The storm came quickly. A week after the party, Mo received a call from an agitated Cormier, who was speaking so fast that Mo barely understood him. Heading to his apartment, Mo found Cormier shouting that he needed to leave Winnipeg immediately, saying it was urgent that he visit his brother in New Brunswick before he died from his brain tumour. Cormier insisted he would cycle the three thousand kilometres to get there, even though it was mid-November and the ground was thick with snow. The catalyst for his anger had been Danielle, who he accused of having had sex with someone else.

"I didn't kill her, I just punched her right in the mouth for that," he told Mo.

Cormier asked Mo to draw him a map to the highway so that he could return to his childhood home and sit by his mother's grave to talk to her. He said he also had things he needed to say about Tina.

Listening to the conversation live in the audio monitoring room, O'Donovan sensed that they might have reached the point at which Cormier would confess. His suspect was spitting out details about how he had been arrested for Tina's murder, swearing that he had only run away from the cops because he thought they were dirty and trying to set him up.

"You said that Danielle resembles Tina Fontaine?" asked Mo, encouraging him to keep talking. "You must have loved Tina?"

Cormier replied that it hadn't been like that. He had found Tina attractive and wanted to sleep with her, and she had encouraged him back, even though she was only fifteen. But Sarah had told him the truth about her age, and that had made him angry. That was why, the last time he saw Tina, he had thrown his dope at her feet and told her to jump off a bridge.

"I had enough of her ranting and fucking child shit. Because that's what it was, it was child shit," he said, admitting that he now felt bad because he realized that Tina didn't know how to survive on the streets like he did.

Becoming calmer, Cormier told Mo he wanted to see a police report to find out why the police had him under investigation for

Tina's murder. He said he suspected a crystal meth dealer had pinned the crime on him. Though, he conceded, the police had probably arrested him because he "may or may not" have been in possession of a stolen truck which might have been the means used to dispose of Tina's body.

As he said this, he smiled and winked at Mo.

"There's three rules in crime," he told him. "Deny, deny, deny." Then he laughed.

In the monitoring room, O'Donovan willed Cormier to keep talking, sensing he was close to revealing an important detail. But as always, his suspect pulled back at the crucial moment. The detective realised he wasn't going to get the break he needed.

During the next few days, O'Donovan waited for Cormier to contact Mo again to continue their discussion. But Cormier remained holed up in his own apartment, sinking into a morass of meth use and self-pity. It was clear from what he was saying to friends that Tina was still very much on his mind.

"I want to say something to you so bad right now," Cormier said to a male guest who had come over to see him. "I'm gonna go talk to Tina for a long time today," he said, referring to his habit of sitting by Tina's memorial at the Alexander Docks and holding conversations with the dead girl. "She knows I'm angry. You don't think she knows I'm angry?"

Cormier's friend advised him to take time out to think about what was bothering him and whether it had a lesson to teach him.

"I don't care about a lesson. I don't care about nothing. I just gotta get away from what I'm feeling," Cormier replied.

A few days later, Danielle returned for an afternoon visit. What started as a casual chat turned nasty after Cormier accused her of posting a naked picture of him on Facebook. She denied doing it, and Cormier started to scream in anger.

"Unfortunately, there's a little girl in a fucking grave someplace screaming at the top of her lungs for me to fucking finish the job, and guess what?" he shouted at Danielle.

"What?"

"I finished the job."

Cormier's abrupt pivot from the Facebook picture to the girl in the grave was puzzling to O'Donovan. It sounded as if he was threatening Danielle by telling her about how he had killed Tina. But the detective couldn't be sure, and Cormier quickly changed the subject. All O'Donovan could do was add the conversation to a growing pile of transcripts he hoped to use as evidence.

A day later, the detective had another transcript to join them. Cormier had been alone in his apartment, singing and mumbling to himself.

"You think you'll get the murder out of me?" he suddenly shouted. "Hmm. That's fucking it, man. Get away from me. Fuck you. Fuck!"

Knowing Cormier was probably using crystal meth at the time, O'Donovan wasn't sure whether to interpret the outburst as a true confession or dismiss it as a paranoid hallucination.

It was now almost December, five months since the start of Project Styx, and O'Donovan could see that the operation was approaching a crossroads. It could continue as it had been, in the hope that Cormier would eventually make the unambiguous confession they needed. Or his team could gamble everything on one last play to force Cormier to speak.

O'Donovan believed a bold move was needed. It wasn't that he felt under pressure to wrap up the project. The Styx budget was under control, and his superiors were confident in his leadership. Nor was his thinking affected by the continuing demands from Thelma and the Indigenous community to deliver justice for Tina. He knew the entire team was doing as much as it could and was committed to working on the case until it was solved. It was more that he realised Styx had gone as far as it could. Despite his deepening addiction, Cormier had proved himself too guarded to be persuaded to open up. And it wasn't just about getting a confession. The detective had become seriously worried about the safety of Cormier's girlfriends, in particular Danielle. It was chilling how much she resembled Tina. When Cormier first met her she had been wearing a white dress that was similar to the white skirt Tina had been found in. Cormier told a friend it was almost as if he had seen a ghost. Since then he had fawned over Danielle, idolized her, and declared his love to her, then blamed her for everything wrong in his life and assaulted her. O'Donovan didn't think she was tough enough to withstand his temper and believed that she was in grave danger of being badly hurt.

The detective arranged a meeting with the senior prosecutors at Manitoba Justice and spent a morning with them detailing his case, reading out intercepts, and talking them through the witness statements. He wanted to know if they felt the evidence already collected was strong enough for an arrest warrant. The lawyers were divided. Some thought the statements and transcripts were compelling but advised him to try to secure a confession to be certain. Others worried that the case was purely circumstantial. After some debate, they agreed that O'Donovan probably had enough to provide a reasonable likelihood of conviction. The detective told them he would do his best to get his confession, but either way he would call them when the project was over for their authorization to charge Cormier with murder.

———

Later, in the hushed and somewhat rundown surroundings of the Winnipeg Police boardroom, the Project Styx team met to work out their final storyline. Having spent weeks laying the groundwork for Jay's big deal out west, O'Donovan already knew that the showdown would take place in British Columbia. After some discussion, the team decided against situating it in Vancouver, where they felt it would be too easy for Cormier to slip away. Instead, they chose the ski-resort town of Whistler. It had the glamorous playboy appeal they had worked hard to foster around Jay and his criminal network. They also believed the town was small and isolated enough to control.

The undercover officers had already planted the idea in Cormier's mind that Jay was owed nearly $200,000 by an associate in British Columbia. Mo was to tell Cormier that Jay and Chris had flown to Vancouver to get the money and that he and Cormier were to follow as backup. Cormier was told they were going there to scare the associate but not physically harm him unless he put up a fight.

Mo did not mention the ski resort to Cormier at the outset so as to retain an element of surprise. He gave Cormier a fake ID in the name of Sebastian Roy and told him to head to Winnipeg Airport on December 8. "Don't bring any metal and don't bring any drugs," Mo warned him. Once Cormier was in Whistler, the plan was to let him know that detectives had new evidence that connected him to Tina's killing. Jay would tell Cormier that the police interest in him was threatening the safety of the entire gang and that way, put pressure on him to confess.

Cormier arrived at the airport in Winnipeg pumped full of nervous energy. He was anxious during the flight because the attendant omitted to serve water to his row, an oversight he found suspicious. In the baggage claim area in Vancouver, he scanned the crowd and pointed out a real undercover officer, who was there for Mo's protection, saying that he thought the man had followed them from Winnipeg. Mo brushed him aside, telling him to go out for a cigarette while he waited for their luggage. But Cormier remained on high alert. Outside the terminal, without prompting, he picked out the Vancouver officer who was playing the part of Mo's old girlfriend and contact in the city. Later that evening, when the officers left Cormier alone in a hotel near the airport, he walked miles back into the city centre to scout out the yachts and prime real estate and to steal a screwdriver from a Canadian Tire store. He told Mo he needed it for protection.

The next morning, Mo told Cormier there had been a change of plan and they were now expected in Whistler. Under a crisp, blue December sky, they began their drive into the mountains. Halfway there, Mo stopped the car so they could smoke and take in the breathtaking scenery of evergreen forests and snow-covered peaks. They marvelled at how bright the landscape seemed after the dull greys and browns of the prairies.

"Look what the cat dragged in," Jay said when Mo and Cormier finally arrived at his suite in Whistler's Westin Resort and Spa.

In a room across the hall, O'Donovan and half a dozen homicide detectives had set up their surveillance operation and were gathered around a monitor, wearing headphones and watching a live feed of pictures from inside Jay's room.

Chris was already with Jay, lounging on the sofa and boasting about how much he had drunk the night before. For a while, the conversation was light. Cormier joked about his sex life and chatted about hockey. Jay encouraged him to order room service. Outside, the snow reflected the bright sunshine, and the men discussed skiing and how good the girls looked, especially the Australian hotel staff.

After a while, Chris moved the discussion to the job they were about to do. Cormier said he was amazed that an outfit as sophisticated as Jay's would be interested in an old-timer like him, obsessed with stealing copper. But Jay reassured him that although he found Cormier unusual for his scrap metal obsession, he had passed their loyalty tests and was good for this job. If he played it right, it would set him up for a long time to come.

"After today, the world's a stage," agreed Cormier.

Across the hallway, O'Donovan nodded to his team that it was time to set the finale in motion. As the lunch orders arrived at Jay's suite, Mo received a call from Candace. He made it clear she was in distress.

"Put her on speaker," ordered Jay, when Mo asked Candace what was wrong. The men gathered around as Candace described how she had been in the Logan Avenue apartment when the police started banging on her door, saying they were looking for Cormier.

"They want him for murder," she said. "And I was like, 'What do you mean, murder?' And they just said that Tina broad, you know, that we heard about before."

In Jay's room, the undercover officers started to act as if they were freaking out. Jay told Chris and Mo to leave him and Cormier alone so he could figure out, one on one, what was going on. He phoned Brad, his supposedly dirty cop, to ask why the police had suddenly appeared, suspecting that they had found new evidence. Cormier looked panicked, and Jay reassured him that he would do everything he could to keep him out of jail. All Cormier needed to do was tell him exactly what had happened and he would sort it out.

"I did not have nothing to do with Tina's death," said Cormier, his voice taut with worry.

Jay told him to stay calm. He was a powerful man who could easily produce a fake ID and get Cormier far away if needed. But first he had to know what he was dealing with.

Cormier was shaking his head. "There's some things that don't add up here," he said, waving Jay away as if he wanted to be left alone with his thoughts. "How far would the Winnipeg Police Service go? How much money would they invest if they think I did it?"

Jay called Brad again, who told him the Winnipeg Homicide Unit had found a new witness from the Alexander Docks who had identified Cormier as the driver of a stolen truck that had been parked by the river shortly before Tina's body was found.

Cormier said the information didn't make sense. "I happen to believe that some of the Winnipeg Police Service are involved in Tina's murder," he told Jay. He said he needed to return home straight away to sort the situation out.

"You're starting to piss me off," replied Jay. He demanded that Cormier tell him the truth so he could deal with the issue before it escalated and damaged his entire criminal network.

But Cormier was still working things through in his mind. "Who are you, Jay?" he asked. "And how far will the Winnipeg Police Service go to try to fucking get me to fucking admit something that I didn't do?"

Cormier continued to mumble his thoughts out loud. For a while, he said, he felt that something dirty had been going on in Winnipeg. It didn't make sense that so many Indigenous women were going missing and turning up dead. Now he was questioning how he had met Mo and how easy it had been for their friendship to develop. "Too easy," he said with suspicion.

Jay was looking at his laptop, studying the security camera pictures Brad had sent and asking more questions about the truck. Cormier admitted he had spent a lot of time at the docks—he liked to sit alone by Tina's memorial—but he was furious that Jay could believe he had something to do with her death.

Jay said he was angry as well. "I feel like this is a fucking slap in the face!" he shouted at Cormier. He didn't like it when his inner circle kept secrets from him, he said.

But Cormier was too busy working through his theories to be intimidated. He muttered about the attendant on the plane who had forgotten to serve him water, and the man waiting by the luggage carousel, who he was sure he had seen before. He remembered reading about the two Winnipeg patrol officers who had pulled Tina up on a traffic stop the week before she died but had quickly let her go. There was something not right about all of it.

Jay had gone back to Brad's email and was reading that the police had forensic results from the stolen truck and a tent they had found on Alexander Avenue. He listed the details aloud: where the swabs had been taken, how many tests had been done.

"And what was the result?" asked Cormier.

"Nothing," admitted Jay.

"Exactly, 'cause it's a fucking smokescreen," Cormier said triumphantly. He asked if he could leave.

But Jay wasn't satisfied. It wasn't just about Cormier, he said; it was about the whole gang. They had all been put at risk because of this investigation.

"Did you wipe down the truck?" he asked.

"What truck?" said Cormier, refusing to be drawn in.

"I'm not a fucking miracle worker. I can fucking pull things, but I'm not fucking God. We need to work at this together," Jay said, looking away from Cormier as he spoke.

It was Jay's refusal to meet his gaze that clinched something in Cormier's mind.

"I didn't do it. How many times have I got to tell you that?" he said. He stood up and asked Jay to call Mo so he could retrieve his jacket from his car.

"Ray, you can't fucking just walk out!" Jay shouted.

"I just did," said Cormier, picking up his cigarettes, striding out of the room, and slamming the door behind him.

In the corridor he bumped into Mo, who asked where he was going.

"Never mind," said Cormier.

Picking up speed, Cormier made his way out of the hotel and onto a patio, where tourists were enjoying the sun. He casually picked up a backpack belonging to a couple having coffee and slipped it onto his shoulders. Now he was moving fast, heading out of the hotel grounds and onto the street beyond. He passed a bicycle chained to some railings and tried to pull it free. But the lock was too sturdy, so he let it go and kept going, trying to lose himself in the crowd.

Mo managed to stay behind him, keeping him in sight as Cormier hurried away from the hotel. Conscious that Cormier was armed with a screwdriver and that he was on his own, unarmed and without a radio, the undercover officer maintained some distance. He phoned O'Donovan to give his location. Meanwhile, the head of the Homicide Unit had dispatched all his detectives and half a dozen patrol officers to bring Cormier in. His team was working alone, without the help of the local RCMP division, and the officers were unfamiliar with the geography of the town. Because of this, it took at least ten minutes to find Mo. After several more minutes spent combing Whistler's main streets, two detectives finally caught sight of Cormier heading into the ground floor of a parking garage. Inside, they saw Cormier walk from car to car, trying the doors to see if any would open. Hearing people behind him, Cormier turned. When he saw the detectives, he stood with his shoulders hunched as if about to fight. Unable to see if he was holding a weapon, the officers pulled their guns, shouted that they were from the Winnipeg Police, and ordered Cormier to lie down. For a few seconds Cormier did nothing, as if considering his options. Finally, he slumped to his knees and lay face down on the ground, stretching his arms and legs out in a gesture of surrender.

"Raymond Joseph Cormier, you are under arrest for the murder of Tina Fontaine," said a detective, cuffing Cormier's hands behind his back and advising him of his rights.

By then, the entire Winnipeg police team had screeched into the parking garage in their fleet of rented SUVs. Cormier was bundled into the back of one while O'Donovan and his detectives prepared to follow behind in convoy. As he was driven to Vancouver, Cormier sat in silence, staring out of the window. When offered a phone to call a lawyer, he shook his head, saying he wanted to return to Winnipeg. He was told he would be taken to the Vancouver Police Homicide Unit, where he would be interviewed by the same team that had captured him in Whistler.

O'Donovan knew he had only twenty-four hours to secure a confession and charge Cormier before he would be legally required to release him. When his suspect had been placed in an interview room, he chose the same detectives who had first questioned him in Winnipeg to interrogate him now. Detective Sergeants Wade McDonald and Scott Taylor were familiar to Cormier, and O'Donovan sensed they intimidated him enough to lay on the pressure. But it would be a difficult task. Cormier was saying nothing. As before, he curled up in the fetal position under the table and refused offers of food and water. He said yes to a blanket but was using it to shield his face from the detectives. As they asked him questions, his only reply was "Fuck off," which he repeated so often that O'Donovan started to call him "the crow." After two hours, the detective had to concede that McDonald and Taylor were getting nowhere.

Next, O'Donovan sent in Detective Sergeants Jeff Stalker and Matt Freeman in the hope that they would fare better. But again, Cormier refused to answer. It was getting late, and O'Donovan, conscious of the passing hours, called the senior prosecutor in Winnipeg to ask if he could issue the arrest warrant without a confession, explaining what Cormier had said to Jay before fleeing. The prosecutor made notes and told the detective he would get back to him as soon as he could with his decision.

For an hour, O'Donovan and his team waited nervously, unsure of what the outcome would be. The prosecutor would need to review the entire case before he could make his decision, and it was by no means certain that he would support them. Then suddenly, the call they were hoping for came through. O'Donovan relayed the prosecutor's instructions back to his office in Winnipeg, where a detective was waiting to expedite the paperwork. It wasn't long before McDonald and Taylor were walking back into the interview room with a printed copy of the arrest warrant in their hands.

"Raymond, take a seat. I have something to tell you," said McDonald.

Cormier sat up but stayed on the floor, the blanket still wrapped around him.

"A senior Crown has authorized the charge of second-degree murder in the case of Tina Fontaine," said McDonald, handing him the warrant to read.

For the first time since leaving Whistler, Cormier looked defeated.

14.

"NOT A CASE OF
TUNNEL VISION"

O n December 8, 2015, the same day Mo and Cormier flew to Vancouver to provide muscle for Jay's big deal, Canada's new prime minister, Justin Trudeau, stood in front of an audience of First Nations chiefs and announced that his government would launch its much-anticipated National Inquiry into Missing and Murdered Indigenous Women and Girls.

"The victims deserve justice, their families an opportunity to heal and to be heard," Trudeau told the special assembly in Gatineau, Quebec, who greeted his announcement with applause and a standing ovation.

Trudeau said that those touched by this "national tragedy" had waited long enough and that his government would make the inquiry a priority. Later, his ministers explained that the first phase would be a consultation with the families of victims to find out how they wanted the inquiry to move forward. The information-gathering process would be detailed and far-reaching, and a final report was not expected for several years.

In British Columbia, O'Donovan noted how Trudeau's announcement coincided with the culmination of his own project to deliver justice to Tina's family. But the detective did not share the prime minister's sense of occasion. When Cormier's arrest warrant had finally arrived, late at night in the Vancouver Homicide Unit, the only emotion he could feel was relief, mixed with trepidation about what would happen next. Without a confession, he knew the case against his prime suspect was still uncertain. With this in mind, early the next morning he instructed his detectives to interrogate Cormier once again in the hope that they might be able to break him.

At around 8 A.M., Cormier was taken to an interview room in the same jail where he had been remanded the previous evening. As usual, O'Donovan positioned himself to watch the live feed as his suspect paced up and down like a caged tiger. When Detective Sergeants McDonald and Taylor walked into the room, Cormier stood within inches of their faces and yelled abuse at them. When they asked questions about the stolen truck and the last time he had seen Tina, Cormier continued to pace and shout, denying his involvement.

After a couple of hours of listening to Cormier rant obscenities, O'Donovan replaced McDonald and Taylor with Stalker and Freeman. Rather than probe for information, this pair of detectives decided to inform Cormier about Project Styx. They told him about the mics in his apartment and the camera placed in the hallway outside. They said it wasn't just Jay who had been an undercover cop but also Chris, Jenna, Candace, and Mo, and they had all recorded their conversations with him.

"I hope you remember everything you said over the past six months," Stalker said.

"Fucking bad actors, I knew all along," Cormier snapped back, defiant and angry. "How did prosecutors allow you to do that? Was Danielle a fake as well?" he asked, clearly unnerved by the realization that his life for the past six months had been built on a charade.

Later, when he'd had time to absorb the full extent of Styx's activities, Cormier said it had been obvious that Jay and his gang were a setup because of the way they had thrown their money around and inducted him so easily into their circle. He felt there had been red flags all over the place, but the crystal meth had a way of making the shadows move, and at the time he hadn't been sure if he could trust his instincts. Now it was clear. Nobody was brought into a gang at that level without having to earn his way up there. He had always suspected that the attack on Jenna was staged. He boasted that he was a twice certified first-aider who knew the difference between real blood and the fake theatrical paint they used on her face.

Mo's deception was harder to accept. Cormier had regarded both him and Candace as true friends, and even months after he had been told the truth, Cormier couldn't quite believe that their connection wasn't real. But he directed most of his outrage at what he saw as the ultimate betrayal by the police: the violation of his privacy.

"Everything was recorded. Every girl I got intimate with . . . everything," he later protested from prison as he awaited trial.

In the Vancouver monitoring room, listening to Cormier scream in response to the Styx revelations, O'Donovan willed him to blurt out a confession. But true to form, Cormier held himself together. By 11 A.M., the detective had run out of time. Cormier needed to be taken away to a courtroom to be formally remanded and officially turned over to the custody of the Winnipeg Police. O'Donovan's priority became how to get him home. With Cormier's history of aggression, he considered a commercial flight too risky. Nor did he fancy the twenty-five-hour car journey over the Rockies and across the treacherous ice-bound roads of the prairies. He relayed his concerns back to his superiors, who in turn contacted the RCMP to arrange for Cormier to be flown back on a private eight-seater twin-propeller plane.

O'Donovan would not be on the plane with him. He was told that he needed to leave immediately, because the press conference to announce Cormier's arrest would take place the next day.

While O'Donovan was flying back to Winnipeg, a female police constable phoned Thelma Favel to tell her to prepare for important news. The following morning, an hour before the press conference was due to start, O'Donovan called Thelma himself to say that sixteen months after Tina's body had been found in the Red River, the police had finally arrested a man for her murder. Thelma cried when she heard.

"Tina didn't suffer," O'Donovan said, feeling that it was a comforting thing to say but wondering how anyone could know what the last minutes of her life were like. "I just want you to know that we have him, and he's not going to hurt anyone else anymore." Thelma struggled to thank him through her tears.

In Winnipeg, Superintendent Danny Smyth, the deputy chief of police, joined O'Donovan to face reporters.

"Today I'm informing the public that Raymond Joseph Cormier has been charged with second-degree murder in the death of Tina Fontaine," said Smyth, as a drawn and tired-looking O'Donovan sat silently beside him. Smyth made a point of listing the names of the internal departments and other police forces who had helped, as if to stress the distance between this investigation and the police's well-publicized failure to protect Tina in the days before her death.

"We in the police community are also members of the general community," he said. "We are just as shocked and outraged by the violence we observe directed against women in general, and the violence we observe directed at Indigenous women and children in particular."

Then it was O'Donovan's turn.

"This has been an extremely long and complex investigation. I couldn't even count the number of man hours that have gone into it," he began. He detailed how his team had been able to build its case only because of the information given to them by the public. "It's definitely not a case of tunnel vision," he said, addressing a common criticism of such focused investigations. His team had looked into numerous suspects, he stressed, before Cormier emerged as the most likely.

When a reporter asked if O'Donovan believed his work countered long-standing criticism of the Winnipeg Police Service for its failure to investigate other missing and murdered Indigenous women, the detective looked pained.

"We worked on this every day, and when I say we worked on this every day, I don't just mean me, I mean my whole squad," he said. "It's not because it's high profile—it's because there was work to be done on it. We would do that for every single case that we have."

In making its announcement, the Winnipeg Police chose not to release a photo of Cormier, leaving reporters to dig up the one they had sent to the "Crime Stoppers' Most Wanted" section of the *Winnipeg Sun* the year before. It was the police mug shot showing Cormier with long, unkempt hair and a zoned-out stare, a photo he himself referred to as his "Charles Manson look." Even before the press conference was over, the picture was leading news bulletins across the nation. Two thousand kilometres away, in Ottawa, the Indigenous activists Nahanni Fontaine and Bernadette Smith were in a hotel conference room attending a pre-consultation session on the national inquiry when Fontaine received a heads-up from an official that an arrest was about to be made in the Tina Fontaine case. Minutes later, seeing Cormier's photo on their phones, the women hugged each other and cried. Fontaine called the official back and asked him to thank O'Donovan personally for her. "Our community needed this," she said. "Every single family deserves that same sense of justice and responsibility."

Thelma Favel was also deeply affected when she finally saw the face of the man allegedly responsible for killing her baby. "I've seen bad things my whole life, but I've never seen anything as evil as that man," she said.

Over the next few months, Thelma and her family spent hours drafting a victim impact statement, which they hoped to read during Cormier's trial. Thelma found it an impossible task, torn between not wanting to rake over the pain of Tina's loss and needing to let the man accused of her death know exactly how badly it had broken her family's heart.

"What do I say to the monster that stole my baby?" the statement began. "Abused her, then killed her and threw her away like she was garbage."

Thelma described how Tina had become lost and confused after her father was murdered but had always been protective of her younger sister, Sarah, and was a sweet, kind, funny girl. She demanded to know what Tina had done to deserve such a terrible fate, warning Cormier that she did not want to hear the excuse that he'd had a difficult upbringing.

"I know hundreds of both men and women who were abused and neglected in the residential schools and now have severe addictions from drugs and alcohol. But you don't see them here, charged with the murder of a sweet, tiny girl," she wrote.

In Winnipeg, the provincial corrections body decided to transfer Cormier out of the city to a smaller prison in the prairie town of Brandon, Manitoba, two and a half hours to the west. It would be easier to protect him there against possible revenge attacks by Indigenous inmates, who made up the majority of Winnipeg's incarcerated population.

Brandon also happened to be home to the general counsel slated to prosecute the case. James Ross was an experienced and well-regarded senior Crown who had the reputation of never losing a murder case, though he'd once had to settle for a manslaughter verdict. Ross teamed up with Winnipeg prosecutor Breta Passler and waited for O'Donovan's Homicide Unit to provide them with the official disclosure: the dossier of evidence collected by the police that they would use to build their case. There were so many intercepts that still needed to be listened to and transcribed that the material arrived in batches, with a constant stream of questions and clarifications ensuing between the Crown and O'Donovan's office. When all the evidence was finally gathered, Ross noted that it was enough to fill thirty-four large ring binders. The volume was so great that it took him and Passler nine months just to read it.

For much of his time in the Brandon Correctional Centre, Cormier was placed in the Rotation Unit, where prisoners were kept in solitary confinement for twenty-three hours a day and, when allowed out, restricted from socializing with other inmates. Here, he struggled to cope with an overwhelming sense of paranoia and victimization as he came to terms with what lay ahead. Cormier said it was as if he'd been thrown down a rabbit hole, and the only way out was to go through the terror of facing a murder charge. The prison doctors treated his crystal meth addiction with a high dose of Seroquel, an anti-psychotic medication, and he was grateful that it kept him asleep for most of the day and slowed his racing mind.

As the months passed, Cormier began to put on weight, replacing the gaunt, half-starved look of an addict with that of a portly middle-aged man. He spent the hours alone in his cell creating a fantasy world of medieval characters, which he drew in elaborate pencil sketches, inventing a language for them to speak. He thought back to his early life for inspiration. Growing up in New Brunswick, he was the youngest in a family of eight boys and five girls, and his childhood had been marked by violence, abuse, and family illness. He had felt closest to an older brother who had taken him under his wing, letting him play hockey with the bigger boys. But that brother had died of cancer, and the young Cormier reacted by acting out, desperate for any sort of attention. He was twice sent to the Kingsclear Youth Training Centre, a reform school that later gained national notoriety for the widespread sexual abuse of boys by its staff, including the convicted pedophile Karl Toft. By the time Cormier was a teenager, he had discovered that alcohol could boost his courage to fight back. It wasn't long before his behaviour was gaining the attention of the police, marking the start of his long career in crime. But despite his criminal activity, Cormier had never stopped wanting to learn. His father had told him it was important to read the newspaper from front to back and his mother had inspired in him a love of crosswords. Whenever he was locked up he would read, especially the Bible and fantasy books, and his prison artwork reflected this passion. In his private world Cormier invented mythic heroes who would fight dragons and finally reveal that consciousness was nothing but an illusion. His thoughts were dark, and he told fellow inmates that if found guilty he would hang himself. The drawings and writings were an expression of his epic struggle. It was Raymond Cormier against the world.

Cormier reserved most of his anger for what he saw as a political conspiracy to frame him. In his mind, the fact that his arrest coincided with Prime Minister Trudeau's announcement of the National Inquiry into Missing and Murdered Indigenous Women and Girls was not accidental; it was a carefully orchestrated plan to present a scapegoat for the problem. In particular, Cormier blamed the New Democratic government of Manitoba, making a connection between the high number of Indigenous youths in care in the province, the failure of Child and Family Services to protect Tina, and the need to find someone to blame for her death. As he learned more about Project Styx, Cormier's belief in an orchestrated conspiracy intensified. If Tina was the poster child for missing and murdered Indigenous women and girls, he was the sacrificial lamb framed as the national villain.

"I wasn't able to piece it all together until after I read the executive summary, then everything seemed to fit into a really good John Grisham novel," he said with anger after he saw the prosecution's argument for his case.

Cormier's paranoia meant he had difficulty trusting anyone, not least his own legal counsel. He fired the first two lawyers assigned to him by Legal Aid, suspecting them of collusion with the provincial political elite because they were based in Winnipeg. They were women, and, he believed, probably feminists, which would mean they would be biased against him. By June 2016 he had decided to find his own counsel locally in Brandon, where it was unlikely there would be the same political connections. After searching through the local phone book, he left a message with the assistant to a junior defence lawyer in a law firm based in town.

At thirty-four, Andrew Synyshyn was a relatively young and

inexperienced criminal defence lawyer who had defended only one jury trial, on child protection, in Brandon and had no experience in dealing with murder cases. When he first read the message left by his assistant, he was curious about why a prison inmate had called his firm directly. Later, when he googled Cormier's name, he almost dropped his phone in surprise that such a high-profile suspect had chosen to contact him.

The following evening, as the summer rain fell hard, Synyshyn arranged to meet Cormier at the correctional centre, hoping for two or three hours of uninterrupted time before the nighttime curfew. Cormier seemed impressed that Synyshyn had shown up so quickly and approved of the T-shirt the lawyer was wearing, which had a motif of numbers on it that he felt were auspicious. Synyshyn later said the meeting was like being drenched by a waterfall of information. Cormier spewed out everything he knew about the case: the Mr. Big operation, the apartment on Logan, his arrest, his relationship with Tina and the people who were conspiring against him. Not much of what he said made sense, and Synyshyn wondered how stable the manic, wild-eyed man sitting in front of him was. At the same time, he was conscious of the professional opportunity he was being presented with. The lawyer returned the next evening to demonstrate his consistency, this time armed with a box of Tim Hortons doughnuts to help sweeten the guards.

Over many more evenings, Cormier and Synyshyn's connection deepened. The more Synyshyn listened, the more Cormier opened up. The accused drew up a grid to demonstrate how he felt about their growing relationship. On one side he listed his enemies: Sergeant O'Donovan and the Winnipeg Police Service, the prosecutor, the NDP government, Manitoba Housing, and the shadow people who dominated his nightmares. On the other side, he wrote down his own name and that of his lawyer. Throughout their conversations Cormier insisted he was innocent, and Synyshyn was impressed by his repeated denials. Over time, he began to believe in his client's innocence. He found himself feeling sorry for him, and just before Christmas he bought him a radio so that he could feel connected to the outside world. Without sharing Cormier's belief in a political conspiracy, Synyshyn was also beginning to feel that it was just him and his client against the world. After their long face-to-face sessions, Synyshyn would often return home and stand in his kitchen, his head buried in his hands, overwhelmed by a crushing sense of responsibility and panic at the difficult trial he knew was ahead.

"We had this bond," he said. "It felt that there was no one else who was going to listen to him or fight for him."

Because of his junior status, Synyshyn was required to pair up with a senior supervising lawyer to qualify as Cormier's Legal Aid–appointed counsel. By the end of the summer, Anthony Kavanagh, an experienced litigator and law lecturer based in Winnipeg, was brought onto the team. Although Cormier seemed happy with his representation, he would threaten to fire his counsel whenever he felt challenged, writing them long letters detailing the ways in which they'd let him down. One point of friction was an official complaint Cormier had made against the police for issuing him with the fake ID used to travel to Vancouver. Cormier believed it had been part of a bigger plan to frame him. The complaint had been dismissed, but Cormier was appealing, despite his lawyers' advice to drop it.

When they first took the case, the Crown prosecutors, Jim Ross and Breta Passler, had scheduled a preliminary trial to take place in May 2017. Typically, a "prelim" was the chance to discover if there was enough evidence to proceed to a full trial and for the defence to hear the prosecution's case. But by the fall of 2016, the Crown had decided to dispense with this stage. A number of key witnesses were vulnerable addicts, and they were concerned that they might not all live long enough to testify in both trials.

Ross knew it would be a challenge to try the case in front of a jury, particularly in the era of TV crime shows, which tended to wrap things up neatly with forensic certainty and confessions, two elements that were lacking in this instance. But the prosecutor was confident that the evidence he did have tied together into what he called a compelling "constellation of circumstances." "It's a series of things that add up," he said. "Each piece of evidence in isolation proves nothing, but together they can be very significant because of the fact pattern."

Ross informed the provincial attorney general that he felt he had a viable case that a jury would convict on, and the attorney general agreed. But wading through the same files that made up the disclosure, the defence strongly disagreed.

"I had never seen so much material say so little," said Synyshyn. He had spent hours trawling through the information, looking for scenarios of guilt into which he could inject an element of doubt. When he first found out about the Beardys' identification of the Chloe Green duvet cover, his reaction had been, "How can this not be him?" But then he read that the witnesses were shown only one photo by Detective Sergeant Stalker and their testimony became less certain. As the lawyer continued to work through the disclosure, he had the sense that each trail of evidence would peter out inconclusively or meet a dead end. It was true that the intercepts from Project Styx revealed Cormier as an unsavoury character with a predatory sexual interest in young women. But that was far from an admission of guilt.

Synyshyn's senior partner, Tony Kavanagh, was equally unconvinced. "I had read, like everybody else, the executive summary produced by O'Donovan," Kavanagh said. "He does a great job of putting together the narrative, and he threads together all the evidence of what Cormier's done. But then I started drilling down into it, and I noticed that there were, let's just call them errors."

To Kavanagh and Synyshyn, the most glaring of those errors was the isolation of Cormier as a suspect so early in the police investigation. They believed O'Donovan had excluded other important leads and felt he should have delved far deeper into Winnipeg's drug and gang underbelly, from where much of his information emerged. Perhaps there was more to be learned from Tina's visits to the Furby Street rooming house, her association with the Kenyan and Nigerian men, the time the police identified her as the passenger in Richard Mohammed's truck, the sighting of her in the Windsor Hotel. Although O'Donovan had explicitly denied operating with "tunnel vision" during the press conference announcing Cormier's arrest, this was exactly what the defence team was accusing him of doing.

"It seemed like a ripe situation for a miscarriage of justice: a high-profile murder, the lack of a suspect, some pretty tenuous evidence, and someone who just everybody would look at and conclude he had to have done it," said Synyshyn.

The defence lawyers' belief was strengthened by the sudden elimination of the Mere Hotel security camera footage as evidence. O'Donovan had considered this a central pillar of his case, believing it showed the stolen truck behaving suspiciously on the night Tina's body was dumped in the Red River. But in 2017, the year before the trial, one of O'Donovan's own detectives had ruled that the truck seen in the grainy footage was not the same as the one allegedly stolen by their suspect. From what the officer could make out, the headlights were different from the Ford F-150 and the colour was paler than the stolen truck's dark blue. The Crown agreed that the footage was inconclusive. In Ross's opinion, even if the truck was the same make and colour as the stolen one, it had been parked too far away from the river to make sense for it to have been used to dispose of a body.

Although the exclusion of the footage was disappointing for O'Donovan, his team had continued to search for evidence, identifying and interviewing people who spent time with Cormier at 400 Logan Avenue in case they had information that Styx may have missed. Then, in the summer and fall of 2017, the detectives were alerted to two startling testimonies that, if true, would prove Cormier's guilt beyond a doubt. Two separate informants who had been imprisoned with Cormier in the Brandon Correctional Centre told the police that their accused had confessed to them while waiting for his trial.

The first informant was a white man in his forties who was serving the tail end of a long sentence for the exploitation of teenage girls. In August, the Brandon Correctional Centre had intercepted a letter from him in which he had written about Cormier and Tina's murder.

O'Donovan sent a team of detectives to Brandon to interview the man, and they were immediately struck by how he seemed not to want any concessions for his information. For two weeks over the summer, he had been housed in the same isolation unit that contained Cormier. The prisoners were kept apart, but in the few hours they were allowed out individually in the common central area of the block, it was possible for them to chat with each other through the cell doors.

Initially, Cormier and the man spoke about sports and other prisons they knew. Cormier told the informant he was drawing pictures for a fantasy novel and would slide these under his door to show him. After a few days, Cormier started to open up about Tina Fontaine, describing how he had met and hung out with the teenager. According to the informant, Cormier admitted to having sex with her and said they got into a fight when he found out she was only fifteen. He said she retaliated by reporting him for stealing a truck.

When the informant asked if this meant he had killed Tina, Cormier replied yes and described how he had lost his temper in an argument. Cormier held up his hands to the glass window high in the cell door to mime how he had suffocated the teenager. When the informant asked what Cormier had done with her body, he replied that he put her into a duvet cover with rocks to weigh her down but obviously had not used enough to keep her submerged.

The second informant was identified a few months later, in November 2017. He was an Indigenous man in his thirties who had mentioned Cormier in a phone call to his sister. Prison guards eavesdropping on the call had alerted the police. This informant also said he did not want anything in return for his information. He described how, since October, he had been housed in a cell opposite Cormier and they had struck up an uneasy acquaintance.

Cormier had a habit of using Bible references and sliding handwritten notes about his thoughts under this man's cell door for him to read. He chatted about stealing bikes and selling crystal meth for money, and about how he would give the drug to young girls and wait until they passed out so that he could do what he wanted with their bodies. Cormier also related how he liked to choke girls from behind so that they would faint and become compliant. The informant said he was getting a weird feeling about their conversations, but Cormier wanted to keep talking, especially about Tina. Cormier said that he and Tina had injected crystal meth together. When he suddenly discovered that some of his drugs were missing, he had lost his temper and started to choke Tina in his rage. According to the informant, Cormier said he blacked out, and when he woke up he found he had put a plastic bag over Tina's head. The informant wanted to know what had happened next, but their conversation was disturbed by a guard.

Although the two descriptions of how Tina had been killed differed in their details, O'Donovan felt he was finally hearing the truth about what had happened to the schoolgirl. He was determined that the men's testimonies should be used in court as evidence. But after years of hearing similar sensational revelations from other prison inmates, Crown attorney Jim Ross was wary. Ross wasn't averse to using the testimony of jailhouse informants. Earlier in his career, he had called one to the stand in a murder trial. But in this case he was convinced that the contradictory accounts were untrue. Neither inmate had revealed information they could not have gleaned from press reports or from Cormier's own conversations, even the detail about the duvet cover, which very few people knew. Ross was aware of the temptation to rely too heavily on informants in weak cases. They were often proven to be liars.

"They tend to be quite manipulative people, and they often tend to be quite clever," he explained. "They will gather what can be known about the case from the media and then present to police the answer they wanted to hear."

This was another blow for O'Donovan. Without the security camera footage of the truck or the informants' statements, the Crown's case would have to hinge on the identification of the duvet cover and the intercepts from Project Styx. O'Donovan assigned a detective to listen once again to the often poor-quality recordings from the Logan apartment and transcribe them as accurately as he could, knowing that they would be crucial to the trial.

In the final months of 2017, the defence counsel brought a number of motions attempting to limit what evidence could be admitted in the trial, raising the suggestion that another person might have been responsible for Tina's death and asserting that the police investigation had been inadequate. They lost every one of them.

As the weeks counted down to the trial's start in January 2018, Ross and Passler continued to prepare their "tough circumstantial case," working out the narrative they would present. The Crown attorneys believed they could convince the jury that the odds of one person both owning a Chloe Green duvet cover and having reason to argue with Tina were extremely low, and that Cormier had killed the runaway schoolgirl then panicked and ineptly disposed of her body.

In their offices in Winnipeg and in Brandon, Kavanagh and Synyshyn were also preparing to put their interpretation of the evidence forward. They both admitted to having sleepless nights.

"You don't have many cases where you truly believe that a wrongful conviction would occur if you don't do your job properly," Kavanagh explained. Unlike Synyshyn, who, said Kavanagh, had developed a strong emotional bond with Cormier, Kavanagh believed in Cormier's innocence from a detached, academic point of view. As the trial date drew near, the weight of his responsibility became intense.

"I did not want a wrongful conviction on my conscience," he said.

15.

JUSTICE FOR TINA

O n January 29, 2018, the trial of the Queen versus Raymond
Joseph Cormier opened in central Winnipeg. Cormier was
charged with the second-degree murder of Tina Fontaine.
He entered a plea of not guilty.

Earlier that brittle, freezing morning, Thelma Favel gathered
with other relatives and family friends outside the Law Courts
Building with red ribbons pinned to their coats in a gesture of
love and remembrance. They stood with their heads bowed
and faces heavy with sadness. For the duration of the trial, which
was expected to take at least four weeks, Thelma had chosen to
stay in the same Best Western hotel from where Tina was last
reported missing. "Looking around the lobby and the parking lot,
I feel closer to her," she said. "That's where I get my strength to
go to court."

Inside the courthouse, Tina's family was joined by reporters,
journalism students, and a crowd of public spectators. The number was too great to fit in the allocated trial room, so proceedings

were moved to the majestic surroundings of the marble-clad court-room in the Old Law Courts Building.

It was in this same impressive room that jury selection had taken place the week before. Potential jurors were asked to stand in front of the judge, while Crown and defence counsels were permitted to object to up to fourteen people each, without having to give a reason for their decision. In preparation, the defence team had googled every name in the jury pool, hoping to find out occupations, political views, and whether members had had any dealings with the legal system before. The team put together a spreadsheet that ranked names according to the qualities they preferred. At the top were people with analytical professions, who they felt would be curious and independent-minded. At the bottom were those from the compassionate sectors—teachers, healthcare workers, and anyone who worked for the government—who might be more predisposed to take the side of the Crown.

Cormier had also been present for the selection. He had shaved his head and wore a black and grey sweatshirt that Andrew Synyshyn had picked out especially for the trial. Cormier had wanted to wear all black, but Synyshyn persuaded him that grey was less intimidating. As each potential juror was called, the defence counsel checked for Cormier's reaction. In the final selection, the twelve people chosen were ethnically diverse and predominantly female: eight women and four men.

The same freezing morning on which Cormier's trial opened in Winnipeg, another jury selection was taking place across the Canadian Prairies. Gerald Stanley was a fifty-six-year-old farmer accused of the second-degree murder of an Indigenous youth named Colten Boushie. Boushie was a twenty-two-year-old Cree man who, in the summer of 2016, had been shot in the head by Stanley as he sat in an SUV parked on Stanley's Saskatchewan farm. It had been a warm day, and Boushie and four friends had been out swimming and drinking. They were driving home to the Red Pheasant First Nation reserve when one of their tires had blown out and they had driven onto Stanley's property looking for help. While there, two of them had got out of the car and attempted to break into a truck. One of them sat on an all-terrain vehicle parked in the yard and tried to start it up. According to Stanley and his son, who was with him, they believed the young people were there to rob them, prompting Stanley to go inside and grab his semi-automatic pistol. He told police that he fired two warning shots and ran to the SUV to turn off its engine. Somehow the gun discharged, shooting Boushie at point-blank range. The young man died instantly.

In the aftermath of the killing, the already strained relations between Saskatchewan's Indigenous community and its predominantly white farmers flared up. On one side, Indigenous leaders accused the RCMP of issuing a statement that focused more on the fact that Boushie's friends had been accused of theft than it did on the young man's killing, making the shooting look as though it was somehow justified. They accused the police of failing to conduct a proper forensic investigation and of insensitive treatment of Boushie's family. On the other side, the local white community rallied around Stanley, raising money for his defence. "His only mistake was leaving three witnesses," wrote one rural councillor on a Facebook group page. The councillor later resigned over his comments.

That morning, the jury selection in Battleford, Saskatchewan, concluded in just over two hours. The defence counsel used its power of veto to make sure that, out of the five men and seven women chosen, not one was Indigenous. A spokesperson for

Colten Boushie's family said it felt as if the trial had already been decided. Although there were no protests that day in the sub-zero temperatures, the hashtag #JusticeforColten began to trend on social media.

The coincidence of both trials being conducted at the same time had the effect of making it seem that Canada itself, and in particular its Prairie provinces, was in the dock for its treatment of Indigenous peoples. In Winnipeg, the chief justice of the Court of Queen's Bench, Glenn Joyal, told the jury members that their job was to hear the evidence dispassionately and decide on the facts of the case. He asked them to use their common sense and life experience and to listen with an open mind without being influenced by public opinion. It was not Mr. Cormier's responsibility to prove his innocence, he said. Instead, it was the jury's task to decide if the Crown had proven Cormier's guilt beyond a reasonable doubt.

After the chief justice had finished speaking, Jim Ross stood up to make the Crown's opening address.

"Tina Fontaine was a fifteen-year-old girl who made a series of poor choices," he began. He explained how Tina had left the safety of her home in Sagkeeng for the Winnipeg streets without fully appreciating the danger she was in. Tina had used drugs and alcohol and worked in the sex trade, Ross continued, but that was not what had killed her.

"The Crown's theory is that what led to Tina Fontaine's death was her friendship with Raymond Cormier," he said. He outlined the witnesses he planned to call and explained that this was not a case that could be proven or disproven by forensic evidence. If the jury was hoping for the certainty of television shows like *CSI*, they would be disappointed. The evidence against Cormier was indirect, but it would point towards him as the killer if they considered all the circumstances.

As its first witness, the Crown called Thelma Favel. Her voice loaded with emotion, Thelma described how Tina had been a sparkling, happy, and polite girl who had always tried to lift everyone's spirits. When Ross asked about Tina's final visit to her biological mother in June 2014, Thelma's voice began to crack. As the court heard Tina's 911 call to report that "Sebastian" had stolen a truck, Thelma's sobs echoed through the courtroom.

"That was Tina," she said, confirming the identity of the speaker.

In their preparation for the trial, Ross and Passler had considered a number of different strategies. One option was to go straight to the duvet cover and Project Styx intercepts and wrap up their argument quickly, hoping the jury would be convinced. But the prosecutors believed they needed to explain the lack of forensic evidence. They knew this ran the risk of overwhelming the jury with days of dry and often academic testimony, all of which essentially led nowhere. But they wanted to emphasize that everything that could be done to solve Tina's case had been done.

After Thelma's emotional opening testimony, the jury heard a list of expert witnesses testify about how Tina's body had been found and recovered, how medical, DNA, and forensic tests had been conducted, and how the results had been analyzed. When it was their turn to cross-examine, the defence team of Kavanagh and Synyshyn tried to inject doubt wherever possible.

When the captain of MS *River Rouge* described how his boat engines had churned up the riverbed when he had moored at the Alexander Docks—an action that had likely freed Tina's body from the mud underneath—the defence asserted that no one knew for certain exactly where Tina had been put in the water. When forensic expert Constable Susan Roy-Hageman described how she made cuts in the duvet cover to drain out the water, then tested it and other pertinent materials, the defence team asked her if any of the results had pointed to Cormier. Roy-Hageman replied that she had not found anything to suggest Cormier or any other individual had been the perpetrator.

When the toxicology expert told the court that drugs and alcohol had been found in Tina's blood but not at a fatal level, the defence argued that it was possible the prescription drug gabapentin might have also been there but didn't show up on tests. It was a possibility they raised again with forensic pathologist Dr. Dennis Rhee, who described the cause of Tina's death as "undetermined." When Rhee stated that Tina had likely died from being smothered or drowned, Kavanagh suggested it might have been possible for Tina to have self-smothered by rolling over onto a blanket.

After the opening day, the trial was moved back to the smaller, more intimate space of the original courtroom. The numbers watching had dwindled until just Tina's family, reporters, and a handful of public spectators were left. Thelma attended on most days, sitting in the same seat on the front bench with her children and a foster daughter who had known Tina growing up. Tina's biological mother, Valentina Duck, was also present, choosing to sit away from Thelma at the back of the public seating. Despite the smaller audience in court, interest in the case remained high. When a number of newspapers headlined the fact that Tina had been found with drugs and alcohol in her system, social media flooded with outrage. The papers were accused of victim blaming and not holding the real perpetrator to account. Summing up the anger, the Assembly of Manitoba Chiefs called out one newspaper for a "sensationalistic headline" that gave the impression that Tina "had it coming."

On the fourth day of the trial, Ida and Chantelle Beardy were scheduled to testify that the Chloe Green duvet cover that Tina had been wrapped in belonged to Cormier. The Crown were hoping this would be a compelling day of evidence, but the Beardys proved challenging witnesses. At first, they failed to turn up, forcing the Crown to notify O'Donovan, who in turn dispatched a team of detectives to find them. Jim Ross suggested that Chief Justice Joyal switch the order of witnesses, as he had spoken to Ida Beardy on the phone and thought she sounded intoxicated. But after Joyal agreed to a brief pause, Ross was able to tell the court that detectives had located both women and they were on their way in.

Ida Beardy was the first to take the stand. When Crown attorney Breta Passler asked her to identify the man who had stayed in her garden, she pointed across to Cormier and said, "That sick bastard over there." Ida recalled how, when she was shown the photo of the duvet cover and recognized it as belonging to her former lodger, it "sent shivers up my spine and still does."

Under cross-examination by Tony Kavanagh, Ida Beardy's conviction turned to irritability as she was asked the same questions repeatedly. When she referred to Cormier as a "sick bastard" for a second time, Chief Justice Joyal intervened, telling her she needed to be polite and patient. For his part, Kavanagh seemed to be enjoying himself, pointing out how much Ida disliked Cormier and throwing doubt on her memory. Ida raised her voice and seemed rattled but stood firm on her identification, insisting she was not confused at all.

When it was Chantelle's turn, she recalled how Cormier used to hang his bedding on the fence and that she remembered a dirty white bedcover with a pattern of leaves. She described it as having burn holes, a detail she had not mentioned in any previous interview. During his cross-examination, Synyshyn picked up on this immediately. Chantelle repeated that she remembered two thumb-sized burn holes on the front of the fabric, as if Cormier had fallen asleep holding a lit cigarette. Although she insisted that her recollection was accurate, she also admitted that her memory often suffered because she smoked weed "all the time."

The Beardys' testimony was reinforced by Detective Sergeants Jeff Stalker and Myles Riddell, who walked the jury through the process of showing the women the photo of the Chloe Green duvet cover. Stalker described the emphatic response of both mother and daughter and how he had been taken aback by the strength of their conviction. But in a long and detailed cross-examination, Kavanagh threw doubt on Stalker's methods, pointing out that he had failed to follow the police procedure of showing a full lineup and that this meant the identification had not been neutral. In his defence, Stalker replied that no one in his office had done anything like this before and that he had been dealing with a piece of property, not a person. Kavanagh pointed out that because Stalker had already visited the Beardys in connection with Tina's murder, his mere presence might have prompted them to connect the duvet cover with Cormier.

Chantelle's description of the burn holes raised an exciting possibility for the Crown. If they actually existed, they could prove to be the smoking gun the prosecution lacked. As the trial adjourned for the weekend, Ross returned to the disclosure to study the duvet cover photos. Early on Saturday morning, he emailed Kavanagh at home.

"Gentlemen, you may wish to take another look at the forensic photographs of the duvet as we intend to have them submitted as evidence on Monday," he wrote.

Kavanagh immediately forwarded the email to Synyshyn, who downloaded every photograph he could of the cover onto his home computer. After an hour of scanning the images, he noticed two small indents that looked exactly like the burn holes Chantelle had described. But on closer inspection, he wasn't sure. Chantelle had said the holes were on the front of the cover, but these were on the back, and they appeared more like frayed cuts. Synyshyn sent the images back to Kavanagh, who also studied them carefully, knowing that what he was looking at could lose him the case. Early on Monday morning, he met Ross to discuss what he had found. Kavanagh pointed out that the brown discolouration at the side of the holes was perhaps not from a burn but from river mud and that the edges looked clean, as if made by a knife. Studying the pictures himself, Ross agreed that what they were looking at were the two cuts made in the fabric by Constable Roy-Hageman when she drained the water out of it. Chantelle's recollection had been wrong.

In the trial's second week, the Crown walked the jury through Tina's final days. They called family and friends who had seen the teenager in Winnipeg in the weeks before she died. In often emotional testimony, Tina's uncles and aunts remembered how she had dropped by if she needed something, sometimes just to say hello. The prosecutors made a point of asking if they had given Tina food or noticed if she changed her outfits often. They replied yes, that Tina had been loved and looked after whenever she had wanted to be.

More witnesses were called to describe the last days Tina was seen alive. The jury heard how she was found asleep in the University of Winnipeg car park on the morning of Friday, August 8, and taken to hospital in an ambulance. Thelma sobbed loudly as the court heard that Tina was tested for drugs and alcohol before being released into the care of a CFS worker and taken to the Best Western Charterhouse hotel, where no one had prevented her from walking out into the night alone.

The jury also heard how, earlier that Friday morning, Tina had been briefly apprehended by Winnipeg patrol officers while in a truck with an older man, and how the officers had let her go. The driver, Richard Mohammed, had tried to keep his name out of court, but Chief Justice Joyal dismissed his request. He ruled that the public stakes were too high, as Tina's killing had become the focus of a national debate on how the justice system dealt with cases of missing and murdered Indigenous women. Mohammed testified that he had asked Tina if she wanted to party and she had got into his car, but they had not gone far before being stopped. The officers, former Constables Brock Jansen and Craig Houle, both recalled how Mohammed had become abusive and said that this had distracted them from studying Tina's details properly.

"Hindsight being twenty-twenty . . ." Jansen replied when asked why he had not reacted to the missing persons alert that had been placed on Tina's name. After failing to protect the teenager he had been dismissed from active service, but continued working for the police in a civilian role. Houle had been allowed to retake his field training but later was found to have stolen from police lockers and left the force. He said he had been traumatized by what had happened with Tina.

As the witness statements progressed, Cormier was conducting intense, whispered conversations with his counsel over the side of the prisoner's box, telling them he was desperate to take the stand himself to say that he had not killed Tina. Both Kavanagh and Synyshyn worked hard to dissuade him.

"I would be failing miserably as a lawyer if I put you on the stand," Tony Kavanagh told his client. Cormier's criminal record and tendency to lose his temper would not come off well, he explained. Instead, he reminded Cormier that the jury would have the chance to hear him deny killing Tina in the video the police had made of his first arrest interview in October 2014. This was the interview in which Cormier had lain on the floor in the fetal position, refusing to answer questions, and then stripped naked. As the video was played to the court, Cormier sat with his head bowed and his face devoid of expression. Chief Justice Joyal reminded the jury that Cormier did have the right to stay silent during the police interview and told them not to view his refusal to speak as an admission of guilt.

The day after the tape was played, a small group of Indigenous activists gathered outside the Winnipeg courthouse, writing the words "Justice for Tina" in the snow. They were there in part because across the Prairies, in Battleford, Saskatchewan, the jury was already deliberating in the trial of the man accused of killing Colten Boushie. That Friday afternoon, the Saskatchewan jury announced that it found Gerald Stanley not guilty of second-degree murder. The verdict was met with disbelief and anger across the country, with Boushie's supporters saying they felt Canada's reputation for fairness and tolerance had been undermined. Thousands gathered in rallies to denounce the decision. "Little about the Stanley investigation and murder is exceptional," read a joint statement by the Native Studies faculties at three Canadian universities. "It needs to instead be understood as yet another link in the centuries-long colonial chain of injustices that Indigenous peoples—and, in this instance, prairie Indigenous peoples—are well aware of." Now all eyes were focused on the Tina Fontaine trial in the hope that it would deliver a different outcome.

Meanwhile, in Winnipeg, the jury number was reduced to eleven after one member was forced to leave because of a personal emergency. For its final week of evidence, the Crown called on those who had spent time with Tina at 22 Carmen Avenue. Sarah Holland was the first to testify. Since Tina's death, she had kicked her addiction and seemed to be putting her life back together. On the stand, she insisted that the accused had had a predatory sexual interest in Tina. Listening from across the courtroom, Cormier shook his head. When she got up to leave, Holland was careful not to meet his gaze.

Tyrell Morrison gave a straightforward account of what he could remember about the activities at the house. The defence had been planning to suggest he could be a suspect himself, but Kavanagh judged his testimony less hostile than they were expecting so had left him alone. When Ernest DeWolfe recalled how Cormier told him he had slept with Tina, Thelma, who was sitting in the front row of the public gallery, burst into tears and quickly left the room. In his cross-examination, Andrew Synyshyn reminded DeWolfe that he had told police he was not "a hundred percent sure" that Cormier owned the Chloe Green duvet cover. DeWolfe replied by flourishing a tissue and saying that he wasn't "a hundred percent sure" it was the same as the next tissue in the box, but it looked pretty much the same. When Synyshyn questioned his motives in coming forward, pointing out that he had an extensive criminal record, DeWolfe insisted he had acted because "it's a little girl dead here."

Finally, at the very end of its case, the Crown presented the recordings from Project Styx. Although the Mr. Big operation had spanned six months, Ross had allocated it just one day in court, saying there was no point in giving it more time because it had not produced a confession.

Mo was the first officer to be called. Despite still working undercover, he testified openly. As he walked into the courtroom Cormier eyed him with hostility, his arms crossed defensively against his chest. Mo explained how his friendship with his target had been set up and how he had played out a number of scenarios designed to manipulate him. The Crown played a recording of the conversation in which Cormier threatened to cycle home to New Brunswick and ranted about Tina.

With his evidence given, Mo privately mused that part of him felt bad about tricking Cormier, who had viewed him as a true friend. "But it's my job, and these aren't good people," he said.

Jenna was the next witness to testify. The jury listened to the recording of Cormier trying to calm her down as she banged on Mo's door, pretending to be distressed. Ross had chosen it because he wanted to show how charming and seductive Cormier could be.

"He was right close to my face, in my personal space," Jenna told the court.

Finally, the Crown called the police officer whom O'Donovan had asked to transcribe the often scratchy-sounding intercepts. After the officer described how he had used high-quality headphones and listened over and over until he was sure of what he was hearing, the Crown played a selection of Cormier's recorded conversations. The jury were handed the transcripts to follow as they listened, though were cautioned to remember that the recordings themselves were the evidence and the transcripts were merely the police's understanding of them.

"*When I found out, that was it. Said I'm not gonna bang her no more,*" Cormier was heard saying in one.

"*Don't overdose here 'cause then your body's going be wrapped up in a fucking carpet and thrown in the river,*" said another.

"*It's right on the shore. So what do I do? Threw her in.*"

"Tina finds a knife . . . She got angry and . . . get the fuck away from me."

"By sunset she died. That's why I don't joke."

"Unfortunately, there's a little girl in a fucking grave someplace screaming at the top of her lungs for me to fucking finish the job. And guess what? . . . I finished the job."

"You think you'll get the murder out of me?"

When the final recording had played, Ross asked the police officer to confirm that all the clips were original. In cross-examination, Synyshyn questioned the officer's work, asking him whether he was sure that everything he had written was accurate. The officer replied that he was, and if he had not understood something, he had not included it in the transcript. When Synyshyn said he had no further questions, Ross stated that the Crown had concluded its case.

The next day, Cormier's defence counsel entered a motion for a directed verdict, asking the judge to instruct the jury to acquit Cormier. Synyshyn argued that the Crown's case was based on "inference over inference over speculation," and that even the forensic pathologist's opinion on how Tina had died was based on a suspicion rather than fact. But Joyal disagreed, saying there had been other successful convictions where no body had been found and that circumstantial cases often drew on inferences. He dismissed the motion. When he did, Cormier appeared extremely agitated, shouting out that he wanted to speak to his lawyers. Kavanagh and Synyshyn crowded around him, trying to calm him down. They had already voiced their decision not to call any witnesses of their own.

———

For the final day of the trial, the courtroom's public gallery was once again packed. Not only was Thelma present with her family and friends, but Valentina Duck had also returned to take her seat at the back. When everyone was present, Jim Ross stood up to give the Crown's closing argument to the jury.

"This is a real whodunit," he said.

The Crown believed that Tina had either been smothered or drowned and that Cormier's own words had identified him as the killer. Ross argued that the intercept in which Cormier had spoken about being right on the shore and throwing a woman in was enough on its own to convict him. Cormier had a clear motive for killing the fifteen-year-old, who had threatened to go to the police over the stolen truck. With the truck, he also had the means to transport her body to the river.

Ross continued by summarizing the circumstantial evidence. As he repeated Ernest DeWolfe's testimony about Cormier's sexual interest in Tina, Valentina Duck shouted out "Sick bastard!" from the public gallery. Chief Justice Joyal reacted sternly, calling for a break and warning Duck that she would have to leave if she couldn't control herself.

"William Shakespeare said in his play *Macbeth*, 'Murder will out,'" said Ross, wrapping up his long and detailed address. "Mr. Cormier, obsessed with and haunted by what he did, and not knowing a recording device was in his apartment—he has revealed himself to you. Believe what he says, and convict him for what he did."

When it was his turn to speak, Tony Kavanagh picked up on Ross's literary reference. The defence lawyer had noticed during the trial that several jury members liked to read in the lunch break, which had given him the idea to describe his closing argument in terms of a book.

"We don't convict on a mystery or a whodunit," he said. "This is not an Agatha Christie mystery." He reminded the jury members that they needed to be convinced of Cormier's guilt beyond a reasonable doubt.

Kavanagh argued that the intercepts from Styx were not as damning as they first appeared. Cormier spoke fast and tended to mix up the tenses and meanings of his words. When Cormier said he was not going to "bang her no more," Kavanagh argued, what he really meant was that he had changed his mind about wanting to sleep with Tina after finding out her real age. When Cormier said he had "finished the job," he was actually talking about finishing the job of trying to find her killer.

"It is undisputed that Tina Fontaine had a tragic life," Kavanagh concluded. "It is not justice for Tina Fontaine to convict the wrong man."

After each side had summed up its case, Chief Justice Joyal spent four hours instructing the jury members on how to apply the rule of law before they began their deliberations. They were told that they needed to answer two questions in order: Was Tina Fontaine's death caused by an unlawful act, and if so, did Raymond Cormier commit it?

While they waited for a verdict, the Crown and defence teams had dinner together, something that may have surprised the courtroom onlookers.

"Trials are conducted in the wrong way if they are personal and the lawyers aren't speaking to each other," said Ross, after spending the evening with his opponents discussing the minutiae of the proceedings and speculating about the jury's decision.

The lawyers did not have to wait long for an answer. The following afternoon, shortly after lunch, the court clerk sent out a text message announcing that a verdict had been reached. It would be given in the same imposing surroundings of the green and grey marble courtroom where the trial had opened three weeks earlier. As news filtered through the press corps and to Tina's family and supporters, seats started to fill up. An informal, self-imposed order separated those present: Tina's family and Indigenous dignitaries, each wearing their hand-beaded medallions of office, sat on one side of the room; journalists and reporters settled into the other. At the back, beside a marble column, Detective Sergeants Wade McDonald and Scott Taylor tried to look inconspicuous in their grey work suits. In the front row, Thelma cried as, one by one, friends and well-wishers walked up to greet her. She appeared exhausted and nervous, clutching the hand of her foster daughter as she waited.

After half an hour of waiting, Cormier was led into the court-room. His legs and arms were in shackles, his face grey and haunted-looking in the pale glow that filtered in through the courtroom skylights.

The court was ordered to stand for the arrival of Chief Justice Joyal and then the jury. As the jury forewoman informed the judge that they had reached a verdict, several jury members bowed their heads, clearly in tears. Joyal was handed a folded piece of paper on which they had written their decision. As he read the words, an almost imperceptible shadow of concern flitted across his face.

"How do you find the defendant?" Joyal asked the jury fore-woman.

"Not guilty," she replied.

Her voice was low and thick with emotion, so it took a second before the room registered what she had said. Suddenly there were loud gasps, and then the wrenching sound of Thelma's sobbing. Joyal gave instructions for Cormier to be discharged. As he was led out, a shout was heard from the back of the room.

"Fuck you! You think you can get away with it!" yelled Valentina Duck, storming past the public gallery and heading for the door.

In the front row, Thelma was calling out "My baby!" over and over.

"I hope you rot in hell," she cried, before crumpling with grief as friends formed a tight, protective circle around her. Someone began to recite the Lord's Prayer.

For a moment, both the Crown and defence teams appeared stunned. Jim Ross and Breta Passler quickly left the room. Tony Kavanagh stared at his feet and Andrew Synyshyn grabbed the side of a marble desk as if he were about to keel over.

Slowly, Tina's family and the Indigenous leaders moved out into the corridor. For a while the group stood in silence, still absorbing the verdict, under the portraits of white men who had founded the city's legal system. In whispered conversations, they discussed what to do next. Then someone brought a wheelchair to take Thelma back to her hotel, and the chiefs signalled that they would make a public statement outside on the steps of the court.

In the fading light of the winter afternoon, Keewatinowi Okimakanak Grand Chief Sheila North eloquently summed up how her community felt.

"This is not the outcome anyone wanted," she said solemnly. "The systems—everything that was involved in Tina's life—have failed her. We've all failed her." If Raymond Cormier had not killed Tina, she continued, then someone else had taken her life, and the city needed to find out who was responsible. "This is not the Canada I want to be part of," she concluded.

Sergeant John O'Donovan had made the decision not to be present in the courtroom. In all his years as a homicide detective, he had attended only one verdict, and even though it had gone his way, he didn't think he could stomach the nervous anticipation again. Earlier that afternoon, when he heard that a verdict was imminent, he had left work to be at home with his wife. It was Detective Sergeant Taylor who broke the news, texting the words "not guilty" to O'Donovan's phone.

"I called out to my wife, who put her arms around me and said she couldn't believe it," he later said, describing the emotional moment when he realized his work had been in vain. "I told her I could."

When the Colten Boushie not guilty verdict had been delivered two weeks earlier, it had prompted mass protest rallies across the country. But that evening, after Cormier was acquitted and set free, Winnipeg remained quiet. In their speeches outside the courtroom, the Indigenous leaders had called for calm and understanding. They spoke out about the Third World conditions they endured and the disproportionate number of Indigenous children in care. But they also stressed how much they wanted to honour Tina and her family by focusing on healing and justice.

The next morning, the freezing weather that had held the city in a stranglehold since the beginning of the trial broke to reveal a sunny, clear blue sky. Hundreds of mostly Indigenous Winnipeggers gathered outside the courthouse to begin marching in honour of Tina's memory. To shouts of "We want justice!" their orderly procession weaved its way through the city, under the rail tracks and past the Canadian Museum for Human Rights. For an hour they walked, carrying placards with slogans of support. "Lady Justice is murdered and missing," read one. "Love for Tina," read another. Finally they came to a stop at the Forks, at the sacred site of the Oodena Celebration Circle at the confluence of the Red and Assiniboine Rivers. Here, the marchers observed a minute of silence. There was anger at the child welfare system, at the police who had failed to identify Tina as a missing person, and at all the professionals who had let Tina down and were continuing to let down so many other Indigenous women and girls.

But there was also a sense of celebration and love.

"My heart is just overflowing with love and gratitude for each and every one of you," said Thelma, who was greeted with rapturous applause when she stood to speak.

For a while, the group lingered in the bright sunshine, listening to speeches, praying and sharing their grief. Whereas the focus of the past few weeks had been the trial, it now shifted to the future. Many spoke of Tina's legacy as a turning point. They acknowledged the changes that would need to come—from the country as a whole, as well as from within their own community. They looked forward to a time when their daughters could live free from the shadow of violence.

A few feet away, the polished granite of the monument to missing and murdered Indigenous women reflected the white of the snow. To the north, almost within sight, ice engulfed the spot where Tina's body had been found. Between the two points, the wide, frozen snake of the Red River curved through the city's landscape, a timeless witness to all that had gone before and all that would ever come.

EPILOGUE

On the evening that Raymond Cormier received his not guilty verdict, the Winnipeg Police Service released a statement saying that they understood that it was a difficult time for Tina's family and all those affected by her loss, and that they would be examining the court proceedings to determine whether an appeal was possible. In reality, the decision whether or not to pursue an appeal lay with the Manitoba Prosecution Service. Three weeks later, it released a statement saying that, after a critical review, it had determined that "there are no grounds to base a successful appeal."

The Crown counsel, James Ross, says he was satisfied that the trial was fair and that the jury "did what we asked them to do." Cormier's trial was the last major court appearance for Ross, who retired shortly thereafter.

Following the verdict, Raymond Cormier travelled east to be reunited with his sister Gabrielle, with whom he had not been in contact for twenty years. The two spent several months together until they fell out and Cormier returned to his childhood home of New Brunswick. In 2019, he gave a television interview in which he admitted to giving Tina weed, but not hard drugs, and once again insisted on his innocence. Cormier says he has made a promise to Tina to find out who killed her, and is hoping to bring a case against the Winnipeg Police Service and the Manitoba Prosecution Service for wrongful imprisonment and malicious prosecution.

Among the Winnipeg Police Service, the reaction to the not guilty verdict was one of sadness, frustration, deflation, and anger. The Homicide Unit firmly believed Cormier was guilty, and that they did everything they possibly could to bring him to justice. The case has had a profound effect on those involved, especially the undercover officers who spent months building relationships with Cormier. A year after Project Styx concluded, Jenna gave birth to a baby girl whom she named after her undercover character, saying "To me, this project was that important."

Tina's case was one of the last for Sergeant John O'Donovan, who left the Homicide Unit a month after the verdict. (He was replaced by Detective Sergeant Wade McDonald.) At the end of 2018, O'Donovan retired from the Winnipeg Police after nearly twenty-five years of service. He is now working for Manitoba Justice as a team commander of one of their investigative units. In his spare time he is writing a memoir of his years as a homicide detective, a process he describes as "great therapy."

While deeply disappointed in the outcome of the trial, O'Donovan understands why the prosecutors did not present all the evidence he collected. In 2018, together with the now Police Chief, Danny Smyth, he travelled to Sagkeeng to brief the band council and community on the investigation. The men took the opportunity to visit Tina's grave and O'Donovan noted she was buried next to her cousin, Jeneanne Fontaine, whose killing he had also investigated. "I was blown away," he says of the emotions he felt standing there. "I spoke to both girls, but especially to Tina. I told her 'I did the best I could.'" He says the police are not looking for anyone else for Tina's killing. Of Cormier, he says, "He has to live with his demons."

Tina's killing has had a significant impact on the policy and practice surrounding Canada's treatment of its Indigenous peoples. Her case was instrumental in the establishment of a National Inquiry into Missing and Murdered Indigenous Women and Girls which, in June 2019, found that the country was complicit in a "race-based genocide" against Indigenous women. Blaming the crisis on deep-rooted colonialism and state inaction, the inquiry put forward more than two hundred "calls for justice" to the police, government, and Canadian public as a whole. It urged immediate action, saying those who had opened up and told their story feared the report would "gather dust on a shelf" and that the recommendations would be left unanswered.

A few months earlier, a long-awaited report by the Manitoba Child Advocate found that Tina was repeatedly failed by the systems meant to protect her, including Child and Family Services. The report listed five recommendations: improving victim-support services for children; developing safe, secure, home-like treatment facilities where children and youth could be placed involuntarily if needed; improving the care of sexually exploited children and youth; improving mental health support; and conducting a review on how school absenteeism is dealt with. Following Tina's death, the Manitoba government began the process of shifting control of child welfare services to Indigenous bodies, in an effort to reduce the number of Indigenous children in care. In 2019, it announced proposed changes in the way Child and Family Services is funded to move away from the practice of paying per child towards block funding. It is hoped the move will encourage a stronger focus on prevention and early intervention.

On the streets of Winnipeg, grassroots organizations are already working to make a difference following Tina's death. There have been several initiatives to protect Indigenous youth in the North End, including the community-based patrol, the Bear Clan. Its executive director, James Favel, says that volunteers walk the streets each evening to prevent women and children from becoming sexually exploited and to restore a sense of safety to the community.

For Tina's family, the pain of losing the teenager persists. Tina's biological mother, Valentina Duck, says that her daughter's death continues to hurt, telling journalists that she wished Tina was "still with me, right here." Coming to terms with Tina's fate has been a particular struggle for her younger sister Sarah, who was thirteen when Tina died. In the following years, Sarah gave birth to a daughter whom she named Victoria Tina after her sister.

Thelma says that the family hopes to press charges against Raymond Cormier for supplying Tina with drugs. She wants his name placed on a child abuse registry to protect "all other children from him." Thelma and other family members have been involved in fundraising to turn the Ndinawe shelter, where Tina spent a few nights before disappearing, into a round-the-clock safe space for youth in Winnipeg. "It was Tina's dream to work with children, and that's why we decided a safe haven would be good in her honour," Thelma said at the opening ceremony of the Tina Safe Haven in November 2018.

Thelma says that her family has been deeply moved by the love and support they have received since Tina's death. In 2018 Tina's school unveiled a mural of the teenager painted on a wall close to where the school's graduation pictures are displayed. For

Thelma it was a bittersweet experience to see the painting, knowing that Tina's picture would never be among the graduation photographs. She says she feels that part of the family will always be missing, but that she hopes to do as much as she can to help other children in need.

"I don't want to hear any more stories about kids being found murdered like that anymore," she says. "I want all kids to be safe."

ACKNOWLEDGMENTS

RED RIVER GIRL OWES A DEBT OF GRATITUDE TO MANY who opened their lives, work and emotions to me. In Sagkeeng, I am thankful for the warm welcome and cooperation of Thelma and Joe Favel, their family and foster children. I'm also grateful for the knowledge shared by Liliane Cook, Marilyn Courchene and Cindy Guimond and residents of the reserve. In Winnipeg, Nahanni Fontaine and Bernadette Smith helped guide me through the issue of violence against Indigenous women with passion and eloquence. James Favel and the Bear Clan showed me the strength and compassion within the North End community. Samantha Lynn Chief, Jennifer Roulette and Candace Neal inspired me with their resilience and forgiveness.

John O'Donovan was my main source for police information and I'm hugely grateful for his patience, openness and sense of humour. When I arrived into a freezing winter, his wife, Mary, made sure I had thick enough gloves and was always a kindly presence. I would like to thank the entire O'Donovan family for allowing me to dominate so much of John's time over the past few years. I'm also grateful to a number of Winnipeg Police Service officers, especially Mo, Candace and Jenna who provided a fascinating insight into the world of undercover policing. Danny Smyth, Wade McDonald, Esther Schmieder, Tracy Oliver, Kevin Pawl provided vital details, as did forensic pathologist, Dr Dennis Rhee.

I'm grateful to Jim Ross, Tony Kavanagh, Andrew Synyshyn and his colleagues for taking the time to explain the complexities of the legal case against Raymond Cormier. At the University of Guelph, Kate Puddister was an invaluable expert on Mr Big operations. From the University of Manitoba, Lorna Turnbull and Marnie Brownell provided useful background on child welfare in the province.

As a stranger to Winnipeg, I relied on the generosity of local journalists, in particular Gordon Sinclair, Nancy Macdonald, Brittany Greenslade, Katie Nicholson and Jillian Taylor. I want to say a special thank you to the CBC's Caroline Barghout for her friendship and impressive investigative skills. Matthew Komus, Christopher Trott and Sandy Riley helped fill in my historical knowledge and Martha Troian provided research. Finally, I couldn't imagine spending so much time in Winnipeg without the love, hospitality and home-cooking of my old friends, Sylvie Houghton and Mark Carriere.

Writing this book has brought new Canadian friends. I'm grateful to Stephen Maher for his early support and introduction to Penguin and to Shannon Masters for sharing her experiences as an Indigenous writer—and for an awesome road trip across the prairies.

Red River Girl began life as a BBC story. I'm grateful to Micah

Laidlow for her comment which became the spark that set the process in motion. I'm deeply indebted to David Botti and Lynsea Garrison whose brilliant, creative talents made Red River Women both an online and radio success, Paul Kerley for production, and my editors—Ben Bevington, Stephen Mulvey and Bridget Harney— for having the foresight to commission the story. At the BBC, Keith Blackmore was an encouraging mentor. I'm grateful to Michael Dwyer from Hurst Publishers for setting me on the road to writing. The Shorenstein Center at the Harvard Kennedy School provided a welcome respite from daily news and the chance to conceive of a longer project. I thank Tom Hundley and the Pulitzer Center for their financial support and the Royal Society of Literature Giles St Aubyn Award for Non-Fiction for their commendation.

At Penguin Canada, I would like to thank Diane Turbide for her wisdom and patience in guiding me through the process of writing. I'm extremely grateful to Alex Schultz for providing an intelligent and thoughtful copy edit. Here in the UK, Sarah Savitt at Virago gave much needed insight and encouragement. I feel extremely lucky to have the support of my brilliant and positive agent, Toby Mundy.

Writing is hard and I feel blessed to have many writer friends— Lisa Woollett, Jill McGivering, Ann Tornkvist, Solitaire Townsend and Minka Nijhuis—to sympathize with when times were tough. Thanks to those who read early drafts, especially Vibeke Venema, Claire Lowman and Simon Ponsford. And to the friends who held my hand, spirited me away and reminded me to laugh; Jake Morland, Ali McConnell, Mark Sainsbury, Stefan Kyriazis, Tara McKelvey, Sarah Faber, Teresa Clifton and all the swimmers in our "Daphne du Maurier" squad lane.

Finally I want to say a huge thank you to my family who saw me through the long days of writing. To my mother, Marian, who read everything, including my roughest notes, and told me how good they were even when they weren't. To my father, Pran and his wife, Jenny, who kept me going. And to my wonderful sister, Anita, her partner, Ioan, and my nieces and nephew, Nel, Nona and Inigo—I couldn't have done it without you.

INDEX

Note: TF = Tina Fontaine

Aboriginal Justice Inquiry of
    Manitoba, 20–21, 24, 58
African Mafia, 77
#AmINext?, 163

Bailey, Doug, 137, 160, 163, 164,
    183, 184
Beardy, Chantelle, 115, 116–17,
    166, 167, 168, 259–60, 261
Beardy, Ida, 115–16, 118, 166,
    167–68, 169, 259
Beardy, Tracey, 114–15, 116
Bennett, Carolyn, 4–5
Best Western Charterhouse
    hotel, 94–95, 100, 102, 116,
    253, 262
#BlackLivesMatter, 27

Boushie, Colten, 254–55, 263, 271
Bowman, Brian, 172
Brad (undercover cop), 221–22,
    230, 231, 232
Brown, Michael, 2, 27
Bruyère, Fonessa, 60–61

Canadian Human Rights
    Commission, 123
Candace (undercover officer),
    179–80, 182, 191, 192, 193,
    194, 199, 221, 223, 230, 238
Capri Hotel, 90, 93
Child and Family Services,
    34–35, 37, 44, 45, 46, 47,
    60, 79, 90–91, 92–93, 94, 96,
    244, 262, 275

Chris (undercover cop), 205, 206, 216, 228, 229, 230

Chute, Kimberly, 93–94

Clunis, Devon, 99, 172

Cody. *See* Mason, Cody

Complete Care, 94

Cormier, Raymond (Sebastian, Frenchie)

    accused of confessing, 249–51

    acquittal, 269

    aftermath of trial, 274

    argument with TF, 125, 129, 135, 138, 144, 147, 148, 149, 152, 170

    arrest for TF murder, 234

    attraction to young women, 195, 203, 205, 218, 219, 247

    and Beardy family, 114–16

    behaviour as threat to Project Styx, 218

    belief about Project Styx, 244

    and bike for TF, 94, 95, 105

    and Candace, 192

    capture and arrest of, 127–28

    charged with murder of TF, 4, 235

    claim to know TF killer, 164

    conspiracy theory of, 244

    convicted of theft, 172–73

    and criminal gang ruse, 176, 205–6, 222–23, 228–34

    criminal record, 117–18

    demeanour during interview, 144, 145, 147, 150–51, 153

    denies killing Fontaine, 2

    describes other suspects, 149, 151, 183

    desire to take stand at trial, 262–63

    DeWolfe information about, 124–26

    DNA sample taken, 160

    and domestic violence scenario, 207–13

    drug use, 113, 116, 130, 132, 135, 143, 149, 187–88, 191, 195, 206, 207, 220, 226

    early life and background, 243

    feelings toward TF, 149–50, 151, 164

    friendship with Mo, 187, 188, 189–90, 191–93, 194–96, 200, 214, 215–16, 223–25, 231, 238

    and Holland, 132–35

    interest in religion, 188

    interest in young women, 204–5

    interview with author, 1–2

    interview with police, 141–50

    introduced into 22 Carmen, 131

    involvement in solving case, 183–84

    and Jenna, 198–99, 202–5, 220

    jury selection, 254

    lack of DNA match, 165

    last sighting of TF, 147

    and lawyers, 244–46

    learns about Project Styx, 237–38

    meets TF and Cody, 111–13

    misunderstanding about bike, 143–44

as Most Wanted, 122

as object of Mr. Big sting, 175–76, 177, 179, 180, 181, 182–83

ownership of duvet cover, 167

police questioning of, 234–35, 237–38

press conference about arrest of, 239–40

prison conditions, 242–43

recounts meeting DeWolfe, 146

recounts meeting with TF, 143

relationship with Danielle, 227

sent to Milner Ridge, 159–60

sexual interest in TF, 105, 125, 129, 148, 149–50, 151, 186, 200, 220

as source of drugs, 129

and Synyshyn, 245–46

talks about TF in bugged apartment, 185–87, 189, 206–7, 220, 224–25

theft charges, 146, 158

theft of bicycles, 187

theories about TF murder, 144–45

trial, 5, 253–54, 256–71

and truck, 103, 105, 120, 121, 125, 151, 152–53, 156, 159, 160, 165, 169, 225, 231, 232, 267

visits TF memorial, 183, 225, 231

volatility, anger, and paranoia, 133, 156, 188, 206, 218, 219, 220–21, 225–26, 239, 244

Cunningham, Alexander, 9, 10–11

Dahmer, Jeffrey, 100

Danielle (Cormier girlfriend), 199, 200, 206, 216, 218, 221, 222, 224, 225, 226, 227, 238

DeWolfe, Ernest (Ernie)
asked to be informant, 159

brings Cormier to 22 Carmen, 131

Cormier anger with, 214–15

friendship with Holland and Morrison, 131

identifies duvet cover, 169

questioning of, 128–30

talks with police about Cormier, 124–26

testimony at Cormier trial, 264, 267

and TF relationship, 109

TF's feelings about, 129, 134

DNA testing, 70–71, 150, 160, 165

Duck, Angie, 80–81

Duck, Valentina, 36, 43, 44, 46–47, 75, 81, 83, 258, 267, 270, 276

Dumas, Larry, 45, 81, 84, 87, 110

duvet cover, 14, 63, 66, 68, 69, 71–73, 87, 120, 132, 165–69, 171, 201, 213, 214, 247, 250, 251, 252, 257, 258, 259–61, 264

education systems, 34. *See also* residential schools

Favel, Brian, 45, 46

Favel, James, 275

Favel, Joseph, 35, 37, 38, 40, 41, 47

Favel, Samantha, 45, 46

Favel, Sarah, 276
Favel, Thelma
  anger over police missteps,
    99–100
  attendance at trial, 258
  background of, 34–36
  becomes TF's guardian, 37
  commemoration gathering for
    TF, 48
  cooperation with author, 6
  and Cormier trial, 253_
  death of Eugene, 39–40, 41
  desire to charge Cormier as
    drug supplier, 276
  fostering of children, 37
  informed of arrest, 239
  popularity of, 29–30
  queries police progress, 158
  reaction to arrest, 241
  reaction to verdict, 269, 270
  reports TF missing, 90
  searches for TF, 47
  TF's desire to see again, 82
  victim impact statement of,
    241–42
  as witness at trial, 257
Foley, James, 2
Fontaine, Doug, 34
Fontaine, Eugene, 15–16, 34,
    36–37, 39–40, 41
Fontaine, Jeanenne, 83
Fontaine, Lana, 82–83, 105
Fontaine, Nahanni, 18–19, 23–24,
    25, 61, 241
Fontaine, Phil, 33
Fontaine, Robyn, 83

Fontaine, Sarah, 36, 37, 39, 40, 45,
    46, 47
Fontaine, Tina
  activities with Cody, 110–13
  alcohol and drug use, 65, 82,
    92, 94, 96–97, 110–11, 112–13,
    137, 143
  ambitions, 39
  argument with Cormier, 129,
    135, 144, 147, 148, 149, 151, 152,
    170, 220
  arrest in murder of, 239–40
  autopsy and state of body,
    63–68
  at Beardy property, 113, 116
  becomes rebellious, 43–44
  Bennett on, 4–5
  birth of, 36
  cause of death, 5
  character and personality, 6,
    38, 41–42, 44, 47–48
  commemoration gathering,
    26–27
  confrontation over bike, 138,
    144
  Cormier denies killing, 2
  Cormier theories about
    murder, 144–45
  date of death, 121
  death of, 2–3
  death of father, 39–40
  description of last days, 261–62
  desire to meet biological
    mother, 43
  discovery of body, 11–12
  and Dumas, 84

education, 38, 42

effect of death on nation, 123, 275

effect of father's death on, 41, 42

elimination of suspects, 170–71

family background/conditions, 83–84

feelings about Cormier, 129, 134

funeral of, 48

gets tattoo, 42–43

Holland recognizes photo, 136

impromptu memorial to, 123

injuries to, 16

leads and tips, 86–87, 88, 91, 96, 101, 120, 124, 170

love of small children, 38–39

meets Cody, 109

meets Holland, 133

online postings, 44, 46, 47

paramedic and hospital treatment, 91–93

phone call to 911, 104–5, 121

physical description, 15

reported missing, 46, 47, 85, 90, 91, 95–96

resemblance to Danielle, 200, 224, 227

response to Cormier, 129–30

runs away from home, 43, 45

selling of drugs, 111

as sex worker, 96, 97, 98–99, 100–101

suspects in the death of, 119

Thelma becomes guardian, 37

use of false names, 97, 98, 133

visits with mother, 44–46

Francis, Cory, 131, 139

Freeman, Matt, 235, 237

Frenchie. *See* Cormier, Raymond (Sebastian, Frenchie)

gangs, in Winnipeg, 77

George (brother of T. Favel), 34

Guimond, Cindy, 40, 41–42

Hall, Faron, 8–9, 11, 12, 16, 26, 67, 190

Harper, J.J., 20, 58

Hart ruling, 176–77

Highway of Tears, 24–25

Holland, Sarah, 125, 126, 128–29, 130, 131–37, 138, 139, 145, 146, 147, 148, 169, 170, 214–15, 264

Houle, Craig, 98, 99, 172, 262

Ikeh, Ngozi, 94–95

Indian Posse, 77, 87

Indigenous people
assimilation attempts, 32–33

prostitution among, 78–80

protest over Cormier verdict, 271–72

relationship with Winnipeg Police, 57–58

and residential schools, 32–33

segregation experience, 32

support for, 26–27

support for TF, 263

treatment of, 256

treatment of in The Pas, 20–21

in Winnipeg, 57, 271

Indigenous women
  deaths in Manitoba, 21–23
  as victims of strangers, 24
  violence against, 3
Ingram, John, 56

Jansen, Brock, 98–99, 172, 262
Jarrett, Holly, 163
Jay (undercover cop), 196, 200,
    201, 205, 209, 211, 212, 213,
    215, 216, 217, 221–22, 223, 228,
    229, 230, 231–32, 235, 238
Jenna (undercover cop), 193, 194,
    196, 198–99, 200–204,
    207–11, 212, 213, 214, 215, 217,
    219–20, 222, 238, 265, 274
Joyal, Chief Justice Glenn, 256, 259,
    262, 263, 266, 267, 268, 269

Katrina, 96–97, 98, 100–101, 102
Kavanagh, Anthony, 246, 247–48,
    252, 257, 258, 259, 260, 261,
    262, 264, 266, 267–68, 270

Laurie (Thelma's daughter), 42, 44

Macdonald, Nancy, 171–72
Maclean's, 171–72
Mad Cow gang, 77
Manitoba Warriors, 77
Margaret, Princess, 10
Mason, Cody, 81, 82, 83, 84, 85, 90,
    102, 107–8, 109–14, 125, 137,
    143, 145, 165
McDonald, Wade, 126, 127–28,
    141–43, 145, 146–47, 148,
    149, 150, 152–56, 234–35,
    237, 269, 274
McMillan, Dale, 175, 176, 177–78
Mohammad (Mo; undercover
    officer)
  background, 178–79
  and criminal gang ruse, 180,
    181, 182, 221, 228, 229, 230,
    231, 232
  and domestic violence scenario,
    207–13
  friendship with Cormier, 187,
    188, 191, 194–96, 200, 214,
    215–16, 223–25, 231, 238
  introduces Jenna to Cormier,
    198–99
  and Jenna disappearance, 220
  meets Cormier, 184
  testifies at trial, 265
Mohammed, Richard, 98, 100, 102,
    248, 262
Morrison, Tyrell, 125, 126, 128, 129,
    131, 133, 134, 136, 137–39, 146,
    150, 151, 170, 264
Mr. Big stings, 175–77. *See also*
    Project Styx

Nanacowap, Joseph, 81–82, 110
National Inquiry into Missing and
    Murdered Indigenous
    Women and Girls, 236–37,
    244, 275
Native Women's Association of
    Canada, 23
Ndinawe group home/shelter, 85,
    86, 90, 110, 276

Nelson, Earle Leonard, 56
North, Sheila, 270
North End Blood, 77

O'Donovan, John. *See also* Project
    Styx
   aftermath of trial, 274
   anger with constables, 99
   applies to become police
    officer, 55
   attack on second young
    woman, 161–62
   begins investigation, 25, 27–28
   case-building strategy, 128
   concern for Fontaine family, 61
   cooperates with author, 4, 5
   and Cormier verdict, 270–72
   and DNA testing, 70–71
   duvet cover, 71–73, 87, 169
   early days of investigation, 14,
    15, 16
   early years, 50–51
   eliminates suspects, 84–85,
    170–71
   emigrates to Canada, 51–52
   Holland interview concerns, 139
   importance of stolen truck, 121
   informed of body discovery,
    12, 13
   instructions on Cormier arrest,
    127
   interest in Cormier, 119
   introduction of Jenna, 197–98
   Kavanagh's opinion on, 247–48
   leads and tips, 86–87, 88, 91,
    96, 101, 120, 124, 247

   moves to Winnipeg, 54
   opinion of Sebastian, 117
   and possible suspects, 101
   press conference about
    Cormier arrest, 239–40
   press conference about TF's
    death, 17–18, 19
   and Project Echidna, 173–74
   Project Styx progress, 226–27
   promotions, 58–59
   and questioning of Cormier,
    234–35, 237–38
   reaction to Cormier, 155–56
   researches Winnipeg, 52–53
   review of timeline, 102, 121
   reviews Cormier interview,
    150–51
   reviews Project Styx, 190–91
   and TF 911 phone call, 104–5
   and TF autopsy, 63, 66–67
   T. Flavel queries progress, 158
   timeline of TF's last days, 130
Oliver, Dwayne, 11, 164
Oliver, Tracy, 137, 138
Osborne, Claudette, 21–22, 26
Osborne, Felicia Solomon, 21
Osborne, Helen Betty, 19–20, 21

Passler, Breta, 242, 246, 252, 257,
   259, 270
Pawl, Kevin, 67–68
Philippot, Marc, 131, 133, 135, 136,
   139
Phoenix Sinclair Inquiry, 39
Pickton, Robert, 24, 32
Project Devote, 26

Project Echidna, 173–74

Project Styx. *See also* Cormier, Raymond; Mohammad (Mo; undercover officer)
 budget, 177, 218, 222, 226
 Cormier behaviour as threat to, 218
 Cormier informed of, 237–38
 Cormier's view of, 244
 criminal gang/Mr. Big ruse, 175, 176, 205, 216–18, 221–22, 228–34, 238
 crucial juncture of, 226–27
 domestic violence scenario, 207–13
 duvet cover ploy, 201
 evolving friendship between Mo and Cormier, 187–97
 final storyline, 228–34
 implementation of, 183–84
 importance of recordings, 251–52
 introduction of Jenna, 197–99
 and Jenna, 200–205
 Mo and Cormier meet, 184–85
 naming of, 174
 planning of characters, 181–82
 role in trial, 257, 264–66
 structure of, 175–76
 team, 178–80

prostitution
 arrest of johns, 80
 in Winnipeg, 77–80

racism in Winnipeg, 58, 171–72

residential schools, 32–33, 41

Rhee, Dr. Dennis, 14–15, 16, 63–67, 258

Riddell, Myles, 114, 115, 117, 118, 124, 125, 128–29, 159, 167, 169, 260

Riel, Louis, 52

Ross, James, 242, 246, 247, 248, 251, 252, 256–57, 259, 260, 261, 264, 266, 267, 268, 270, 273

Roy-Hageman, Susan, 13–14, 69–70, 71, 119, 257–58, 261

Sagkeeng First Nation, 30–31, 32, 33

Salvation Army, 80

Sango, Richard, 103–4, 126

Sarah, 113

Saunders, Loretta, 3, 163

Schmieder, Esther, 108, 109, 111, 113–14

Sebastian. *See* Cormier, Raymond (Sebastian, Frenchie)

Smith, Bernadette, 21–22, 26, 241

Smyth, Danny, 4, 16–17, 162, 239–40

Southeast Child and Family Services, 85, 90

Stalker, Jeff, 114, 115, 116, 117, 118, 124, 125, 128–29, 159, 166, 167–68, 169, 235, 237, 247, 260

Stanley, Gerald, 254–55, 263

Stephanson, Rob, 108, 109, 111, 113–14

St. Theresa Point, 106–7

Synyshyn, Andrew, 244–45, 247, 248, 252, 254, 257, 259–60, 260–61, 262, 264, 266, 270

Taylor, Scott, 126, 127, 141, 148,
     149, 150, 152, 154, 155, 158,
     234–35, 237, 269, 271
Thundersky, Raven, 23
Tina Safe Haven, 276
Toft, Karl, 243
Treaty 1, 31
Trudeau, Justin, 219, 236, 244
Truth and Reconciliation
     Commission, 33
Tyrell, 113

Whitehurst, Steve, 82, 85, 108
Wilkie-Gilmore, Dr. Andrea, 92
Wilson, Hillary, 22

Winnipeg
     early police force in, 56
     gangs in, 77
     history of, 55–56
     homicide record, 57
     missing and murdered women
          in, 4
     North End in, 76–78
     prostitution in, 77–80
     racism in, 58, 171–72
     relationship between police
          and Indigenous people, 57–58
     winter in, 54–55
Woodhouse, Anthony, 59